P9-DUD-916

CONTENTS

CONTENTS

INQUISITION AND
LIBERTY

INQUISITION AND LIBERTY

BY

G. G. COULTON

Beacon Press   Beacon Hill   ·   Boston

First published in 1938 by William Heinemann Ltd.
First published as a Beacon Paperback in 1959
by arrangement with William Heinemann Ltd.
Library of Congress Catalog Card Number: 59-10732
Printed in the United States of America

ILLUSTRATIONS

From woodcut illustration to *Das buoch der heiligen altvätter* (German translation of *Vitaspatrum*) printed by Anton Sorg in 1482. (A. Schramm. *Bilderschmuck IV*. No. 962.) The text tells how this "most famous hermit in Lower Egypt" held his hand in the flame, under temptation, so that his fingers were found in the morning to be fully consumed. (*Vitaspatrum* in *P.L.* lxxiii. 833.)

From this same book. (Schramm. No. 992; *P.L.* lxxiii. 916.) This story is worth translation in full. "The Ancient Fathers said of Abbot John the Little that he spake once unto his brethren: 'I would fain undertake a life as safe as that of the angelic hosts; they labour not, but serve and praise God without ceasing.' So he drew off the clothes that he wore, and went into the wilderness. And when he had spent a week there, then he came back to his brethren. And when he knocked at the door, the brother said before opening: 'Who is there?' Then said the other: 'I am thy brother, John.' Then his brother answered, saying: 'John is become an angel, and cometh henceforth no more among men.' But John, hearing this, knocked again and said: 'I am John': yet he opened not, but let him suffer until morning without the cell. Then indeed he opened unto him and said: 'John, if thou art a man, then must thou work and earn thine own meat.' Then he begged forgiveness of his brother, saying: 'Forgive me, brother, for I have sinned.'" These are two of the woodcuts lending themselves best to illustration; but a far stronger example might be found in the story of St. Simeon Stylites. (*P.L.* lxxiii. 325-334.)

Traced from a photograph supplied by Bernon & Cie.

Frontispiece to Vol. III of Townsend's *Journey Through Spain*.

Twelve full-page illustrations which appeared in the original edition have been removed in the present edition.

PREFACE

ONE of Macaulay's best-known epigrams is among the least accurate. In his Essay on Ranke, he describes how the Church of Rome "thoroughly understands, what no other Church has ever understood, how to deal with enthusiasts. . . . The Catholic Church neither submits to enthusiasm nor proscribes it, but uses it." This is a very misleading half-truth. It is true for many conspicuous cases, from the Friars to the Jesuits and beyond: but it is false for a multitude of other cases which had not come within Macaulay's reading at the age of forty. Darwin, for some time, wondered why the meadows round his house, among fir-woods, produced no self-sown firs. Yet careful observation finally showed that the fields were in fact full of such seedlings, struggling upwards but steadily cropped by the cattle. The Middle Ages were equally full of heresies, but so steadily cropped that few grew to anything like maturity. The greediest devourer was, of course, the Inquisition. To understand that institution, we must try to visualise the society in which it was born and exercised its powers. That was a society younger than ours, therefore less experienced, and thus more liable to unfortunate experiments, unless we are to suppose that successive generations are incapable of learning from the failures of their predecessors. We must expect, therefore, to find our far-off ancestors still groping in the dark, here and there, for truths which we have learned from their bitter experiences. We must expect this; and the recorded facts seem to prove it beyond dispute. It is no Pharisaical sense of superiority which prompts the conviction that, thanks to great and good men in the past, our own generation has emerged, or at least is struggling to emerge, from material and moral quagmires which earlier ages scarcely even realised in their full significance. Not only we may say, but often we must say, "So-and-so did wrong in the past," even while we are most ready to own that, in his place, we ourselves might have done as ill or worse. We must judge the individual by what we can learn of his social surroundings: but also we must reverse the process and judge that surrounding society by what we know of individual human nature. A man is not necessarily a barbarian for living in primitive and semi-barbarous circumstances. Yet in some sense those surroundings are truly part of himself, except in the rarest possible cases. They form the atmosphere of his globe: or, as the Psalmist puts it, "they come into his belly like water, and like oil into his bones." Even those who have resisted most heroically have been to some extent warped by that resistance; a man's own age may dominate him by repulsion as definitely as by attraction. It is in the face of these considerations that the present work has been undertaken.

At first sight, a fresh book on the Inquisition may seem superfluous. Dr. H. C. Lea's first three massive volumes on the subject were hailed with the warmest praise by Lord Acton, most learned of all English-speaking Roman Catholics. They are at the base of all that has been since written on the subject, even by those who differ most from Lea's point of view; and they have rendered possible two such excellent summaries as those of Abbé E. Vacandard and Professor A. S. Turberville. The present volume does not compete directly with these, but attempts to approach the subject from a rather different standpoint. The story of those far-off struggles has been told, naturally enough, from above, as from a secure mountain height. Here, I attempt to view it from below, at the level of the participants themselves. This is, therefore, not constitutional but social history; it aims at helping the reader to visualise how he would find himself if anything of the kind were again introduced into English life. Though we have ceased to think of history as a schoolmaster commissioned to teach us certain "laws" of life, yet it may most legitimately strive to convey at least the sort of practical guidance which we can pick up, for instance, from a business man with whom we talk on a railway journey. Therefore I have attempted here to give far more prominence to authentic individual cases, and to keep in view, from beginning to end, the practical question of censorship and physical coercion as against freedom of thought. At as many points as possible, I have translated my documents in full. This, I have reason to believe, satisfies an increasing number of present-day readers, who like to judge for themselves and who can often form from the original documents a better idea of these old-world social or religious conditions than the most brilliant summary would give them. I give references, in my Appendix, to those points alone which might seem disputable without documentary vouchers, or which some reader with a first-rate library at hand might wish to pursue further.

CHAPTER I

The Growth of Nonconformity

THE elasticity of man, both in body and in mind, is not least among the marvels of this universe. No machine has ever been comparable to the human heart in accuracy and length of service. It will work steadily, perhaps for more than a century, night and day, with a power which, reckoned in foot-pounds, reaches an astounding total. Even when we are old and rheumatic, our joints still move with an independence of outside help which the most costly machine can scarcely rival for a week on end. And the mind is still more marvellous in its elasticity and adaptability. In our medieval Colleges, the Founder's statutes sometimes make allowance for a little formal relaxation round the fire after supper; men may sit and tell each other authentic histories and marvels of the world—*Mirabilia Mundi*. Such is the aim of this present volume; to present the reader with trustworthy pictures of human thought in the remote past, and of the actions conditioned by that thought. We shall see men starting from presuppositions quite alien to our own, and shaping their deeds accordingly. We shall admit at every turn that we ourselves, believing as they did, should probably have acted as they acted. And when we ask ourselves further how those men felt in their hearts, journeying under such conditions from the cradle to the grave, the answer must be that man is always a miraculously adaptable animal. The most you can give him will not really satisfy; yet, if he sees no other remedy, he will content himself with the least. It is equally encouraging and humiliating to consider what we are willing to endure so long as bare life is left to us. The long-suffering of man is truly among the *mirabilia mundi*.

Let us begin by going back nearly a thousand years, to that time which, even when all exaggerations have been cleared away, must still be called "The Dark Ages of Europe."

One of the very few Dark Age chroniclers who puts real life into his story is Ralph Glaber, monk of Cluny, patronised by two of the greatest abbots of his time. He claims with some justice to be reviving a flame which had smouldered for nearly two hundred years; he admits no true-bred predecessors since Bede's *Ecclesiastical History of the English Nation* and Paul Warnefrid's *History of the Lombards*. Under the year 1017, he describes a fateful scene at Orleans, one of those Gallic cities which had retained some remnants of their Roman greatness. We get fitful glimpses of this greatness under Clovis. Orleans had witnessed the first Church Council that was attended by prelates from the whole of Gaul. In 830 a great lawsuit had been transferred by the King from Paris to Orleans, because it had more distinguished Doctors of Roman Law. Later, in the twelfth century, it became perhaps the most prominent school of classical literature outside Italy; in the thirteenth century it possessed the greatest Law University of France, and was counted by St. Thomas Aquinas among the four first Universities of Europe. Hither, then, in 1017, came King Robert of France and Queen Constance to judge a batch of heretics, the evil savour of whom had spread as far as Paris. The two leaders were "reputed among the worthiest of that city in lineage and in learning." One "was held the dearest of the clergy at the Abbey of Ste-Croix; and the other ruled as head over the school of St. Peter's Church." But a woman-heretic came from Italy, "filled with the devil and seducing whomsoever she would; not only the unlearned and simple but even many who seemed among the most learned in the clerical order." Finding her way to Orleans, she infected these two intellectual leaders, men who were in the highest favour with the pious King and his Court. These, with all the proselytising fervour of sudden converts, spread the poison busily, proclaiming that the whole world would soon come over to this new religion. At length, however, one of their missionaries approached a priest "of sound understanding" at Rouen, who at once appealed to "the most Christian count of that city, Richard," our own Conqueror's grandfather. Richard reported in all haste to the King, who "as a most learned and Christian monarch, was very sad and mournful, fearing the very ruin of his land and the destruction of souls." He hastened to Orleans, and there convoked a council of bishops, abbots and religious layfolk. The two heresiarchs made no secret of their opinions. The King and his prelates "interrogated them more closely, since they had been hitherto most edifying in all probity of morals. . . . Yet they answered thus: 'It is long since we embraced this sect which ye so tardily recognise; but we have waited until ye and all others, of whatsoever law or order, should have fallen in with it: nay, we believe even now that this will come to pass.' Whereupon they proceeded to put forth the most foolish and miserable and self-deceiving of all ancient heresies." They maintained that the orthodox proofs of the Holy Trinity, culled from the Old and New Testament, were "mere ravings"; again, Creation is a fable, since this universe has always existed; their morals were those of Epicurus; they denied future rewards and punishments. None at that Council or in this colloquy was able to answer adequately their blind and erroneous assertions; so our Glaber himself proceeds to confute them, to his own complete satisfaction, in three folio columns. The King, however, wielded more effective weapons. When all argument had failed, he explained bluntly that "with the consent of the whole population" he must burn them, unless they reverted instantly to the true and universal faith. They remained obdurate; and the rest of the story must be told in Glaber's own words.

"The King, and all the men there present, saw that they could not be recalled from their madness; therefore he bade kindle, not far from the city, a vast fire, that perchance they might be terrified thereby and desist from their wickedness. Yet, when they were led thither, impelled by raving madness, they proclaimed themselves quite willing, and offered themselves freely to those who drew them towards the fire. At length, when they had all been cast therein, thirteen in number, and they began to burn more bitterly, then they commenced, with such voice as they could, to cry from the flames that they had been abominably deceived by the devil's arts; that hitherto they had erred concerning our God, Lord of all things, and that they must be tormented now and for evermore in vengeance for that blasphemy against Him. Then many of the bystanders, moved with pity and humanity, came near and would have torn them, half-dead, from the flames; yet this availed nothing, for the avenging fire consumed them and they were reduced forthwith to ashes. Such followers of these perverse opinions as were found afterwards, in any place, were destroyed with like retaliatory vengeance. Thus, when the madness of these abominable fanatics had been uprooted, the worship of the venerable Catholic Faith shone more brightly throughout the earth."

This is a tragic story on the very surface; but its further significance is greater still. Even this scene, which to us seems so disorderly, was in one true sense a step forward in law and order. For it is a dizzy world that Glaber describes, a world that yearned for any redemption from its own chaos; and he himself realises this to the full. The lurid stories of earlier chroniclers—the wild excesses of Frankish kings and nobles and queens and princesses in Gregory of Tours—Bede's picture of The Yellow Plague and Paul's story of Alboin's compelling his wife to drink at a great feast from her father's skull—are not more bewildering than Glaber's descriptions of disorder in nature and in society at his own day. Michelet points out how, in the seventy-three years from 987 to 1059, there were forty-eight of famine or pestilence—two of them, at least, were marked by cannibalism. Here, again, nothing short of Glaber's own words can tell the story: "It is horrible to relate what corruptions then prevailed among men. I grieve to say an almost unheard-of thing, that rabid hunger compelled men to devour human flesh. Wayfarers were seized by their stronger fellows, and torn limb from *should man accept such grave times and burdens upon him as a sign from the divinity? If so, does he accept the fate of suffering and dying during this time?*

limb, and cooked and devoured. Many also, fleeing from one place to another that they might escape the famine, were taken in at hostelries and slain in the night, as food for those who entertained them. Many also enticed children with an apple or an egg, and led them far away to kill and devour them. The bodies of the dead were torn from their graves in very many places, as a defence against famine. Yet it grew at length to such a pitch of madness that beasts were safer from the ravisher than men. For, as though the eating of human flesh had now become customary, one man at Troyes brought it cooked for sale in the market, as though it were the flesh of cattle. When men seized him, he did not deny the nefarious crime; so they bound him and burned him in the fire. Another, who disinterred this man by night and devoured him, was burned also in like fashion. There is a church some three miles from the city of Mâcon, solitary in the uninhabited forest, dedicated to St. John. A certain murderous man had built a hut there, who slew a multitude of wayfarers that came to him and made them his accursed food. But it befel one day that a man with his wife came thither to lodge. There he rested awhile; but then, scrutinising the corners of this hut, he saw the severed heads of men, women and children. He grew pale, and would have gone forth; but his pestilent host strove with him and would have retained him by force. He, however, fearing this death-trap, prevailed and hastened with his wife to the city, where he told his tale to Count Eudes and the citizens. A band of men was then sent to enquire of the truth; and, hastening thither, they found this savage in his hut with forty-eight heads of murdered folk, whose flesh he had devoured in such beastly fashion. They brought him to the city and bound him to a post in a barn; and, as I myself saw afterwards with my own eyes, they burned him with fire."

Add to this the constant warfare between baron and baron, or between barons and king, and Saracen invasions. The latter, however slight compared with those of the past, were still formidable enough to make men wonder whether Antichrist and Armageddon and the end of the world might not be at hand. As to these chronic petty wars at home, which in their totality ran up an account of ravage and slaughter even heavier than the more spectacular wars of later times, the Truce of God, instituted in Glaber's time, had only the modified success which has attended the modern League of Nations. Its main sanction was in the anathema of the Church; but she seldom came forward to pledge her authority in these bloody quarrels; nor was she always, even then, above suspicion of partiality. Here and there, local militias were formed in support of this Truce of God; and these had some effect; but, even in thirteenth-century France, private wars between baron and baron were part of the law of the land; and Götz von Berlichingen's auto-biography shows us the same abuses surviving, on an even greater scale, in the Germany of 1500.[1] Nor could Glaber see much more hope in Church than in State. He dismisses the debaucheries of one contemporary Pope (Benedict IX) as too horrible to relate in detail; and he complains most bitterly that the clergy as a body, and especially the prelates, were de-moralised by greed for money. When St. Peter's at Rome caught fire, he describes the Christian worshippers as threaten-ing God with their vengeance unless He intervened, exactly as the savage hopes to extort what he wants by offering violence to his own idol. Glaber knows that false relics are being manu-factured wholesale, and he is embarrassed by the inescapable difficulty that these also will sometimes work miracles, the Devil having his own hierarchy in competition with Jehovah. Society may sometimes show signs of repentance and amend-ment; yet, too often, it returns as a dog to his vomit. In short, Glaber's world has advanced disappointingly little beyond those earlier generations of orthodox Frankish Christians under Clovis and his successors, whose story has recently been summarised with admirable lucidity by a scholar whom nobody will accuse of anti-religious bias, Professor Ferdinand Lot.[2] He writes: "The form of Christianity which triumphed in the West was not very lofty or pure in quality. Even the best of the bishops were superstitious, believers in omens and haunted by the fear of the devil. Their conception of divinity is too often that of a jealous God, revengeful and favourising His devotees without regard to their morality. What can we say of the mass of believers? Certain practices contributed to the degradation of Christian feeling; for instance, the use of 'penitential books,' imported from Ireland, which are tariffs for the redemption of sins. From this time forward the worship of God yields to that of the Saints. . . . Gradually these Saints were differentiated according to the special effects of their intervention; so that, in effect, the healing Saints are substituted for the gods and heroes of antiquity. . . . Humanity, abandoned to itself, fell back with all its weight into paganism."

On the face of it, the story of the Dark Ages in Europe is painful and even sordid. There is no true escape from this in ignoring the facts; still less in the attempt to deny things which force themselves so plainly upon every careful student. Not only is Glaber's evidence in accord with all other chroniclers who give us living pictures, as apart from a mere skeleton of world-events, but it is borne out by legal and official documents. The real escape from depression here, as elsewhere, is to face the facts on all sides and look into their deeper significance. In the Dark Ages, even more than in the later Middle Ages, nobility is to be found less in men's creations than in their aspirations; less in what was achieved by society as a whole, or even by the Church as a whole, than in what the better spirits sought to achieve. Those spirits were no more typical of the society around them than the Hebrew Prophets were typical of the average Jews in their own day. In both cases, on the contrary, those whom we admire were noble mainly in their attitude of passionate protest; their idealism stood in conscious and studied reaction against the gross materialism that they saw around them. Facing the facts thus, we may constantly bear in mind, throughout this present story, the honour that those few do to humanity in every age, in their refusal to accept the lower standards of their day. Where history can be most easily described by the superficial reader as a mere chronicle of follies and crimes, there we may take heartiest encouragement from those who steadily refused partnership with the fools and the criminals:

> "What I aspired to be
> And was not, comforts me:
> A brute I might have been, but would not sink i' the scale."

Yet Glaber has another side to show: he is one of the very few medieval writers who seem to believe their own day better, or at least no worse, than the days of their forefathers. He describes how, after a period of suspense around the year 1000, which suggested the coming of Antichrist and the end of the world even more definitely than usual, the earth awoke to fresh life. "It seemed as though the world shook itself and cast off its hoary age, and clad itself everywhere in a white robe of churches." And certainly, if we look at the actual facts, Europe did take a fresh start about this time. No barbarian ravages after 1000 were comparable to those invading hordes of earlier generations; and there did come a general revival which, gathering force in the twelfth century, went far to anticipate what we call the Renaissance. From that point of view, there is a double significance in this Orleans story. It marks, on the one hand, a serious revolt, however sporadic and partial as yet, from the authority of the One Church. We see here how some of the most learned and respectable citizens, in one of the most civilised cities of Europe, deliberately repudiated the current traditions, and convinced themselves that this repudiation was destined to be victorious. On the other hand, the King now comes in and treats this ecclesiastical revolt as one of the weightiest matters of State; the King's Peace is infringed by those who attack the Pope's Peace. Not, of course, but that other sovereigns had acted on this same principle, especially in France. Yet hitherto there had been, so to speak, only guerilla warfare; henceforth there will be pitched battles: war will be engaged along the whole front. Glaber had already recorded three heresies in earlier years. In the year 1000, or thereabouts, a "legate of Satan" appeared near Châlons in the person of a mad peasant, who believed he had a swarm of bees in his belly, which he sent forth in the shape of Scripture quotations and crude theological arguments. One of his tenets was the unlawfulness of tithes; and thus, naturally enough, "he drew to himself no small party from among the common folk." The bishop, an old and prudent man, exposed his folly; and the heretic, deserted by his followers, cast himself into a well. In Lombardy, again, the walled town of Monforte, "full of folk of nobler birth," frankly revolted from Christianity. "They adored idols after the fashion of pagans, and sought to celebrate their foolish sacrifices with the Jews." The Marquis of Asti and his brother, the bishop, tried vainly to storm the town, and had to content themselves with burning those prisoners whom they took in skirmishes. About the same time, in the diocese of Ravenna, a grammarian called Vilgardus preached a sort of Renaissance neo-Paganism until "at last he was found to be a heretic, and condemned by Peter, bishop of that city. Many also of this pestilent creed were found throughout Italy; but these perished either by sword or by fire. Moreover, at the same time, certain men went forth from Sardinia, which commonly aboundeth in such folk, and corrupted part of the people of Spain; these also were exterminated by the Catholics. This is a presage in accordance with the prophecy of St. John [in the Apocalypse], who hath told us how Satan shall be loosed at the end of a thousand years."

Thus, then, the clouds are gathering for a storm which will shake Europe for centuries to come. As the world revives, so also does heresy; and the citizen's theological opinions now become one of the weightiest matters not in Church only, but in State.

CHAPTER II

The Crime of Nonconformity

CHRISTIANITY, from the very first, had in itself the germs of conflict between authority and criticism; and this conflict developed rapidly with the development of an organised Church. Within a century of the Crucifixion, it was already possible for the main body to proclaim itself Catholic, or Universal, and to ignore or repudiate other men's claims to be followers of Christ. Already in the New Testament, we find St. Paul pronouncing a curse upon all who teach the Galatians what he condemns as a false Gospel (Gal. i. 8); and the First Epistle to Timothy delivers two dissentient teachers over to Satan (i. 20). Strong convictions necessarily produce violent reactions in minds of different constitution. Yet, on the whole, the earlier generations of Christianity were marked by a spirit widely different from what we have seen at Orleans in 1017. In the Apostolic Age, the main bond was that of brotherly love. During the next three centuries, this was gradually exchanged for the bond of organised authority, wielding the sanctions of worldly, and even bodily, punishment.

A movement can afford to be liberal in proportion with its essential truth and greatness; therein lies the main distinction between genuine progress and those reactionary movements which make equally bold claims upon us. Christian faith, at first, was concerned mainly with the present and future. Is Jesus indeed the long-promised Messiah? Are His promises true of a new Kingdom of Heaven? Have we indeed a better world before us, into which every man may press who is bold enough? —a Brave New World of the Spirit—"the Kingdom of Heaven suffereth violence, and the violent take it by force"? In those days, then, the Christian was any man who was willing to

10

co-operate with Jesus, and to press onward in His footsteps. "He that is not against us, is for us." That was His answer to those who grudged that an outsider should go about doing good after his own fashion. When Christ said the apparent opposite, "He that is not for us is against us," that was in the face of men who ascribed undeniably good works not to God's inspiration but to that of Beelzebub. The former saying was a blessing upon all good done in good faith: the other branded it an unforgivable sin to discover evil motives even in patent good: that was the Sin against the Holy Ghost—*Der Geist der stets verneint* —cloaking mean envy under the claim of orthodox zeal. Among His definite disciples, there was little divergence so long as they enjoyed His daily presence. After the Crucifixion, however, men began to form different ideas of His presence, His work and His promises. The future lay before this new society, to be moulded after His Spirit but without that daily oracular guidance of the earliest days. To the most earnest of these disciples, the one certain and overwhelming truth was that He had given them new life; that He had brought them into a new world of thought and feeling which none who had once entered could ever dream of leaving. But with converts made after the Crucifixion the case was necessarily different. To them, it was not merely a matter of present and future, but also of the past. Before they could accept the Gospel gift, they must needs look into the credentials of the Giver. A minority might be convinced at once by the intrinsic beauty of this ideal; but most men needed some further guarantee. Therefore, at a very early stage, the Christian question became to a very great extent an historical problem, in which all future hopes must depend upon past events. And, as usual when so vast an issue depends upon any historical question, people began to demand from history a clarity which history alone cannot possibly give. Intuition may indeed give convincing results, when the teaching brings a man into deeper peace with himself and with others, with a growing certitude for all his work towards human progress. So far, every true religion touches all right-minded

persons; in different degrees, of course, ranging from the
vaguest sympathy to the most whole-hearted conversion, but
always operative to some extent upon all who value inward
peace and outward harmony with the progress of the universe.
But, from the first, Christianity depended to a great extent
upon something beyond this. Had Christ, after the Crucifixion,
been seen and heard and touched by His disciples? There, it
begins to depend upon the ordinary laws of historical evidence;
and a man who is wholly captured by the ideal message might
feel historic doubt as to the concrete events. Not only would the
most explicit records be insufficient to bear the whole weight of
proof for an event which, in the very essence of its claim, is
unique, but in fact the Gospels are neither so explicit here, nor
so unanimous in their evidence, as we might wish. It would
seem that God never intended the evidence for Christianity to
be mainly historical, in the ordinary sense of that word. And
though, here again, St. Paul does emphatically and passionately
claim that historical basis, yet in that sphere there was sometimes a startling latitude of tolerance among early Christians.
Justin Martyr, the first of the apologists whose works have
come down to us, claims in so many words that philosophers
like Socrates and Heraclitus were essentially Christians, since
they lived for the truth and Christ is truth. In other words, he
welcomes as fellow-Christians all who strive whole-heartedly for
the truth.[1] And, when we come to St. Augustine, we see clearly
how far the centre of gravity has changed in Christian apolo-
getics. In his day there were already about ninety different
sects, most of whom anathematised each other. Again, there
were philosophers like Celsus, emphasising many of the
objections which are most definitely formulated against
Christianity at the present day, because they are the most
important. Celsus, in especial, lays great stress upon the
weaker links in the chain of historical evidence. To such
adversaries Augustine replies from a point of view from which,
in strict logic, that historical question is irrelevant. He writes:
"There are here three things incredible and yet true. It is

incredible that Christ rose again in human body and ascended
with that body to heaven. It is incredible that the world should
ever have believed a thing so incredible as this. It is still more
incredible that this incredible thing should have been persuaded
so effectually to the world, and even to learned men, by a set of
low fellows of the humblest extraction, a mere handful in
number, and quite destitute of worldly experience. The first
of these three incredibles our adversaries refuse to believe; yet
the second forces itself upon their bodily senses; and this second
cannot possibly be explained but by admitting the third." He
goes on to rehearse the miracles claimed for the first Apostles,
and adds: "If our adversaries will not believe these miracles,
wrought to enforce conviction of the Resurrection and Ascension
of Christ, yet, for us, this one vast miracle may suffice, that the
world has believed in that Resurrection and Ascension without
the aid of corroborative miracles." There we find the natural
exaggeration of an apologist; yet, in the main, St. Augustine has
taken a far firmer apologetic standpoint. The weight of proof is
here transferred from the past to the present. We are now more
on the ground of the author of the Epistle to the Hebrews, for
whom faith is far less a matter of belief in past events than in a
grasp of present spiritual suggestions and a reaching forward to
the future—a violent and forceful seizure of the Kingdom of
Heaven. We are now no longer dependent so much upon
written records or Church tradition, as upon matters of common
daily observation, and a mind willing to seize upon proffered
possibilities for good—the mind that moves with Christ, if only
because it moves on a parallel rather than a contrary line. Here
(argues Augustine) is a creed which has fought successfully
against such odds and inspired so many lives: can this victory
possibly be ignored by any truly scientific mind? Science, after
careful enquiry, may indeed reject it: but to reject it without
careful examination is patently unscientific. So far, Augustine
has certainly taken strong ground; but his argument raises
further important issues in another direction. We may see this
in the form which Dante gives to the Augustinian argument:

"If the world actually did turn to Christianity without [the persuasion of] miracles, then that [one miracle, in itself] is such that the others are not worth the hundredth of it." (*Paradiso*, XXIV, 106.) If this be indeed so, that a non-miraculous Christianity would in itself be a greater miracle than miraculous Christianity, then it may logically be argued that the higher faith is independent of particular miracles, and therefore comparatively independent of historical testimony. That conclusion, in a tentative form, was drawn independently by Augustine himself. He freely admits that miracles are a lower form of evidence. The early Church needed them to convert rude minds, "for in no other way could they be convinced: but it is their conversion which has rendered miracles unnecessary to their posterity. For, now that the Catholic Church has spread and taken firm root over the whole world, those [earlier] miracles have not been permitted to endure to our own days, lest men's minds should always seek after visible things, and the human race should cool down into frigid familiarity with such events as, in their first freshness, kindled it to enthusiasm."

These thoughts of Augustine echoed down the earlier Middle Ages; and we find St. Odo, the practical founder of the great Cluniac Order, writing much the same in about 940. The Church (he argues) "needed visible miracles in those days when a handful of fishermen and artisans were striving to convert emperors and high priests; but the faith is now settled upon a foundation firm enough to dispense with them. . . . If miracles are ceasing in our own day, this is because God wishes to search men's hearts: for the followers of Antichrist shall work miracles [in support of their own false doctrines], in order that those who revere the Church only for the sake of her miracles may cease to venerate her, transferring their allegiance to Antichrist." That argument, followed to its logical consequence, would have revolutionised medieval religion. But nobody did follow it to its logical consequence, although other great churchmen spoke as Augustine and Odo did. Thus the Church was content to suffer contradictory doctrines on this, as on other important *to Gregory the Great there is a continuing of Augustinian thought, w/certain additions*

subjects, so long as they were not too crudely opposed to each other. St. Gregory the Great, in one of his homilies, commits himself definitely to the doctrine that physical miracles cannot by themselves establish the truth of a religion: that a true creed must base itself upon the moral miracle of its actual hold on mankind, and its elevating influence over men's minds. Yet that same Gregory, in his still more influential *Dialogues*, did almost more than any other writer to encourage the rage for miracles—even for the most childishly improbable—and to give official approbation to the popular belief in purgatorial fire.

Such being the dubious and inconsistent attitude of the greatest minds, the revival of European thought at the end of the Dark Ages was naturally accompanied by a revival of religious quarrels. The West began now to take up in earnest a series of struggles which had long been familiar to the East; and these civil wars within the Christian Church—for they were no less—will be conducted with more systematic brutality and on a greater scale, in these ruder and more warlike populations of recently-converted barbarians. Eastern and Western Christianity had, for centuries past, contrasted with each other as Athens had always contrasted with Rome. To the Eastern, his religion had been a matter for nimble thought and lively discussion; to the Western, rather a matter of strictly imperative law. The Western aim had been to stand firmly upon the old traditional ways—*stare super antiquas vias*—while the Greek had pushed his zigzag exploring trenches in all directions, pursuing each article of his creed into every stage of philosophical refinement and subtlety.

In the East, therefore, violent differences began very early; and, with them, the spirit of persecution. Even in the early days when Christians themselves were persecuted by the State, they were not always tolerant of each other. Constantine, who first decreed toleration for Christianity and then adopted it as the religion privileged by the State, came forward soon as a persecutor. Heretical priests were punished; indeed, more stringent measures were taken against them and their services than against the pagan sacrifices, although paganism, in the eyes of the law, was now condemned as a *superstitio*. When the Council of Nicaea had decided against Arius, Constantine banished him, commanded the surrender of all copies of his books under pain of death, and sent him into exile with the two bishops who had maintained his cause to the very end of the Council.

There were still great churchmen who believed in tolerance. St. Hilary of Poitiers, in 365, deplored the gradual revolution which had brought an Apostolic brotherhood of sufferers into a newer institution of persecutors for the Faith. "The Church terrifieth with threats of exile and dungeons; and she, who of old gained men's faith in spite of exile and prison, now brings them to believe in her by compulsion. . . . She, who was propagated by hunted priests, now hunts priests in her turn. . . . This much must be said in comparison of that Church which was handed down to us, yet which we have now lost: the fact itself is in all men's eyes, it cries aloud." Yet, not many years later, St. Jerome held that Vigilantius, by his campaign against the adoration of relics, would have been justly punished with death. His contemporary, St. Augustine, though at first he disapproved of corporal penalties in matters of belief, expressly revokes this in his *Retractations*. Experience (he said) had convinced him that men may thus be brought to see the true faith; and this he reinforced by theological arguments based upon an allegorical interpretation of Christ's parable of the lord and his supper: "Compel them to come in" (Luke xiv, 23). For, wild as such a distortion of Christ's words may seem on the face of it, this was a perfectly logical consequence from the exclusive spirit which has increased from generation to generation among the Catholic majority, and from their equally exaggerated doctrines of heaven and hell. It is quite impossible to understand those ages in which the Inquisition formed one of the most important institutions of European society without starting mentally from those doctrines, which affected the ordinary man even

more deeply than the more exalted teachings of which
Christianity is justly proud.

While many of Christ's sayings, and especially His parable ✳
of the tares, were either explained away or more or less ignored,
His words about future punishment were interpreted not only
with cruel emphasis, but with exaggerations not warranted by
the actual text. It was perfectly natural, however essentially
unchristian, that those who had seen their own innocent
companions submitted to abominable tortures should emphasise
the idea of future retribution. Tertullian, writing less than two
centuries after the Crucifixion, exclaims: "how shall I laugh,
how shall I rejoice! . . . [I shall see] the magistrates who
persecuted God's servants melting in fiercer flames than those
wherewith they themselves raged against the Christians. . . .
What prætor or consul or quæstor or priest, however free of his
money, can afford you such a sight for your exultation? Yet
already, in a certain sense, we ourselves possess this through
faith, depicted in spiritual imagination."[2]

Centuries later, when wave after wave of barbarians had
swept over the Roman Empire, and missionaries like St.
Columbus and St. Boniface gradually converted them to
Christianity, it was long before these wild men were really
changed at heart. Their new religion was only skin-deep. St.
Gregory himself, writing to his first missionaries in England,
was obliged to advise a minimum of outward breach with the
past; let the heathen temples be now used as churches; let the
feasts to their "devils" be continued in honour of the True God.
St. Vitus converted the heathen of Rügen in the Baltic: but, a
few generations later, fresh missionaries found a population of
relapsed heathens, who honoured their earlier apostle rather in
breach than in observance of his teaching. They had erected an
idol which they called Swantovit; this they worshipped with
human sacrifices, preferably of Christians. Such folk were far
more likely to be impressed by Tertullian's hell than by milder
Gospel precepts; in their rough hands it became an even more
grotesque idol; and, far outlasting the Reformation, it enabled

an Anglican divine to boast that "the hell described in the Gospel is not with the same particularity to be met with in any other religion that is or hath been in the whole world."[3]

Perhaps the greatest mission-preacher of the whole Middle Ages was Berthold of Regensburg, whom his contemporary and fellow–Franciscan, Roger Bacon, singles out for especial praise. Berthold, in many other ways so robust in common sense and so modern in his points of view, is never weary of preaching hell-fire. He bids his hearers imagine themselves white-hot in the midst of a white-hot Universe for all eternity. Let them count the sands of the sea-shore, or every hair that has grown upon man and beast since the days of Adam; let them reckon a year of torment for each of those hairs and, even then, the sinner will be only at the outset of his unending agony. Worse still, Berthold has no doubt that those souls which will escape this fate are only a small minority: for did not Christ say "many are called, but few are chosen"? (Matt. xxii, 14). That doctrine, again, must be fully grasped if we are to understand those ages. Among the points which would be singled out on the spur of the moment as most exclusively characteristic of the Roman Catholic creed, there is perhaps none which has such a long and unblemished pedigree as this of the paucity of saved souls. A Redemptionist Father, F-X. Godts, has published an unbroken catena of evidence from the earliest times to mid-eighteenth century, when a book was condemned at Rome for pleading a majority of saved over damned.[4] No such unbroken catena could be compiled in favour (for instance) of Papal Infallibility, or the Immaculate Conception, or Indulgences, or Purgatory, or Image-worship, or Pilgrimages, or Transubstantiation. Moreover, this fatal disproportion is often calculated with startling crudity: three saved, perhaps, to a thousand damned; or again, the story of the Deluge is interpreted in this sense; Noah's own tiny company as compared with those that perished in the Deluge. St. Thomas Aquinas, who is always among the most balanced of the Schoolmen, takes it as axiomatic that "a few" will be saved as compared with "the multitude" of those who go to hell.* Whatever may be pleaded as discount for theological rhetoric, and however impossible it would be for the ordinary man to put these points coldly together and draw the inevitable logical conclusions—let alone act consistently upon them—we cannot escape from the certainty that they did, on the whole, influence men's thought very deeply: reflectively in the Universities, and temperamentally in the market-place or even in the pothouse.

Let us therefore trace it among the high-brows, where its course is clear and conspicuous. St. Gregory the Great is commenting on PS. LVII, 11, vulg. (LVIII, 11, A.V.). He finds in his text the words which run in the Roman Catholic (Douay) translation "the just shall rejoice when he sees the revenge." This he interprets as meaning that the blessed souls in heaven will rejoice to see the pains of the damned below them in hell.  Then, in the twelfth century, comes Peter Lombard, Bishop of Paris, whose *Sentences* were the foundation-stone of scholastic discussion, and became a textbook so universal as to out-rival the full Bible text. Peter discusses St. Gregory's words fully and agrees definitely with him. The parable of Lazarus and Dives proves clearly that the Blessed do in fact look down from their bliss upon the Damned; and that bliss is heightened by the reflection that we have here a visible and conspicuous instance of God's justice upon sinners, as contrasted with His mercy to the elect. So far the *Sentences*, upon which nearly all the great Schoolmen commented, each in his turn. Two of the earliest, Albert the Great and Alexander of Hales, left this question alone; it was a mystery of God, not to be solved by the human intellect. But St. Thomas Aquinas, arguing the matter out in greater detail and more systematically than Peter Lombard, is entirely of his opinion. The Blessed "will have no pity on the Damned," since their conviction of God's justice does not

joy in revenge of God over evil

---

* One of the assertions solemnly condemned as heretical in Raymond Lull, by Gregory XI, was: "God hath such love for His people that almost all men in the world shall be saved; since, if more were damned than saved, Christ's mercy would be without great love." (Eymeric, Directorium, pars. II., quæstio IX; ed. 1585, p. 275b.)

permit this: "it will not be possible to pity their sufferings according to right reason." Nay, they will positively rejoice at the sight (not, of course, directly, for it would be fiendish to rejoice in a fellow's torment as such) but indirectly. "A thing may be a matter of rejoicing in two ways. First, directly, when one rejoices in a thing as such; and in this way the Saints will not rejoice in the punishment of the wicked. Secondly, indirectly, by reason of something annexed to it, and in this way the Saints will rejoice in the punishment of the wicked, by considering therein the order of Divine justice and their own deliverance, which will fill them with joy. And thus the Divine justice and their own deliverance will be the direct cause of the joy of the blessed: while the punishment of the damned will cause it indirectly." St. Bonaventura, his contemporary, puts it even more strongly: so do other Schoolmen. St. Bernardino of Siena, writing about 1420, insists that heaven would not be perfect without this: just as the skilful musician needs the bass for his effects, so the harmony of the universe is perfected by a due admixture of groans from the Damned. It is a popular error to imagine that Calvin, or even his followers, who are too often confounded with him, painted hell oftener or in greater detail or with more lurid colours than Roman Catholic preachers before and after them. This story of the Blessed and the Damned affords a crucial example of the mischief that relentless logic may work when based upon arbitrary premisses. The Aryan Race Legend itself has not led to more unhappy philosophical results than this perversely accurate deduction from a misunderstanding of a few Bible texts.[5]

Side by side with such developments as this came others which gave them even greater significance. The exaggerations of hell-fire aided those of sacerdotalism. The Elder of original Christianity, whose character and age made him natural leader in the congregational worship, had now become a Priest with sacrificial powers, whose person counted far less than his office. The escape from everlasting torment (or, as time went on, the mitigation of such torment in Purgatory) depended now to an enormous extent upon the hierarchy. [*Charitas* was necessary for salvation: but, whereas in St. Augustine *charitas* still means being right with God, in St. Bernardino, a thousand years later, the emphasis is rather upon being right with the Church.] Everything depended upon the man's dying moments: was he, at that supreme crisis, right in his faith and in unison with the Catholic Church? The salvation even of the most virtuous Jews or Pagans was admitted only as a remote hypothesis by the Schoolmen, with refinements of logic which the multitude naturally ignored. Heretics, therefore, however well-meaning (in so far as men could imagine a well-meaning heretic) were decoys who enticed their fellow-Christians to everlasting torments. In these conditions the wonder is less that orthodoxy should have been intolerant, than that we should find such instances of tolerance (apart from mere indifference) as we do.

[handwritten margin note: dying moment — right "w/ God/church"]

CHAPTER III

The Penalties of Nonconformity

THE greater intellectual activity of Christians in the East and South led naturally to greater friction between Orthodoxy and Heresy. The very birth of a State Church (in the sense in which Constantine may be said to have made a State Church of Christianity) was signalised, as we have seen, by penalties against heretics; and in Greece and Asia Minor and Africa the quarrels amounted, in fierceness and duration, to actual civil war. The State could not ignore this: therefore we find a succession of imperial laws against heresy. In fifty-seven years sixty-eight penal clauses were enacted against nonconformists, ranging from expulsion and confiscation to death. This extreme penalty, however, was mostly reserved for the two most dangerous. The Donatists in Africa waged open civil war against the Catholics. We must not believe too implicitly that it was they who first took up arms or who committed the worst atrocities; but civil war there certainly was, bloody and unrelenting, quite sufficient to explain imperial severity in this case. Again, the Manichæans touched only the fringe of Christianity; they were, as we shall see later, an essentially hostile sect and, what was more dangerous, they had their own hierarchy and sacraments, organised in definite rivalry with Catholicism. They were accused also of anti-social tenets; a law of A.D. 428 describes them as "fallen to the lowest degree of criminality," and the State decreed death against these also; sometimes, indeed, bracketing them together. But none of these laws attempted to encroach upon the inner domain of conscience: they condemned only outward manifestations or acts.

It is in Spain that the first conspicuous case can be found of a heresiarch put to death officially for heresy pure and simple: in that sense this story begins with Spain, as in Spain it will culminate and in Spain it will end.

Priscillian was a theologian whose attainments impressed his contemporaries and whose writings, in the fragments which have survived, are studied with sympathetic interest by modern orthodox scholars. "His erudition and critical spirit were so remarkable that one serious historian does not hesitate to assert that we must now put him by the side of St. Jerome." But he was accused of Manichæism,* in spite of his repudiation of such doctrines; and of sorcery, in spite of his vehement protest that he agreed with the Hebrew verdict: "Thou shalt not suffer witches to live" (Exodus xxii, 18). A Council at Saragossa condemned him; yet he was raised to the bishopric of Avila, the town where, centuries later, St. Teresa was born. Thence he travelled Romewards to justify himself before Pope Damasus, who, however, refused to listen to him: so, again, did St. Ambrose. In 385 a Council was convened at Bordeaux to judge him: to escape judgment by these bishops he appealed to the Emperor, who was then the tyrant Maximus. The trial was held before the court at Trier, his accusers being two Spanish bishops, Ithacius and Idacius. St. Martin of Tours, who was then at Trier, adopted an attitude of protest which is thus described by his biographer Sulpicius Severus: "He ceased not from pressing Ithacius to abandon his accusation: he also besought Maximus not to shed the blood of these poor wretches: it would be enough and more than enough for the bishops to condemn the heretics to expulsion from the churches: it would be a cruel and unheard-of breach of God's law to make the earthly power judge in an ecclesiastical cause." So long as Martin remained at Trier, the trial was adjourned; and, even when he left, his great influence wrung from the Emperor a promise not to shed the blood of the accused men. But soon the Emperor, detestably inspired by bishops Rufus and Magnus,

* The Manichæans, as will be seen later on, were dualists, believing in the almost equally balanced forces of Good and Evil, and exaggerating that Pauline contrast between the willing spirit and the recalcitrant body which did so much to stimulate asceticism.

set aside all indulgent feelings and handed over the case to the
prefect Evodius, a violent and inflexible man. Priscillian
appeared twice before him and was convicted of sorcery. He
also confessed that he had given himself to abominable studies
and held nightly meetings with immodest women and had been
accustomed to pray stark naked. Evodius declared him guilty
and placed him in ward until the report was presented to the
Emperor. This was transmitted to the palace, and Maximus
declared Priscillian and his accomplices worthy of death.
Ithacius, seeing how odious he would make himself to his fellow-
bishops if he maintained his part as accuser down to the last
formalities of capital punishment, desisted from the prosecution
and thus avoided appearing in court; for the case was now to be
tried afresh. This artifice could work no real change, since all
the evil was already done. Then Maximus appointed one
Patricius as public prosecutor. At his demand Priscillian was
condemned to death with several of his accomplices." The rest
were driven into exile.

It was natural enough that a pagan contemporary should
express horror for these bishops "who themselves looked on
upon tortures, feasting their eyes and their ears with the pains
and groans of the accused"; and nobody can pay serious
attention nowadays to the record that Priscillian, under such
duress, confessed to the same secret abominations with which
the early Christians had been credited by their persecutors. But
the really important point is the horror expressed by the best
minds of the time at this incident which formed so close a
precedent for the future Inquisition. In that fourth century,
just as in the thirteenth later on, men are put to death by the
civil magistrate for ecclesiastical offences. In the fourth as in
the thirteenth, the real movers are bishops; but here, as there,
the bishop leaves the actual butcher's work to be done by the
layman: "The Church abhors blood." The main difference is
that, whereas in the full flow of medieval life no great Churchman saw any harm in this, in these earlier days, which preserved fresher memories of Gospel Christianity, the crime

excited profound disgust. St. Martin refused communion with these murderous bishops or with any of their abettors: he yielded at last only because, by thus avoiding a complete and final rupture with the Emperor, he might be able to save the lives of suppliants who had come to Maximus, and to avert further persecution of the Priscillianists in Spain. Even so, however, he felt that spiritual power had gone out of him by reason of this compromise with the powers of evil. St. Ambrose, again, though he had refused to argue with Priscillian, was shocked at this judicial murder. Ithacius, having vainly attempted to shift the responsibility upon other shoulders, was driven from his bishopric by the general reprobation.⌉

Yet, though the crudity of the crime, once committed, forced itself upon the eyes and ears of right-minded folk, the spirit of it was too closely in accordance with the natural policy of a dominant Church for this repentance to be long-lived. The Priscillianists had now not only their missionaries but their martyrs; and, under these inevitable conditions of conflict, they became not only more anti-clerical but more anti-social. St. Leo the Great, in 447, was shocked at the excesses of these heretics; and he spoke out, but without his usual clarity. No man on occasion could be more certain of himself than St. Leo, or bolder in action when he felt justice to be at stake. When a Council was held at Ephesus (449) to decide the Monophysite controversy, Leo would have had it meet in the West, and protested against the necessary Eastern bias of such a meeting. When the Emperor decided otherwise, he did not even trouble to attend personally, but simply sent a bishop, a priest and a deacon as his delegates, with his own *Tome* or treatise, in which he decided as Peter's successor all the points of the controversy. The Council did not even allow this to be read; and, for this and its other irregularities of procedure, Leo stigmatised it as the *Latrocinium*, or Robber Council, a name which has clung to it through all history. At the next regular Council (Chalcedon, 451) his *Tome* was read and approved, the East accepted the authoritative ruling of this Roman bishop. In this controversy

St. Leo decided with a clarity and a boldness which left nothing
to be desired. His words there were among those few which all
modern Roman Catholics, practically without exception,
recognise as having all the notes of an *ex cathedra*, and therefore
infallible, pronouncement. How much hate and suffering
might have been spared to future Europe, if only in this matter
of Priscillianism he had spoken equally clearly and boldly as to
the lawfulness of extracting evidence by torture, and of inflicting death for purely doctrinal differences! But this was not
to be; his words on that occasion were such that it is possible for
two very able and honest men, Dr. H. C. Lea and Abbé E.
Vacandard, to understand them very differently. The latter,
with his usual candour, prints the Latin original in his footnote;
it may be translated as follows:

"Our fathers, in whose times this abominable heresy broke out,
wrought actively throughout the world for the expulsion of this
injurious madness from the whole Church: seeing that the
princes of this world also felt such detestation for this sacrilegious
frenzy that they slew with the sword of public law the heresiarch
with many of his disciples. For they saw that every care of
honesty was removed, and every compact of matrimony
dissolved; that divine and human law would be alike subverted
if such men had ever been suffered to live under this profession.
That strictness [of the lay magistrates] benefited ecclesiastical
mildness which, though it contents itself with priestly judgment
and shuns bloody vengeance, yet is helped by the severe
decrees of Christian princes; since those who fear corporal
punishment sometimes address themselves to the spiritual
remedy." The word here translated "punishment"—*supplicium*
—is one which is very frequently used for the death penalty.

Lea, it may be granted, is too trenchant in commenting upon
this: "Leo . . . not only justified the act, but declared that if
the followers of heresy so damnable were allowed to live, there
would be an end of human and divine law. . . . The final step
had been taken and the Church was definitely pledged to the
suppression of heresy at whatever cost. It is impossible not to

attribute to ecclesiastical influence the successive edicts by which, from the time of Theodosius the Great, persistence in heresy was punished with death" (I. 215). This is one of the few concrete cases which Vacandard gives in justification of his criticism that Lea "though he tries to be impartial distorts the facts" (36 *note*). Yet Vacandard's own summary runs: "St. Leo shows here a certain boldness: he does not yet demand the employment of the sword, but he accepts it in the name of public good. We must fear that, step by step, men will go still farther in future" (32). But why have we no more than this "a certain boldness," in matters which have had far more importance for civilisation and humanity than that other abstruse theological knot which Leo cut with so clear and unsparing a sword? Does not the theory of Papal Infallibility embrace morals as definitely as theology? And might not St. Leo be expected to be as clear on this subject as St. Martin? Is not this one of the many lamentable cases in which Rome, when she speaks at all, has used only oracular language upon questions of the day upon which unprejudiced thinkers are making up their own minds pretty clearly?

There is henceforward a lull in Western persecution. France, Germany and Italy had forgotten too much under the Northern barbarians, and had as yet learned too little beyond a rudimentary Catechism, to breed much heresy, or to shock men with what was bred. As the Penitentials and the complaints of ecclesiastical disciplinarians show us, the ineradicable remnants of heathen superstitions were giving far more trouble than any germs of advanced thought. The orthodox believed in the existence of Thor and Odin as firmly as the heathen did: the only difference was that, while to the latter they were gods, to the former they were demons. Yet the cult of such "demons," and the charms or incantations which reposed upon this cult, enjoyed in practice an immunity which contrasted crudely with Priscillian's experience. It was like the paradox in the East under Constantine and his successors, when it was far more dangerous to be a nonconformist member of this Christianity, this State-protected creed, than to continue worshipping impenitently at those temples which were legally outlawed, if not destroyed. The reason was probably the same in both cases. No man dared to undertake a fight along the whole line against an ignorant multitude wedded to the superstitions of their forefathers. Again, orthodoxy could better afford to play a waiting game against the polytheism of the East or of the North. It was only towards the end of the Middle Ages, as we shall see, that the Inquisition began its formal campaign against witch-craft. Meanwhile the Church could not have burned whole populations, whose religion on the whole was nearer to that of their Germanic or Scandinavian forefathers than to that of the Apostles. Nor, again, could she wage war to the knife against the Arians, the only heretics who flourished then in the West. Arianism had at one time been practically the State creed in the East;* it came into the West with conquering princes; and the orthodox would have had little hope in physical violence against it until Clovis took it as a convenient excuse for destroying rival chieftains and conquering fresh territory.[1] Thus it was that Glaber was able to regard heresy as a comparatively fresh phenomenon in France and Italy and Germany.

This, as we have already seen, was one symptom of a reviving world. Heretical missionaries from the East began about this time to sow their tares in the West: the story of Orleans has its analogues in cities so far apart as Arras, Cambrai, Châlons, Goslar, Liége, Soissons, Ravenna, Monteforte and Toulouse. Most of these certainly, and probably all, held a predominantly Manichæan creed, though the most recent research is inclined to decide against their being Manichæans pure and simple.

This creed had from the first been the most formidable rival of orthodox Christianity: it had excited equal fear and disgust. It combined Christian elements with Buddhist and other far-Eastern ideas: therefore it was more feared and hated than the completely pagan creeds. After the death of its founder Manes, it was to some extent modified by his disciple Paul of Samosata,

* See note in Appendix.

from whom the believers, in later generations, were often called Paulicians. The Emperors often persecuted the Manichees with banishment or martyrdom, but could not stamp them out. John Zimisces, about A.D. 970, reversed the policy of his predecessors; he tried toleration and transplanted a colony of them to Thrace, "where they multiplied greatly, showing equal vigour in industry and war." We find them also numerous and flourishing in adjacent Bulgaria; and it is at this time that they sent their missionaries so busily westward along the trade routes, with the results recorded by Glaber. Like the gipsies of later times, they were named after the land which Westerners regarded as their original home. *Bulgarus* thenceforward became, in several languages, a term of supreme contempt and abomination, gradually losing its original religious significance; but its primary meaning is recorded in the name of a convert from Manichæism who became one of the cruellest Inquisitors, Robert le Bougre.

The two main characteristics of Manichæism were dualism and extreme asceticism. Their dualism, borrowed probably from Persia, led them to regard the universe as dominated by two almost equal powers, the gods of Light and Darkness respectively. From this derived naturally a similar conception of dualism and constant struggle between mind and matter, the Spirit and the Flesh. The powers of Light shall indeed win in the end; but until then the struggle will be fierce and perpetual, needing all the efforts of well-disposed folk to second those of their Deity. These ideas had a decisive effect upon their attitude towards the Christian Scriptures. For these heretics, the Old Testament is not authoritative but reprobate, as the book of a bygone, materialistic, evil age. Jehovah is Satan; the patriarchs and prophets were Satan's servants. The New Testament, again, must be read not as the Church reads it. Christ was no man in human flesh, but a phantasm, born of a virgin not in reality but in appearance, an emanation from God to combat the powers of Darkness here below. The future life, again, is something far different from what the Church imagines;

rewards and punishments come through the transmigration of souls.

In the second characteristic, asceticism, the Manichæan was as excessive as a few among the earlier Christians had been. He reprobated all sexual commerce, even in matrimony; his diet was strictly vegetarian, rejecting eggs or anything that had had life. This, however, was absolutely binding upon the "perfecti" alone; the ordinary flock, the mere "credentes," seem to have differed from ordinary Catholics in strictness of life only as the Quakers did from the ordinary Englishman under the Stuarts. This self-denial by proxy, as it may be called, was strikingly similar to that which obtained in Catholicism; yet that was no easing of the friction, but rather an aggravation. Just as the monk's ideal of celibacy and abstemious diet was held to endow his prayers with special efficacy, so also with the Manichæan "perfectus." In each case, the multitude was encouraged by, and felt itself more secure in, the self-denial of its leaders. But among religious sects imitation is notoriously the parent of loathing and contention: nor were matters mended here by the extent to which these heretics modelled their organisation upon that of the Catholics, just as these latter had borrowed much of their own from Imperial Rome. It was Manichæism therefore which inspired the fiercest zeal of the Inquisitors, and provided them with their most colourable excuses.

Yet the creed had long fascinated the great mind of Augustine; and, in a sense, he never quite outlived its influence. The struggle is fully recorded in his *Confessions*, which may be called the first formal autobiography in all Western literature and which, in a cheap and accessible English translation, still retains much of its original charm. He tells us how, even after his own studies had shown him the patent absurdity of Manichæan physics, he clung to its metaphysics for many years to come. Indeed, reading between the lines, we may ask ourselves whether he would ever have been entirely converted, but for the personal influence of St. Ambrose at Milan. Ambrose was a splendid representative of the old Roman *gravitas*. As an

eminent lay magistrate, elected to the bishopric by overwhelming popular acclamation before he had even been
formally baptized into Christianity, he brought into the Church
all those qualities which had raised him so high in the State.
We see in the *Confessions* how the younger man was dominated
not so much by what Ambrose said as by what he was. Here was
a man always at work, yet never in a hurry, entirely loyal and
devoted to the great spiritual army in which he had accepted a
general's rank, exploiting all its possibilities for influence and,
once, even bringing one of the greatest of the Emperors to his
knees. Augustine had found among his fellow-heretics nothing
comparable to the solid and stately collectivism embodied in
this bishop; from Ambrose he learned that ideal of a Catholic
Church of which he became, it may be said, the chief apostle
throughout the rest of the Middle Ages and beyond. Yet even
there we find strong traces of his early dualism. The eternal
conflict between Light and Darkness, real and inescapable
enough in all conscience, is often painted in his writings with
Rembrandtesque force. Though his famous *City of God* does not
itself actually draw this crude contrast, yet it did lend itself to
Gregory VII's exaggeration that the Church stands for Light
and the State for Darkness. Take the striking passages in which
St. Augustine protests against the theory of inborn human
innocence. Speaking of his own childhood, he writes: "Who
remindeth me of the sins of my infancy? . . . Who remindeth
me? Doth not each little infant, in whom I see what of myself I
remember not? What then was my sin? Was it that I hung
upon the breast and cried? for should I now so do for food
suitable to my age, justly should I be laughed at and reproved.
What I then did was worthy of reproof; but since I could not
understand reproof, custom and reason forbade me to be
reproved. . . . Was it then good, even for a while, to cry for
what, if given, would hurt? . . . to do its best to strike and
hurt, because commands were not obeyed which had been
obeyed to its hurt. The weakness then of the infant's limbs, not its
will, is its innocence. Myself have seen and known even a baby

envious; it could not speak, yet it turned pale and looked bitterly on its foster-brother. Who knows not this? Mothers and nurses tell you that they allay these things by I know not what remedies. Is that too innocence, when the fountain of milk is flowing in rich abundance, not to endure one to share it, though in extremest need, and whose very life as yet depends thereon? We bear gently with all these things, not as being no or slight evil, but because they will disappear as years increase; for, though tolerated now, the very same tempers are found utterly intolerable when found in riper years."[2]

We need go no further than this to understand why St. Augustine has always been the favourite Father of those who would emphasise the doctrine of Original Sin. Again, whereas St. Thomas Aquinas and all the great Schoolmen put un-baptized children into that limbo of hell in which there is no bodily pain, but deprival of the Beatific Vision, yet it was to St. Augustine's authority that orthodox and conspicuous theologians, almost down into modern times, sometimes condemned the unbaptized to bodily torment also, in their un-redeemed responsibility for Adam's fall.[3]

Major conflict b/n east and west
w/ east {Monichaeanism} ~ subscribing
to dualism — no difference b/n the
good and the evil, since both are contained
w/in one.

CHAPTER IV

The Priest's Responsibility

THE creed brought by these Græco-Bulgarian missionaries was not purely Manichæan. Like Catholicism itself, this institution had developed as time went on; so that there was perhaps as much difference between these Bulgarians and the first Paulicians as between the Church in tenth-century France and in fourth-century Greece. Henceforward, therefore, it will be better to call these heretics by their own chosen name of *Cathari*, "the Pure." In this, again, they resembled the Quakers with their self-chosen name of "Friends"; and in both cases it needs a good deal of search below the surface, with some exercise of imagination, to comprehend the fury which these sects excited at first among their contemporaries.

One primary and most obvious cause was that class-jealousy which is a temptation to specialists of all kinds, not in theology alone. The modern scientist, like the ancient Pharisee, may too often be found dismissing outsiders with "This people who knoweth not the law are cursed" (John vii, 49). Human nature being what it is, that cause probably operated even more strongly in medieval persecution than the frequent documentary evidence enables us to prove.

We must recognise, however, that the Christian clergy were far from the first recorded persecutors for differences of opinion. Plato himself wrote in his *Laws*: "Let this then be the law: No one shall possess shrines of the gods in private houses, and he who is found to possess them, and perform any sacred rites not publicly authorised, shall be informed against to the guardians of the law; and let them issue orders that he shall carry his private rites to the public temples, and if he do not obey, let them inflict a penalty until he comply. And if a

33

person be proven guilty of impiety, not merely from childish levity, but such as grown-up men may be guilty of, let him be punished with death." Nor was he the only philosopher who proved thus false to his own mistress. The Arab Ibn-Roschid, whose name (under the distortion of Averroes) became the bugbear of medieval Christian philosophy, was persecuted himself; but he was willing to punish those of the common folk who did not believe as ignorant men are bound to believe. Yet it was the Muslim priesthood who were mainly instrumental in those persecutions which killed the short-lived efflorescence of philosophy under the Saracen rulers of Spain. They found their tools among the masses, and the time-serving politicians or rulers compliant to that multitude; but, naturally enough, the initiative was mainly with the official priesthood. So again in Christianity, as in Priscillian's case, even among those who did not instigate the crime, there were few who fought actively against it. We are reminded of Clough's cynical couplet in his *New Decalogue:*

> "Thou shalt not kill, but needst not strive
> Officiously to keep alive."

Therefore, as Lea writes with no more than epigrammatic exaggeration (I. 215): "Whenever the State or any of its officials lagged in the enforcement of these laws, the churchman was at hand to goad them on. Thus the African Church repeatedly asked the intervention of the secular power to suppress the Donatists; Leo the Great insisted with the Empress Pulcheria that the destruction of the Eutychians should be her highest care; and Pelagius I, in urging Narses to suppress heresy by force, sought to quiet the scruples of the soldier by assuring him that to prevent or to punish evil was not persecution, but love. It became the general doctrine of the Church, as expressed by St. Isidor of Seville, that princes are bound not only to be orthodox themselves, but to preserve the purity of the faith by the fullest exercise of their power against heretics. How abundantly these assiduous teachings bore

their bitter fruit is shown in the deplorable history of the
Church during those centuries, consisting as it does of heresy
after heresy relentlessly exterminated, until the Council of
Constantinople, under the Patriarch Michael Oxista, introduced
the penalty of burning alive as the punishment of the Bogomili.
Nor were the heretics always behindhand, when they gained
opportunity, in improving the lesson which had been taught
them so effectually."

However, many of the clergy had even stronger reasons than
mere class-jealousy. Fielding's *Joseph Andrews* (to choose only
one witness from that time) shows clearly enough the disgust
excited among careless, selfish and not too moral clergy by
"enthusiasts" like Whitefield and Wesley. The medieval priest
was faced here with a still cruder contrast than that of the
eighteenth century, and had proportionately more reason to
hate the nonconformist. I cannot begin better here than in the
words of an absolutely irreproachable witness. Ralph of
Coggeshall, who wrote about 1200, is one of the most valuable
of our chroniclers for such matters as came under his own
notice. He was a monk of St. Bernard's Order, Cîteaux; and at
this time the Cistercians were the most zealous, not to say most
official, of heresy-hunters, the Dominicans not having yet come
upon the scene. Ralph writes:

"In the days of Louis (VII, 1137–1180), father to King
Philip of France, while the errors of certain heretics, who are
commonly called Publicans, spread secretly through many
provinces of France, a marvellous thing befell in the city of
Reims, in the matter of an old crone infested with this plague.
The lord William, Archbishop of that city and uncle to King
Philip, was riding one day for pastime without the city, attended
by his clergy; when one of his clerks, Master Gervase of Tilbury,*
seeing a maiden walking alone in a vineyard, and impelled by
the wanton curiosity of youth, went aside to her, as we have

* "Gervase of Tilbury, an historian of the thirteenth century, whose career
as a wandering scholar is very interesting, was for some time in the service of
Otto IV, and was made Marshal of the Kingdom of Arles by him."—(*Dict. of
English History*.)

heard from his own mouth in later years when he was a Canon. Having saluted her and asked her whence she came, and who were her parents and what she did there alone, having also observed her comeliness for a while, he began at last to address her in courtly fashion and prayed her of love *par amours*. 'Nay,' replied she, with a simple gesture and a certain gravity in her words, scarce deigning to look at the youth; 'Nay, good youth, God forbid that I should ever be thy leman or any other man's; for if I were once thus defiled, and lost my virginity, I should doubtless suffer eternal damnation beyond all help.' Hearing which, Master Gervase forthwith knew her for one of this most impious sect of Publicans, who in those days were sought out on every hand and destroyed; more especially by Philip Count of Flanders; who by an act of righteous cruelty punished them without mercy; yet some had already come over to England, who were caught at Oxford, and ignominiously branded on the forehead with a white-hot iron at Henry II's bidding and banished the realm. While therefore the clerk aforesaid disputed with the maiden, confuting this answer of hers, the Archbishop came up with his train; and, hearing the cause of this dispute, he bade them take the girl and bring her with him to the city. Then, when he had addressed her in presence of his clergy, and proposed many texts and reasonable arguments to confute her error, she answered that she herself was not so well-instructed as to refute such weighty objections, but confessed that she had a mistress in the city who would easily refute all by her reasonings. When therefore she had revealed this woman's name and abode, the crone was forthwith sought out by the servants, and set before the Archbishop. She therefore—being assaulted on all sides with texts from Holy Scripture, both by the Archbishop himself and by his clergy, that they might convince her of so heinous an error—yet she, by a certain sinister subtlety of interpretation, so perverted all the texts they cited, that all understood clearly enough how the Spirit of all Error spake through her mouth. For she replied so easily, with so ready a memory, to all the texts and stories objected to her, whether from the Old or the New Testament, as though she had acquired a knowledge of the whole Scriptures* and had been always practised in answers of this kind; mingling falsehood with truth and baffling the true explanation of our faith with a certain pernicious understanding. Since, therefore, the obstinate minds of both women could be recalled neither by fair words nor foul, nor by any citations or texts of Scripture, from the error of their ways, therefore they were shut up in his prison until the morrow. On the next day they were summoned again to the Archbishop's hall, before him and all his clergy, and in the presence of noble men; where they were again publicly challenged to renounce their errors, and many reasons were again alleged. Yet they would by no means admit his salutary warnings, but rather persisted immovably in the errors they had conceived; wherefore they were unanimously adjudged to the stake. When therefore the fire was already kindled in the city, and they should have been dragged by the serjeants to the penalty to which they had been condemned, then that wicked mistress of error cried aloud: 'O madmen and unjust judges! Think ye to burn me now with your fires? I fear not your doom, nor shudder at the flames ye have prepared.' With these words, she suddenly drew from her bosom a spool of thread, which she cast through a great window of the hall, yet keeping the clue in her hand, and crying with a loud voice in all men's hearing: 'Catch!' No sooner had she spoken this word, than she was caught up from the ground, and followed the ball like a bird through the window, under all men's eyes: for, as we believe, those same evil spirits bore her away who of old lifted Simon Magus into the air.† But what became of that witch, or whither she was spirited away, no man of that company could

---

* This, as will presently be seen, was one main characteristic of the heretics.

† For this legend see Vincent of Beauvais (*Spec. Hist.*, lib. IX, c. 12) and the *Golden Legend* (Temple Classics, Vol. IV, p. 15): "Then said Simon: it is not as thou sayest, but I shall show to thee the power of my dignity, that anon thou shalt adore me; I am first truth, and may flee by the air; I can make new trees and turn stones into bread; endure in the fire without hurting; and all that I will I may do. So Peter disputed against all these, and disclosed all his malefices."

discover. Meanwhile the maiden, who had not yet come to such
a pitch of madness in that sect, remained behind. No persuasion
of reason, no promise of riches, could recall her from her foolish
obstinacy; wherefore she was burned to death, to the ad-
miration of many who marked how she uttered no sighs, no
tears, no laments, but bore with constancy and cheerfulness all
torments of the consuming flames, even as the martyrs of
Christ (yet for how different a cause!) who were slain in old times
by the heathen in defence of the Christian religion."

One of the most significant points, perhaps, in this whole
story is the writer's obvious confidence in the reader's sympathy
not with the girl but with the clergy. That incidents of this kind
were not infrequent we may gather from Peter the Precentor of
Paris, one of the most learned and pious of Ralph's contemp-
poraries.[1] After complaining that the Church of his time dealt
more harshly with heretics than the pagans had dealt with the
early Christians, he goes on: "Moreover, certain honest matrons,
refusing to consent to the lasciviousness of priests 'of the seed of
Canaan' (Daniel xiii, 56) have been written by such priests in
the book of death, and accused as heretics, and even condemned
by a certain notoriously foolish zealot for the Christian faith,
while rich heretics were simply blackmailed and suffered to
depart. One man, because he was poor and pallid, though he
faithfully confessed the faith of Christ on all points, and
sheltered himself under the hope thereof, yet was burned
because he said to the assembled bishops that he would by no
means submit to the ordeal of red-hot iron unless they could
first show him that he could do so without mortal sin and
without tempting God. Hearing this, they abandoned him
with one accord [to the secular arm], telling the king that it was
not lawful for them to be present at a judgment which involved
the shedding of blood." Lea quotes another case (I. 87):
"About 1220 a clerk of Spire, whose austerity subsequently led
him to join the Franciscans, was only saved by the interposition
of Conrad, afterwards Bishop of Hildesheim, from being burned
as a heretic, because his preaching led certain women to lay

aside their vanities of apparel and behave with humility."

It is, in fact, difficult to exaggerate the extent to which
medieval heresy and infidelity were bred or encouraged by the
ignorance and immorality which prevailed (the word is not too
strong) among the clergy. For one of Chaucer's model Poor
Parsons, his friend Gower, who goes more statistically into the
question, implies a score of the sort sometimes satirised in
The Canterbury Tales and *Piers Plowman*. To put it again in
terms of Fielding, there were a score of Parsons Barnabas and
Trulliber to one Parson Adams. We have here not only the
complaints of the most irreproachable contemporaries, for
more than five centuries before the Reformation, but the most
unexceptionable official documents. There is far too little
candour on this subject among modern historians, some of
whom seem more concerned for social charity or for the quiet
conventions of club-life than for search into the naked causes of
events. To write of the Inquisition without plain speech on this
subject is (as Lord Acton complained) as much as "to write the
story of the French Revolution without the guillotine."

Briefly, therefore, the evidence for clerical ignorance in the
Middle Ages is almost beyond belief. At the end of the period,
Erasmus's contempt for his fellow-clerics is well known; but
it is not sufficiently realised that even these of 1530 had im-
proved upon their forefathers, if only a little and by slow degrees.
St. Boniface had to negotiate with Pope Zacharias about the
case of a priest who did not know the simple baptismal formula,
and had said *in nomine patria et filia* instead of *in nomine patris
et filii*. Giraldus Cambrensis (1200) exposes their occasional
ignorance in face of quite simple phrases in their own services.
An official record, in 1222, of the examination of priest-vicars
under the Dean and Chapter of Salisbury shows us, in seventeen
parishes, five priests who could not construe even the first words
of the central prayer of the Mass, beginning *Te igitur clemen-
tissime Pater*. St. Thomas More quotes as proverbial the man
who ludicrously misunderstood those same words, imagining
that Clement was a person. Roger Bacon, wishing to describe

mere parrot-learning, and catching at an example which will be immediately intelligible to his contemporaries, writes: "just as boys gabble through the Psalter which they have learnt, and as clerks and country priests recite the Church services, of which they know little or nothing, like brute beasts." St. Thomas Aquinas makes a similar confession: so do St. Bonaventura, St. Bernardino, St. Catharine of Siena, the Cistercian Cæsarius of Heisterbach and the cultured Florentine citizen Sacchetti. St. Bonaventura (or possibly some almost equally competent contemporary) sent round a circular letter to the Franciscan Order. He wrote: "There are in Italy so many inexperienced clergy that, even if they be well taught in grammar and other knowledge, yet when a hundred or more rectors and vicars are gathered together, there are scarce any who have in fact enough knowledge of the Scriptures to manage either the souls committed to their care, or other things necessary for salvation." The Prelates (he continues), "given up to worldly cares, wink at these faults, so that there is scarce any hope of amendment; nay, even if at times they would fain correct such shortcomings and remove the unprofitable clergy, they have none better to put in their room." We find instances of priests unable to stammer out correctly even those six Latin syllables upon which Transubstantiation depends, *Hoc est corpus meum*, and whose congregations were therefore deluded into worshipping a mere wafer as God. At the end of the Middle Ages, when books were far less rare than they had been before the rise of the Universities, wills and inventories seldom show even a single volume in the possession of an ordinary well-to-do priest. Only a very small proportion, also, had ever been to a University, and a still smaller proportion of those who entered had proceeded to any degree. It had been one of Charlemagne's most difficult tasks to raise the country clergy from their ignorance; and, while he attempted this by sending some of them to study in monasteries, his son was compelled to abandon the attempt as more injurious to monastic discipline than fruitful for clerical education. Erasmus tells us how his contemporary bishop of

Utrecht, after putting all his energies into raising the intellectual and moral standard of his priesthood, finally gave it up in despair.

For here, as so often, ignorance and immorality tended to go hand in hand. No hostile critic has dared, except in petty skirmishes, to grapple with H. C. Lea's *History of Sacerdotal Celibacy*, which may now be bought in a cheap popular edition.[2] More important still, from the evidential point of view, are the two volumes on the same subject, published in 1829 and re-published in 1845, of the two brothers Theiner in Germany. Both were Roman Catholics and scholars of exceptional learning: the younger filled for some years one of the most responsible of all historical posts as Prefect of the Vatican Archives. Not only do these, previously and independently, cite in nine cases out of ten the same authorities as Lea, but they conclude on a still more pessimistic note. The law of celibacy, they say, has never been really kept except at exceptionally favourable times and places; far from strengthening the Church morally, it has been a perpetual canker, worst when it is most secret; and they openly plead for the speedy abolition of a rule which has so patently failed. At the time they wrote, it was notorious that the ordinary priest was often an unmarried husband in Italy, and especially in Spain. In Spain, indeed, the custom still holds.[3] And all this is a legacy from the Middle Ages. Official episcopal visitations, published only since Lea's death, show among the 281 parishes of Hereford diocese eighty priests accused of unchastity, sometimes multiple, or again with married women. This was in 1397, while Chaucer was still alive. The statistics of a similar visitation in Lausanne diocese, the most civilised in Switzerland, give slightly more unfavourable results (1416).

In many other ways, also, the clergy too often set an evil example. Prince-bishops made war on each other or on lay barons. One of the severest Inquisitional judges, later on, was the Bishop of Albi, who had regal rights which enabled him to claim what was elsewhere enjoyed only by sovereigns, a half-ill-repute of high church offices – bishoprics, archbishoprics.

share in the revenues from confiscations of heretics' property. His successor, in 1310, "to settle a quarrel with the Seigneur de Puygozon, raised an army of 5,000 men with which he attacked the royal Château Vieux d'Albi, and committed much devastation." Such instances were rare in England, where "the King's Peace" was much more of a reality: but concerning the Continental prelates a scholar of about 1200 writes: "These mitred bishops are dumb dogs [in the church]; yet they are ready for prey and indecently crowned; they bear the lance in place of pastoral staff, and the helmet for mitre, the shield in place of stole."[4]

Such were the temptations besetting these ecclesiastical barons that it became a serious question among men of real piety whether a bishop could go to heaven. Churchmen of sensitive conscience sometimes repudiated the office as too dangerous for their souls. Thus St. Bonaventura refused the Archbishopric of York; and when Albert the Great, St. Thomas Aquinas's master, accepted the see of Regensburg, the General of his Dominican Order wrote in distress and rebuke: "Who would believe that you, in the very evening of life, would set such a blot on your own glory and on that of the Order which you have done so much to augment? Consider that which hath befallen those men who have suffered themselves to be drawn into such offices; consider what their reputation now is, what fruits they have brought forth, and how they have ended their lives!" John of Salisbury alludes to a debate of his own time— only half-serious, of course—"Can an archdeacon be saved?"[5]

Sale of Church offices.

For not bishops only, but thousands of clergy who had family influence or money, with a smaller number whose abilities and force of character recommended them, amassed pluralities and sinecures which sometimes put them among the wealthiest men in Europe; even, perhaps, above some of the minor princes. The sale of Church offices was constant and unblushing; it was lamented as one of the worst and most notorious of social evils. Glaber complains that the Church of his day is eaten up with this canker: that from top to bottom financial corruption

the hierarchy are infected with greed and avarice. Shortly after his day, Pope Gregory VI bought the tiara for a huge sum, and confessed afterwards the justice of that Emperor's mandate by which he was deposed and exiled. Not long afterwards came Gregory VII, one of the two strongest Popes of the last ten centuries. He set himself seriously to cleanse this Augean stable, but with little effect even in his own lifetime. In later generations, the traffic in benefices became more and more of an open system. In fifteenth-century England we meet with the "chop-church," the holy broker, as a regular profession. The ordinary clergy had scarcely any professional training except the rule-and-thumb method of beginning as parish clerk and gradually passing on to the diaconate and priesthood. Thus, while some of these clerics were among the most eager and selfish capitalists of the age, a multitude of the lower clergy had little or no more than the better-to-do peasants. Such members of the ecclesiastical proletariate were compelled to wrangle with their parishioners for the smaller tithes and the casual fees; thus their poverty, however undeservedly, caused almost as much scandal as the prelate's superfluity and pomp. In proportion as men of the later Middle Ages had grown to fear the priest less, they were apt to dislike him more. In the early thirteenth century, when the priesthood were perhaps at their highest power in Europe, orthodox writers tell us that men regard it as an evil omen to meet a priest by the way. He was already to some extent what Lina Duff-Gordon describes in her *Home Life in Italy* for modern times, the harbinger of death in the cottage, which he seldom entered except for the funeral rites: so that "the Priest has come!"—*è venuto il Prete*—sounds like a knell. St. Thomas More, even when he strives his hardest to make a case for the Church against Tyndale, confesses that there are far too many priests in England, chosen with far too little care, and often employed in menial jobs which naturally brought upon them the contempt of menials. The Spanish envoy reported to Charles V just before the Reformation, from London: "nearly all the people here hate the priests."

For one constant thread runs through the whole documentary evidence, from the time when records become full enough to allow us to judge. Significant beyond all the scandalous incidents recorded, and all the complaints of disciplinarians, is the comparative impunity—too often the absolute impunity— of the sinner. The preamble of Henry VIII's statute for the Dissolution of the Monasteries goes no farther than the most unexceptionable ecclesiastical testimonies, when it points out that the most notorious shortcomings of the last two centuries and more had in no way been amended. The episcopal registers and similar records often show the most notorious clerical offenders not only ending their days in worldly prosperity, but perhaps going on from strength to strength. A little of this evidence has been brought out recently by Mr. Geoffrey Baskerville in his *English Monks and the Suppression of the Monasteries*. I deal with the subject in detail in *Five Centuries of Religion*, Vol. II, Chapters XX–XXII. The scandal of this continual impunity can be read in the writings of the Saints. St. Bernard wrote, just when the Catharist menace was becoming serious, "we can no longer say with Isaiah 'As the people, so is the priest,' for our priests are worse than the people." Worse, that is, not absolutely (since there has probably been no time when the average cleric has not lived more regularly than the average layman) but worse in their neglect of opportunities and in the scandalous contrast with their lofty profession. Four generations later, St. Bonaventura made a similar complaint. St. Catharine of Siena wrote so plainly concerning the Italian priesthood in her day that the English translation published under official Roman censorship discreetly and silently suppresses all her too candid descriptions.[6]

Erasmus's complaints are well known; but too little attention is paid to Dean Colet's Sermon before Convocation, in which he pointed out that all these scandals had long since been condemned, and re-condemned again and again, by Popes and Councils, so that no more was needed for real reform than that the authorities should at last address themselves in earnest to enforce their own time-honoured regulations. And all through these indignant protests there runs the sad refrain: "This it is which affords the most colourable excuse for the heretics who afflict our Church." It is absurd to ignore these testimonies, or to dismiss them, as is often done by well-meaning modern writers, as mere demonstrations of saintly crotchets and ascetic over-sensitiveness. St. Bernardino of Siena, a little younger than Chaucer, was not only the greatest preacher of his day in Europe, but a scholar of distinction and a most conscientious persecutor of heretics. In one of his sermons, taking for his text the slime-pits of the valley of Sodom and Gomorrah (Gen. xiv, 10), he says: "The first pit of slime is infidelity or default of faith. For very many folk, considering the wicked life of monks and friars and nuns and clergy, are shaken by this—nay, oftentimes fail in faith, and believe in naught higher than the roof of their own house, not esteeming those things to be true which have been written concerning our faith, but believing them to have been written by the cozening invention of man and not by God's inspiration; having no faith in the divine Scriptures or in the holy Doctors, even as the Prophet testifieth concerning the unfaithful Christians of this present time, saying: 'Nor were they counted faithful in his covenant.' From hence it followeth that they believe not in virtue, despise the Sacraments of the Church, hold that the soul hath no existence, neither shun vices nor respect virtues, neither fear hell nor desire heaven, but cling with all their hearts to transitory things, and resolve that this world shall be their paradise."

CHAPTER V

Priests and People

IT may be asked: If the medieval clergy were really so defective by modern standards, how had they so much influence upon the persecution of nonconformists as the records show on their very face, and as we can read between the lines of the documents? If the masses disliked the priest, why did they support him in this struggle, often for life and death? How explain this fact?

To begin with, the fact itself is often exaggerated, as I think the documents will show as we go along. Secondly, the nonconformist was often hated and dreaded not for his antagonism to the priest, but (a very different thing) for his inconvenient and suspicious innovations: for his call to a change of heart and a readjustment of moral values. This is universally acknowledged nowadays in explanation of the persecution of the early Quakers; and those same psychological causes operated even more strongly and instinctively in the Middle Ages. St. Thomas More may help us here again. In his defence of the clergy against the lawyer St. Germain he reminds this distinguished layman that, after all, the clerics are drawn from the laity, and are likely to show some of the defects which beset society in general during their own day. The rough and uncultured priest whom we so often find in the records was at his best the cream, and at his worst the froth, on the surface of a rough and uncultured multitude. Therefore there was fellow-feeling between them, even though respect might be wanting. The ecclesiastical baron was hail-fellow-well-met with other barons, who were often his brethren in the flesh or sometimes even his sons: at Rouen, for instance, very near to Glaber's time, the see was occupied by three archbishops in succession who were

46

married or quasi-married men. The parish priest and his brother
the ploughman might form the same model pair as they do in
The Canterbury Tales; or, on the other hand, their fellowship
might be rather that of the ale-house bench. Thus there was a
sympathy between them even while they quarrelled, and parson
or parishioner might well have treated any intruder, however
well-meaning, as Sganarelle and his wife treat Monsieur Robert
in the *Médecin Malgré Lui:* "Je la veux battre si je le veux, et
ne la veux pas battre si je ne le veux pas. . . . C'est ma femme,
et non pas la vôtre. . . . Je n'ai que faire de votre aide."
Moreover, all ages have shown a distinction in men's minds—
perhaps a necessary and wholesome distinction—between the
priest's person and his office. Dr. Dill notes this in the Eastern
cults of later paganism—Mithras, Cybele, etc. The multitude
were fascinated by the ritual with its psychological mass-
suggestion, while they despised the celebrant. When Gregory
VII tried to put down clerical concubinage by forbidding
attendance at the Mass of any notoriously concubinary priest,
this did not purify the churches so much as it emptied them;
therefore, so great was the reaction, that before the Inquisition
was founded, it had already become a heresy to hold that the
miracle of Transubstantiation was in any way affected by the
moral character of the Transubstantiator. Here, again, we may
get sidelights from certain modern populations in which the
medieval tradition survives most completely. A writer in
French Canada tells us how the belief in the priest's supernatural power often overrules all personal considerations. A
farmer, reporting to a friend his heated discussion with the
parson concerning disputed tithes, added: "I would have sent
him off with a kick behind, if only I had been sure my leg
would not wither up!" Travellers in Spain, such as Townsend
in 1786 and Rafael Shaw in 1910, note the faithfulness of the
people to their traditional and picturesque ceremonies, even in
minds otherwise bitterly anti-clerical. The latter writes (p. 16):
"The crucial question of to-day in Spain is the religious question.
Not the belief or disbelief of the people in their religion, but the

relations of the Church—i.e., that of the priests and, far more, of the Religious Orders—to the nation." And again (p. 18): "The steady and continuous efforts made by the Church to upset the existing régime and bring back a reign of absolutism with the proscribed branch of the House of Bourbon, though not continually present in the minds of the people, are not unknown to or ignored by them. But with all this intensely anti-clerical feeling, the mass of the people are untouched by modern scepticism and are deeply and sincerely religious. Their religion is simple in the extreme: many would call it gross superstition: but, such as it is, it suits their stage of intellectual development and undoubtedly has a considerable effect on their conduct. To represent the Spanish working man—as the Church newspapers always do—as an atheist and an anarchist, only to be restrained by force overthrowing the social order, merely proves how completely ignorant the Clericalists are of his real character."[1]

Mr. M. P. Charlesworth, in his Raleigh Lecture for this year 1937 before the British Academy, laid great emphasis upon the extent to which the Roman Empire, even in its decadence, was kept up by imperial propaganda. He warns us rightly against taking that word in its merely insidious sense; "propaganda" includes the propagation of all sorts of ideas—good, bad, or indifferent. One of the most powerful of imperial propagandist methods was through the coinage. "Coins passed through the hands of the highest and the lowest, into the coffers of the rich and under the country farmer's hearthstone; and upon these coins were placed words and symbols that could be understood by the simplest. . . . Thus, wherever a man was and wherever he went, he could find objects that focused his political and his religious emotions alike upon one centre, the emperor and the imperial house." When we turn from that Totalitarian State of antiquity to this Totalitarian Religious State of the Middle Ages, must we not recognise that the latter had one line of propaganda which has never been surpassed in recorded history: the doctrine of Transubstantiation. The commonest village

priest (it was held) could do what the archangels themselves
were impotent to perform; he could daily work a miracle that
was beyond the power even of that blessed Virgin who, in
most men's minds, was almost a Fourth Person of the Trinity.
Anyone, wherever he was and wherever he went, was confronted with this a hundred times a year, if not every day.
Thus, century after century, the Mass bore up the Priest; until at
last, as popular education slowly spread, and when long
experience had borne in upon the lay folk that the clergy were
men of like passions with themselves, then the priest was at
last dislodged from his pedestal, and the Mass fell with him.
It was here as in the last generations of Imperial Rome, when
the Emperor's coins still proclaimed him as *semper invictus*,
and the barbarian hordes were overrunning the Empire.

Thus, on reflection, we have no reason to be surprised that the
earliest heretical manifestations in the West should have
provoked violent popular reaction and frequent cases of lynch-
law. Later, again, when the battle had been raging for generations, and the heretics, defeated in the field, still held out in
guerilla warfare, it was natural that popular feeling should
become more or less reconciled to the persecuted side, if not
definitely and actively favourable. And this is precisely what
the documentary evidence will show us.

We have seen how, in the case of the eleventh-century
heretics, the civil magistrates and the populace were ready to
second the Church authorities, and sometimes to outstrip them.
This phase lasted, in places where the heresy was new, down to
the middle of the twelfth century. At Soissons, in 1114, the
Bishop imprisoned some, and went to Beauvais to consult his
fellow-bishop on the measures to be taken. In his absence the
people, fearing that the clergy might be too lenient—*clericalem
verens mollitiem*—broke open the prison and dragged the
heretics to a fire outside the city. So again, in 1144, at Liége: the
Bishop hoped to convert them, but the mob would have burned
all, and did in fact burn a few whom the Bishop could not
protect. At Cologne, again, a group were burned by the

populace in spite of clerical attempts to convert them by
persuasion. In 1051, heretics were hanged at Goslar in presence
of the Emperor and with popular consent; but this provoked a
memorable protest from one of the greatest bishops of the
century, Wazo of Liége, whose writings did much in later days
to inspire the Church policy of Gregory VII. He condemned the
Goslar executions, as St. Martin had done that of Priscillian.
Again, the Bishop of Châlons, having captured some heretics,
wrote to consult Wazo: should he hand them over to the
secular arm? *No*, replied Wazo: that would be to act against the
Spirit of the Church and even against the Saviour's express
teaching in the parable: "Nay, lest while ye gather up the
tares, ye root up also the wheat with them." For (pursued the
Bishop) those who to-day are tares may to-morrow be converted
to wheat, and reign above us in heaven: therefore let us indeed
excommunicate them at present, but let them live.

We have here, unfortunately, the high-water mark of
medieval toleration, so far as orthodoxy is concerned. For
Wazo, it will be observed, speaks of no civil penalty whatever;
he recommends only that excommunication which is patently
justifiable, since every institution has the natural right of
ejecting those who cannot conform to its laws or its spirit. But
no pope or cardinal or bishop or orthodox schoolman will henceforward commit himself to such an edict of toleration. Even
Peter the Precentor of Paris admits prison for the heretic; and
St. Bernard, a greater man, admits still more. For this Saint's
words are commonly misrepresented by writers who have
evidently not studied the context, nor even read the sentence
immediately following upon that which they quote. He did
indeed heartily reprobate lynch-law for the heretics, and write
"faith must be persuaded to men, and not imposed upon them."
But he immediately adds: "yet it would be better that they
were coerced by the sword of that [magistrate] who 'beareth not
the sword in vain,' than that they should be suffered to bring
many others into their own error. 'For he is the minister of God,
a revenger to execute wrath upon him that doeth evil.' " And

this quotation from Romans, xiii, 4, is reinforced by other passages in those two sermons of St. Bernard's (the sixty-fourth and sixty-fifth of the series on the *Canticle of Canticles*) approving the banishment or imprisonment of all heretics who preach their doctrines openly. Even St. Bernard, therefore, could not go farther in tolerance than this, considering the overwhelming super-importance of dogmatic faith; and no orthodox theologian of his Church ever went beyond him until modern times.

With him, we now reach a point where heresy has ceased to be merely sporadic and has become endemic in the most civilised districts of the West. These pronouncements by St. Bernard were in response to his friend Erwin, Provost (i.e. Prior) of Steinbach in Rhineland. Erwin had described these heretics as apparently inoffensive: they did, indeed, travel about with women, but so, he remembers, had the Apostles done; and he brings no accusation of actual impropriety. Again, it was admitted that in diet and other ways they showed an example of great self-restraint, and Erwin notes that these heretics constantly appealed to Christ's words as a criterion between themselves and the orthodox: "By their fruits ye shall know them." St. Bernard's answer shows how overwhelmingly the question of religious faith outweighs all other social, or even moral, questions. He knows well enough how fateful this question of comparative morals is; he has laid elsewhere his finger on the open sore of the Church, confessing that the priests are worse than the people, if not absolutely, at least relatively to their profession. He admits in these heretics an apparent regularity of life, and even their semblance of belief: "If you inquire into [such a man's] faith, nothing is more Christian: if into his conversation, nothing is more blameless; and he proves by his deeds what he speaks with his mouth. You may see the man, in witness of his faith, frequenting the church, honouring the priests, offering his gift, making his confession, communicating in the sacraments. What can be more faithful? As regards life and morals, he cozens no man, overreaches none, does violence to none. Moreover, he is pale with fasting;

he eats no bread of idleness; he works with his hands for his livelihood. Where, then, is the fox?" The allusion, of course, is to Cant. II, 15, and St. Bernard explains how this man is one of the "little foxes" that must be caught, because they ravage "the Lord's vineyard." This going about with women is very dangerous; he cannot indeed assert (though he suspects) that it has borne fruit in evil deeds, but certainly the Church has forbidden it; and it is wicked to appeal against the Church to the example of Apostles in the New Testament. Moreover, the one sin which heretics themselves cannot deny is that of giving holy things to the dogs. Thus St. Bernard, in his incautious contempt, practically repeats the Jewish argument of John vii, 47: "Are ye also deceived? Have any of the rulers or of the Pharisees believed on him?" For he points out how these men, who presume to set up their ideas against the Church, "are a vile and rustic crew, unlettered and altogether unwarlike"; their converts are "ignorant peasant women, and of such a sort as I have always found all folk of this sect whom I have known as yet." Even their righteousness is but as filthy rags: "They do indeed abstain, but they abstain heretically." How, then, are they to be brought to this one all-saving Faith, without which their good works are vain? Here is the question which will exercise all zealous Churchmen for a full century, until it receives at last a clear answer to the Inquisition.

St. Bernard's contemporary, Abailard, is embarrassed also by the multitude of sects which are forming and setting themselves up against the Church. We shall come to his evidence later on: but meanwhile it may be well to give in detail the life-story of one of the most remarkable among these heretics. It is in many ways typical, though the man himself was the most eccentric-minded of the batch. Here, then, is the contemporary account, from an Augustinian Chronicler of the most orthodox zeal.[2]

About 1145, St. Bernard's pupil Eugenius III held a great Council at Reims: "and, as he sat therein with full session of bishops and nobles, a certain pestilent fellow was brought before him. This man, full of devilish spirit, had by his magic cunning seduced so many people that, trusting in the multitude of his followers, he wandered formidably from place to place, hostile to churches and especially to monasteries. Thus, when he had raged long and wildly (*diu multumque debacchatus*), wisdom at length overcame his malice and he was caught by the Archbishop of Reims, who brought him before the Holy Council. His name was Eudo, a Breton by nation, surnamed *De l'Étoile*; an unlettered and ignorant man, so crazed with demoniacal illusions that, since he was called *Eun* in the Gallic tongue, he believed his own person to be intended in that phrase of ecclesiastical exorcism, "[I adjure thee] in the name of Him who shall come to judge the quick and the dead, and to try the world through fire."* He was so arrant a fool that he could not distinguish between *Eum* and *Eun*; but that in his most stupendous blindness he believed himself to be Lord and Judge of the quick and dead. By his diabolical magic he was so powerful in catching the souls of the simple that, as a spider with flies, so he ensnared and gathered around him a multitude of dupes, who all followed him inseparably as Lord or Lords. Sometimes, also, he moved from district to district with amazing speed; at other times he dwelt with all his followers in waste and inaccessible places, whence at the devil's instigation he would burst suddenly forth, especially as attacker [*infestator*] of churches and monasteries. Oftentimes his acquaintance and kinsfolk (for he was not of plebeian birth) came unto him, either in order to rebuke him with familiar boldness or that they might cautiously enquire how matters went with him. For there appeared around him an immense glory, with royal pomp and pride; and his companions seemed free from care or labour, preciously attired, feasting sumptuously and living in the utmost joy; so that many who came to rebuke him, seeing his false and fantastic glory, were corrupted. For it was devils who made these fantastic shows; devils who fed that wretched multitude in those waste places with no true and solid food,

* *Per* Eum *qui venturus est judicare viros et mortuos, et seculum per ignem.*

but with airy nothings. For (as I heard afterwards from some who had been in his company and who, when he was taken from them, wandered as penitents throughout the world) they found at their bidding, at the prompting of every wish, bread, flesh and fish and all most choice goods. Yet that those same goods were not solid but unsubstantial, invisibly ministered by the spirits of this air, rather to catch souls than to feed them, is clear from this; that, however freely they had eaten to repletion of these goods, then, after but small eructation, there followed forthwith such hunger that they were compelled to turn again without delay to the selfsame viands. But whosoever had chanced to join their company and had tasted even a morsel of their food, that man's mind was changed forthwith, and he adhered to the filthy multitude. Moreover, it was not without peril to receive anything from them, of whatever kind. In short, a certain knight of this pestilent fellow's kindred is said to have come to him and warned him simply to abjure that abominable sect and return to his own family through communion of Christian grace. Éon, keeping the man cunningly in suspense, showed him in manifold sort the abundance of his unsubstantial riches, to catch him with the flattering bait of things seen. 'Thou art my kinsman' (he said), 'take what thou wilt and as much as thou wilt.' The knight, as a prudent man, having poured his words of reproof upon the air, took his leave and departed. His squire, however, saw a falcon of marvellous beauty, and coveted this to his own ruin: he besought and received it, and followed his departing master with rejoicing. The knight bade him cast it without delay from his wrist, saying: 'This is no bird, but a devil in that shape.' The truth whereof was soon revealed. For, when the fool paid no heed to his warning, he first cried out that the falcon gripped his fist too sore in its talons; then the bird caught him up into the air and he was never more seen. Thus, seeing that this pestilent fellow, through the operation of Satan, raged as I have related, an army was sent again and again to seek him out and prosecute him; but in vain, for when they sought him he was not to be found. At last, however, he was baulked of help from the demons; and, since Satan no longer suffered him to rage through their agency (for they can do no more than, by God's just judgment, the higher powers let them loose to do), he was easily arrested by the Archbishop of Reims, and the foolish multitude who followed him were scattered abroad. Further, his disciples were caught with him, who were his closest adherents and fellow-workers. When therefore he was set before the face of the Council, and asked by the Pope who he was, he made answer: 'I am Eun, who shall come to judge the quick and the dead and to try the world through fire.' Now he held in his hand a staff of strange shape, forked at the upper end. When asked what that staff signified, he said: 'It is a matter of great mystery. For when (as ye now see) it looketh heavenwards with its two heads, then God possesseth two parts of the world and leaveth the third unto me. Then, if I bow those two heads of my staff to earth, and raise that lower and single part to heaven, I shall leave only a third share unto God, keeping two for myself.' At this the whole assembly broke into laughter, mocking this man who was so deeply given over to a reprobate mind. So the Council decreed that he should be diligently kept in guard, lest this plague should creep about again; and he lived but a short while afterwards. He had distinguished his disciples with great names, calling one Wisdom, another Knowledge, another Judgement, and so forth with the rest. Seeing that these would on no account accept sound teaching, but rather gloried most obstinately in their false names, so that he who was called Justice, with unhappy confidence, threatened his gaolers with a sentence of vengeance, these men were brought first to the law-court and then to the stake, choosing rather to burn than to be corrected and live. I have heard from a venerable man who was present when these things were done that, when this so-called Justice was being led to his death, he cried again and again: 'O Earth, cleave asunder!' as though at the bidding of his mouth the earth should open and swallow up his enemies like Dathan and

Abiram. Such was the force of this error, once fixed in their hearts."

The value of a contemporary account like this lies in the double light it casts on the mentality of the age. The painting reveals the painter himself; while he tells us about the persecuted heretic, we are taking the measure of this orthodox persecutor, one of the soberest and most trustworthy chroniclers in the twelfth century, which was an age of great chroniclers.

church position re: coporal punishment for heresy was at best ambiguous.

CHAPTER VI

Hesitations of the Hierarchy

RULE OF LYNCH-LAW

THERE was thus nothing even approaching an official and definite Church law as to the punishment of heretics. Lynch law, with or without clerical encouragement, supplied a rule-of-thumb policy: these sporadic tares were violently uprooted wherever they grew up.

But gradually the heresies became something much more than sporadic. The early twelfth century witnessed in France a revival of classical studies more remarkable than any other until the Italian Renaissance: Chartres was here the principal school and Orleans the next. The contemporary philosophico-theological movement was equally remarkable: Abailard with his pupils and his opponents are types of an activity which culminated in the foundation of Universities at the end of the century. And, in proportion as the wheat grew up, so did the tares, after their own nature. The practical problem, therefore, became urgent.

Leo IX, at the Council of Reims (1049), had decreed excommunication against heretics, but added no word for or against further punishment. Calixtus II, at the Council of Toulouse (1119), called upon the secular arm against them. Innocent II, who practically owed his tiara to St. Bernard, invoked the secular arm still more plainly at the Ecumenical Lateran Council of 1139. The Council of Reims in 1148 was presided over by St. Bernard's pupil Eugenius III; it forbade anyone to receive or give even passing refuge to the heretics of Southern France; a decree which would seem to take their forcible expulsion for granted. It is at this point that we find heresy so far advanced and so widespread that the problem of wheat and tares becomes urgent and inescapable. The

temporising policy of the last hundred and fifty years can now
no longer be maintained: the official Church must soon make
up its mind one way or another. Therefore the tide will set
definitely in favour of death for heresy: yet it is not until 1209
that Vacandard finds the first instance of a council openly
claiming this as the Law of the Church: death (it is now
claimed) must be inflicted "according to Canon Law and State
Law"—*secundum canonicas et legitimas sanctiones*.

It must be repeated here—for that is at the root of the whole
matter—that there never has been a time at which the medieval
creed was both thoroughly probed and consistently accepted.
The so-called Ages of Faith were only Ages of Acquiescence:
with rare exceptions, belief was less active than passive. The
brief revival of learning under Charlemagne and Louis the Pious
produced a few thinkers who, if they had not been scattered
voices preaching in the wilderness, might have revolutionised
Church teaching. Such, for instance, was the story of Claudius
of Turin and Agobard of Lyons: both bishops, and one a
canonised saint, yet both preaching doctrines which, under the
Inquisition, would have brought them infallibly to the stake.
Charlemagne himself had led, within his whole empire, the
opposition to that image-worship which had finally fought its
way to the front in Christendom. Under his influence, the great
Synod of Frankfort decided against the adoration of images,
and Charlemagne practically called on the Pope to change his
own mind. A few years later, Agobard and Claudius both fought
against this prevailing custom as a practical revival of idolatry.
Agobard wrote roundly: "Things are (nowadays) believed by
Christians of such absurdity as no one ever could aforetime
induce the heathen to believe." He boldly rebuked again the
"absurdity" of attributing literal verbal inspiration to the
Bible. At the same time he bitterly resented the popularity of
the Jews at Louis's court, and the fact that their preaching was
often more admired than that of the Catholic clergy. In his
contemporary John the Scot (Eriugena) Europe produced one
of the most original of all medieval philosophers, and one of

the most difficult to reconcile with orthodoxy. These men thought and taught among the most advanced city populations, or at the court of intellectually-minded monarchs; but as yet there was no province where the general soil was favourable enough for such seeds to germinate freely. The time and place came at last in the twelfth century, and in Languedoc.

This story is summarised in a page of Macaulay's *Essay on Ranke* which, apart from that specially Macaulayesque glitter for which we must always make allowance, remains in accord with the latest modern research. There was scarcely any other portion of the Roman Empire in which the population had been able to keep so much of the old imperial culture, in comparative security from the Northern invaders, as here under the Southern sun. Some of the southern prelates, in the earlier Christian centuries, had been worthy pupils of those schools of rhetoric and philosophy which, under the later Roman Empire, had sometimes flourished more brilliantly in Provence than in Italy itself. There was a greater mixture of races here than in any other part of what we now call France: Greeks had come in, and Phœnicians, and even Saracens. Luchaire sums up admirably: "On the whole, the South surpassed the North by its culture, its sonorous tongue, judicial customs which retained Roman law, a milder social constitution, freer towns, less lofty fences between class and class and a milder form of serfdom. Moreover (and here was its main originality), the South was tolerant. Jews could live there without persecution or coercion. They were allowed to exercise public functions. Lords, and even prelates, confided to Jews the management of their domains. They grew rich in open commerce and industry: Narbonne counted then more than 300 Jewish houses, represented by branch establishments at Pisa and Genoa. Almost everywhere the synagogue stood freely by the side of the church. How can we be surprised that the heretics profited by this southern mentality? The preachers of new doctrines proselytised, held meetings, and defied the bishops without any protest from the multitude or interference from the authorities."[1]

Thus this Southern civilisation bore in almost every way a far more modern stamp. Their Christianity in the twelfth century differed from that of the newer civilisation of the Teutonic and Scandinavian invaders. In Provence, it had been handed down from father to son almost imperceptibly, and its defects were those attendant upon anything which we inherit without having had to struggle for it. The clergy were more supine here than in most districts, and correspondingly less respected in their persons. In contrast to this, the erstwhile wild men of the North possessed far more of the qualities natural to fresh converts. Freeman has emphasised the overflowing and sometimes turbulent religious enthusiasm of the Normans, "the first Crusaders of the first Crusades." Moreover, their creed bore many traces of the crudity with which a missionary must, of necessity, propound any complicated metaphysical system to a rough and illiterate multitude. As Harnack points out, the Teuton had learned religious obedience and civil obedience in a single lesson. Even when the conversion was not forcible, as it was under many of Clovis's conquests, and in Saxony where Charlemagne deported whole populations to fill their places with men of less obstinate paganism, the missionary was necessarily here, as always, herald of a political conquest. Thus the new convert learned all his duties in the same breath. "Thou shalt not kill" was not a more categorical imperative than "Thou shalt pay the priest his tithe." Both were supported by practically the same sanctions, in money or in person. To those fighting men, this whole sum of commands and prohibitions formed, so to speak, a code of Army Regulations, under which they were to march without any attempt at finer distinctions. To the soldier it matters nothing whether his officer's command rests ultimately on Common Law or on Statute. Thus the Languedocian heresy, bringing two different civilisations into conflict, naturally ended in civil war; and the victory of the North inevitably involved the death, for good or evil, of that distinctive Provençal culture.

Two heresiarchs of St. Bernard's day secured, among this

Southern population, a depth and width of influence beyond the rest. Pierre de Bruys, whose followers were called Petrobrusians, preached the most violent antisacerdotalism for twenty years in the dioceses of Embrun, Gap and Die. God is no more in the church than in the market-place: the forms and ceremonies which to so many folk replace true religion are utterly useless; the Cross should not be prayed to, but loathed as the instrument of the Just One's death. We are told, indeed, that Pierre once roasted his food at a bonfire of crucifixes. The priests lie in pretending that they made Christ's body and give it to the people for their salvation. Against all this, the bishops appealed to the Kings. They finally caught and burned Peter in 1126, but the Petrobrusians still flourished; and Henry, the ex-monk of Lausanne, took up what was practically the same campaign. He was taken and condemned in 1134, but released presently; and St. Bernard in 1147 describes all Southern France as in full conflagration. "The churches are without people, the people without priests . . . the sacraments are no longer held sacred . . . men die in their sins . . . the voice of a single heretic silences all those apostolic and prophetic voices which have united in calling all the nations into the Church of Christ." The nobles would not aid the prelates: they preferred to put Henry's theories of clerical disendowment into practice. St. Bernard himself was prevailed upon to go thither, with the papal legate and the Bishop of Chartres. Here, as always, his eloquence commanded huge congregations and corresponding enthusiasm; and the biographers tell us of his miracles. Henry refused to meet Bernard in public disputation; therefore the nobles no longer supported him; he was caught next year and clapped into prison, where he seems soon to have died. Yet the sect certainly survived him to some extent, and probably helped the spread of the Waldensians in the next generation.

Meanwhile the ordinary ecclesiastical rule of discipline is a sort of lynch law, generally presided by the civil magistrate and encouraged by the local clergy, but resting on no legitimate basis either of Common Law or of Statute. Let us take for

example the English case of 1166, not only because William of
Newburgh is an exceptionally accurate and vivid chronicler,
but because it is the first case of group-heresy in our country.
He writes: "In those days certain false teachers came to
England, of that sect (it is believed) which men commonly call
Publicani.* These took their origin long ago in Gascony from
an uncertain founder, and poured the poison of their false belief
into many regions. Indeed, so many are reported as infected
by this plague in the widest districts of Gaul, Spain, Italy and
Germany that, as the Psalmist saith, they seem more in number
than the sand. At last, seeing that the bishops and the provincial governors deal too remissly with them, these abominable
foxes come forth from their holes and, under a specious pretence
of piety, seducing simple folk, they spoil the vines of the Lord
of Sabaoth the more grievously by reason of their freedom.†
On the other hand, when God's fire kindles the zeal of the
Faithful against them, these heretics lurk in their dens and are
less harmful; yet even so they cease not to harm by spreading
their hidden poison. They are rustic and unlearned men, and
therefore dull to reason; yet so steeped in that pest, when once
they have caught it, that they are obstinate against all teaching;
wherefore we very seldom find that any of them, when dragged
forth from his hiding-place, is converted to piety. In truth,
England hath ever been immune from this and other heretical
plagues, while so many heresies have flourished in other parts
of the world." Britain (he adds) did indeed breed the heretic
Pelagius; but, since the expulsion of the Britons by the English,
"no poison of heretical plague hath ever boiled up there; nor
hath it entered from elsewhere, until the days of Henry II, to
propagate and spread. Then, however, by God's favour, this
pest was so met at its first creeping-in that it hath dreaded
ever since to enter this island. There were somewhat more
than thirty men and women who, dissembling their error, crept

---

* A medieval corruption for *Pauliciani.*

† Song of Solomon, II, 15, the stock text of medieval preachers against
heretics.

in hither under peaceful colour, for the sake of propagating their falsehood. Their leader was one Gerard, to whom all looked up as preceptor and prince. For he alone had some tincture of learning; the rest were ignorant and illiterate, utterly rustic and unpolished, of German nation and speech. After some stay in England, they added to their group one single woman, deceived by their poisoned whispers and (as is reported) bewitched by certain charms. They could not long remain hidden; but, when men began to watch them curiously, since they were of a foreign sect, they were discovered, caught, and kept in public prison. The King, as unwilling either to release or to punish them without enquiry, decreed the assembling of an episcopal council at Oxford. Here the religious question was formally treated; and the man who seemed learned undertook the case for all his fellows and spoke for the whole group, answering that they were Christians who revered the apostolical teaching. Questioned in order concerning the articles of faith, they answered rightly concerning the substance of the Physician on High, but perversely concerning His remedies wherewith he deigneth to heal human infirmities, to wit, the holy Sacraments. They solemnly renounced holy baptism, the eucharist and marriage, and dared nefariously to derogate from the Catholic unity which these divine props support. They were plied with testimonies from Holy Scripture, but answered that they, for their part, believed as they had been taught, and were unwilling to dispute of their faith. When warned to do penance and join the body of the Church, they spurned all wholesome advice. When men pitifully threatened them in order that fear at least might bring them to reason, they answered in derision, falsely pleading those words of Christ: 'Blessed are they which are persecuted for righteousness' sake, for theirs is the Kingdom of heaven.' Then, lest this heretical venom should spread farther, the bishops proclaimed them publicly as heretics and handed them over to the Catholic King for corporal discipline. He commanded that the brand of heretical infamy should be burnt upon their foreheads, and

that they should be scourged forth from the city before the
people's eyes, strictly forbidding all to receive them under their
roof or to succour them with any solace. When sentence had
been pronounced, they were led rejoicing to this most righteous
punishment; their leader strode before them at no flagging pace,
and sang 'Blessed are ye when men shall revile you!' so grievously did the spirit of seduction abuse these minds which he
had deceived! The Englishwoman whom they had misled
departed from them under fear of punishment, confessed her
error and earned reconciliation. On the other hand that
detestable crew, branded on the forehead, was subjected to the
severity of justice: their leader had the shame of a double
cautery, both on his forehead and about his chin, as a token of
his pre-eminence. Then their garments were torn down to the
waist and they were publicly scourged, driven from the city
to the sound of cracking whips. Then the intolerable cold (for
this was winter-time) brought them to a miserable end, since
no man gave them even the least mercy. The pious vigour of
this severity hath not only purged the realm of England from
this pest which had already crept in, but the terror which it
struck into the heretics hath proved a safeguard against future
incursions."[2]

This is fairly typical of what was going on elsewhere about
the same time. Vacandard, following Lea, gives a long list down
to the end of the century and thus summarises the most
interesting of the cases: "The execution of the heretics judged
at Vezelay in 1167 by the abbot and several bishops forms a
veritable drama. When the culprits had been convicted, the
abbot addressed the crowd: 'My brethren, what would ye have
me do with those who are obstinate in their error!' All cried:
'Burn them, burn them!' and so it was done. Two obtained
pardon: the rest, seven in number, were given over to the
flames."[3] For, by this time, the fire was becoming a common
penalty for heresy, especially in Northern France and Germany.

Yet heresy spread at an increasing rate, especially in Italy
and Southern France. Italy was honeycombed with such

organisations. In that peninsula, there was no efficient central control by the civil power, and the clergy could depend upon the secular arm far less than in many other parts; therefore, when stamped out in one city it broke out in another. At Orvieto, seventy miles from Rome, in 1125 there was civil war, and the heretics gained the upper hand until the Catholics rallied and subdued them: they broke out again in 1150. In Viterbo, actually within the Papal States, heresy was publicly rampant; and, in spite of Innocent III's intervention, these rebels carried the municipal elections and chose as governor an excommunicated heretic. But the comparative independence of these separate cities, while it favoured this sort of guerilla warfare, hindered concentration; it was in Southern France that the war had to be fought out over the whole front. Here, for the first time, the stake received definite legal foundation. The magistrates of Toulouse, applying this penalty regularly, pleaded that they did so in virtue of orders from their Count, Raymond V, who died in 1194. Certainly, in 1197, Peter II of Aragon (a district in close connection with that of Toulouse) put the matter beyond all doubt for his own kingdom and his county of Barcelona. Heretics are to be driven out as public enemies: and if, by Eastertide, any is still to be found, the discoverer may claim one-third of his property, while the State will take two-thirds and burn him. Moreover, the King claimed here to be "obeying the canons of the Holy Roman Church." Such, in fact, had been the vacillations and indecision of popes and prelates and theologians as to the principle, while in practice the stake had become more and more habitual, whether by mere mob-law or under quasi-legal sanction, that the King's exaggeration is natural enough. Indeed, it may possibly be no exaggeration at all. For Lucius III, in his decree *Ad abolendam*, drawn up in concert with the Emperor Frederick Barbarossa (1184), had already commanded that heretics should be "left to the judgement of the secular power, to be punished with the penalty that is his due"—*animadversione debita puniendus.* '*Animadversio*,' in this context, is a technical term

of Roman law for the death penalty; it is employed in an edict
of Valerian in A.D. 258. Abbé Vacandard evidently feels that the
King of Aragon, in decreeing capital punishment, was really
going no farther than the natural interpretation of this papal
decree; and he indicates that this is strengthened by the evident
allusion of Lucius to the accompanying imperial decree of
Frederick. Hostiensis, the classical medieval commentator on
these decrees, insists that this phrase *animadversione debita
puniendus* means burning alive; and Eymeric, the fourteenth-
century Inquisitor and jurist, gives his approval to Hostiensis.
The question, however, was still arguable; as yet the official
Church is not definitely and irrevocably committed; but her
legislation is drifting more and more in the direction of popular
severity. The main doubts were at length removed only in the
next century, by Innocent III and Gregory IX, exceptionally
strong popes and great canon lawyers both. Yet even they will
be found to decide less on principle than on grounds of
expediency.

Innocent III, at that Ecumenical Council of the Lateran in
1215 which was a landmark for the rest of the Middle Ages,
prescribed it as the duty of every good Catholic to report to
the authorities any heretic whom he may know, in order that
heretics may be "exterminated": any prince who neglects to
carry out this "extermination" will be deposed, and the pope
will release his subjects from their allegiance. What, then, did
Innocent mean by *exterminare, exterminium*, words which he
uses also on other occasions than this? It is characteristic of
the habitual temporisation that this word, which should have
been crucial, has lent itself to even more discussion than those
of Lucius III.

Pegna, the canon lawyer who published Eymeric's book and
dedicated it to Gregory XIII, with the approval of the Inquisition at Rome, has no doubt that Innocent here pronounced a
sentence of death. But the word *exterminare*, in Classical Latin,
means only to drive out, expel, though with a distinct implication of violence. Therefore distinguished modern writers, not

only apologists but also an agnostic like Julien Havet, and Luchaire who often judges the Church severely enough, argue that in Innocent III's legislation "there is no question whatever of death for heretics." This, with all due respect for really great scholars, seems attributable to the notorious ignorance of the Bible text among scholars in Roman Catholic countries.[4] Great theologians in the Middle Ages did, of course, know their Vulgate well, though there were thousands of ordinary priests who might never have seen the outside of the book. Thus there was probably no book that was so familiar as this Vulgate both to Innocent himself and to the majority of the assembled prelates; familiar to the pope and to his hearers alike. In that book, *exterminare* with its derivatives occurs thirty-nine times; in not one of those cases is it used in the bare sense of *banish*, and nothing worse. This can easily be verified with the help of a Vulgate concordance and the Douay (Roman Catholic) translation of the Bible. In twenty-nine cases, the Douay translators give *destroy*; in five, *cut off*; the other five give *lay waste, make havoc, root out, shoot out* and *disfigure*. The "Destroyer" of the Apocalypse (Bunyan's Apollyon) is in the Vulgate *Exterminator*, so also in I Cor. x, 10. Therefore, to say the least, it was very incautious for a pope, addressing distinguished churchmen in a decree of almost unexampled solemnity, to choose a word which, in the one book which all might be presumed to know best, and which was certainly authoritative in their minds above all others, never once bears the signification of mere "banishment" which, we are now told, he wished to impress at this moment upon his hearers and upon posterity for all time.

Nor can it be pleaded that here the lawyer in Innocent got the better of the theologian. The concordance to Justinian's *Codex* shows that *extermino* is used only once in that great collection of Roman Law, whereas the three more definite words for *banishment* (*expello, exsul, deporto*) occur no less than seventy-five times. Again, in medieval writers contemporary with Innocent, the cases where the word means something more than banishment are commoner than those in which it bears

plainly the milder sense attributed to it by Havet and Luchaire.
William of Newburgh, describing what we may almost call the
"pogrom" of 1166, these fatal cruelties of Oxford, heads his
chapter "Concerning the heretics who came to England, and
how they were exterminated"—*exterminati sunt*. William of
Auvergne, one of the greatest bishops of Paris, wrote about
1230 that these "spiritual beasts" "should be *exterminated* by
fire and sword and all kinds of warfare."[5] Finally, we may
appeal to Innocent's own use of the word elsewhere. Sometimes
it may strictly mean no more than forcible banishment, though
even here his words are always associated with the wholesale
bloodshed which was then going on in Southern France; but
once at least he uses it as synonymous with the other words:
destruction, ruin, and *shattering* (*destruere, pernicies, conterere*).
Thus the attitude of this exceptionally intelligent, learned and
masterful pope is thoroughly characteristic. Abraham did not
primarily desire the death of Hagar and Ishmael; but he sent
them out to what, had it not been for a miracle, was death.
Innocent did not primarily desire the death of heretics, but he
passed upon them what he knew to be practically a capital
sentence; indeed, less merciful in some cases than the sword
itself. Moreover, his words were understood in their darkest
sense by Bishop Doyle, the able and candid Roman Catholic
prelate who worked so hard for an understanding between his
own Ireland and the English Protestants. He wrote in 1826:
"Such a law, in the present age . . . would upturn the very
foundations of society and, instead of benefiting the entire
community, it would drench our streets and fields in blood." [6]
Still, to an ambiguous word we must allow to some extent the
benefit of ambiguity; and it was left to Gregory IX to decide
clearly for the first time, from the Chair of St. Peter, that
heretics were to be burned. Yet, here again (as we shall see
later), it is thoroughly characteristic that the step was taken in
a fashion which enables apologists to plead, with some show of
reason, that he did it less on principle than as a political move:
that Frederick II had already decreed burning from his

imperial throne, and that no pope could suffer a layman to usurp Church authority in a matter so weighty for religion.

Far more unambiguous and fateful than any of these formal legislative acts was Innocent's practice, when he let loose the Northern Crusaders against the South. We may here apply the common-sense principle of Roman Canon Law: "the best interpreter of legislation is custom." Nothing can tell us more plainly how the law was understood than a careful observation of the manner in which it was regularly applied. Innocent's Crusade against the Albigensians put his official seal most unmistakably upon a century of similar acts on a far smaller scale and, in general, by people of incomparably less authority. Deeds speak more decisively than words; and this has been emphasised in the present twentieth century by Cardinal Lépicier, Professor at the Gregorian University of Rome, with the express approval of Pius X. After arguing, in the fashion familiar to medieval schoolmen, for the Church's eternal and inalienable power over the bodies of obstinate heretics, he clinches all these abstract philosophical pleas by a blunt appeal to the *fait accompli*. He insists that the attempts of modern Roman Catholics to ignore or deny this principle are not "compatible with the constitution of the Church or with historical facts." He proceeds: "Perhaps this doctrine [of St. Thomas Aquinas] will seem too severe to our age, which neglects the spiritual order and is prone to sensible goods [*ad bonum sensibile proclivi*]. But why do we require further proof for this point? Ought not unquestioned historical fact to stand for all proof? The fact, I mean, that many heretics have been condemned to death by the just judgment of the Church. . . . The naked fact that the Church, of her own authority, has tried heretics and condemned them to be delivered to death, shows that she truly has the right of killing such men, as guilty of high treason to God and as enemies of society." These things have been *done*; and "who dares to say that the Church has erred in a matter so grave as this?"[7]

CHAPTER VII

The Little Foxes

THE Cathari of Southern France, often called *Albigensians*, because they had their headquarters in the episcopal city of Albi, have left few memorials beyond confessions made under actual or possible torture, and descriptions by their enemies. Among the latter, naturally enough, come a few writers who had left them and gone over to the Catholic side. But, though such descriptions need more cautious scrutiny than they often receive, we may still form a fairly clear picture, in its main details, of these men. For one thing, the modern world can sympathise with them for more than one tenet or practice which their orthodox contemporaries record with blame.

The most valuable of early Inquisitors' manuals, on the whole, is that of Bernard Gui, Dominican Friar and Bishop. He called it *Practice of the Inquisition into Heretical Perversity*, and wrote it between 1320 and 1325. [1] It embodies some of the work of the Franciscan David of Augsburg, half a century earlier. Gui himself was a very active Inquisitor; we have also his *Register*, recording the trials and condemnation of 930 prisoners between 1307 and 1323. In his time, Catharism was on the wane and Waldensianism was more important; but we can trust him on all the main points of fact. Generations of persecution had doubtless gone far to exasperate the Catharists; but their main doctrines and practices, from the very first, contrasted strongly enough with orthodoxy to render the Crusade a conflict of the most violent character between two irreconcilable ideals. To Catharist and Catholic alike, this was a war between Light and Darkness.

In the first section of the fifth book of the *Practica*, Gui

devotes four pages to a summary of Catharist tenets, based in
great part upon the confessions of a heresiarch, Pierre Autier,
when Gui tried him in 1310. They assert two Gods or Lords,
one benignant and the other malignant. The visible universe
was created not by God Our Father but by Satan, the Lord of
this world. Correspondingly there are two Churches; their own
is that of Jesus Christ: as for "the Roman Church," this "they
impudently call the Mother of Fornications, Babylon the Great
Whore, and the Devil's Basilica and Satan's Synagogue. They
despise and revile all its ranks and orders and regulations and
statutes; all who hold by its faith they call heretical and erring
folk; they preach that no man can be saved in the faith of the
Roman Church." They reject all its Sacraments, "and they
invent, like apes, certain others in place thereof, which seem
to have the similitude thereof; imagining, in place of baptism
with water, some other spiritual baptism, which they call the
consolamentum of the Holy Ghost, whenever they receive any
person, sick or whole, into their own sect and order, according
to their execrable rite. In place of the hallowed bread of the
Eucharist, the Body of Christ, they feignedly fashion that which
they call Blessed Bread, or Bread of Holy Prayer, which, at the
beginning of their repast, holding it in their hands according
to their rite, they bless and break and distribute to those
present and to their own believers." Instead of the Sacrament
of Penance, they put the keeping of their own religion, preaching
that this suffices for salvation. They deny all validity to
priestly absolution in the confessional. For carnal matrimony
between man and woman, they substitute a spiritual matrimony
between the soul and God. They deny the Incarnation; Christ
did not take true human flesh or die or rise again; all this was
only in similitude. The Virgin Mary was no woman in the flesh;
but the true Virgin is their own sect, giving birth to Sons of
God. There will be no resurrection of the flesh: it is only the
Inner Man that will rise again. "These errors, and many others
which follow from them . . . they wrap up in equivocal words
and phrases, making inexpert layfolk believe that they believe

truly in God the Father, Son and Holy Ghost, Creator of all things, and in the Holy Roman Church. . . . After they are detected, and can conceal no longer, they defend them openly before the Inquisitors."

This last paragraph we must not apply to the earlier Catharists. Then, in their immediate influence and confident hopes of victory, they were evidently public and self-assertive proselytisers; but in Gui's time they had become a hunted minority, and he lays special emphasis on the importance of catching their few leaders, by way of neutralising the poison. For "the conversion of Manichæan heretics is commonly true, and rarely feigned; and, once converted, they make a clean breast and reveal the truth and discover all their accomplices; whence we reap rich fruit." If they refuse conversion, we hand them over to the secular arm.

Gui was an honest and well-intentioned man: but in one respect his ignorance of Church history, general enough in his time, betrays him into injustice towards these Catharist tenets. Some of their rites, at least, were not "invented" in mimicry of the Roman Church, but inherited from earlier Christianity. Their substitute for the Eucharist, for instance, closely resembles the "Agape," that early Christian commemorative meal in which many scholars have seen the earliest form of Eucharistic service. Again, their treatment of Confession was more in accord with primitive Christianity; except that Gui accuses them of requiring neither satisfaction nor restitution on the penitent's part. This accusation probably rests on the comparative absence of conventional form from their rites, misinterpreted by the Inquisitor's prejudice. In so far as it would imply lax morality, this is rendered improbable by what Gui goes on to tell us in the next section, as will presently be seen.

Meanwhile, however, we may corroborate Gui's description by a summary of one of the fullest recorded trials of a Catharist, in Gui's own *Register*, under the year 1307. Here are the charges against Stephana, daughter of Martin de Praud. She denies the Incarnation of Christ and the Resurrection of the Flesh. The visible world is created not by God but by the Devil; the seven Sacraments are naught; marriage is a carnal and profane act. She believes in the heretics and in salvation through them. The Sign of the Cross is devilish. She condemns "the whole Roman Church" as unholy, "saying that [its priests] cannot loose or bind sinners, being rather sinners themselves." She "asserts [her own heretical ministers] to be imitators of the Apostles, keeping the same life and following as they did: with many other erroneous falsehoods." She has confessed before the Inquisitors to having seen seven heretical Perfecti at Toulouse, and to having "adored" one of them. "Concerning which errors and heresies thou hast oftentimes been admonished and exhorted with reasons and authorities from Holy Scripture, and besought in the Lord's name, with soft words, both by me as Inquisitor and my vicars, and by many Religious of the Friars Preachers and Minors and other Orders, with many other honourable men, clergy and layfolk, of the city of Toulouse, and by your own parents also, that ye should depart from these errors and return with good and pure heart to your Holy Mother the Roman Church, outside of which there is no salvation, and shouldst leave that detestable heretical sect which leadeth souls to damnation and eternal perdition; yet thou wouldst not even so be persuaded, nor be converted to the Catholic faith after long waiting, but rather thou persistest even to this day, with hardened mind, in thine aforesaid obstinacy." She is therefore handed over to the secular arm. "Next day, Monday, she was better advised, seeing that the penalty of fire was then prepared for her, and was imminent that very day. She said that she would be converted to the Catholic faith and return to the unity of the Church. Whether she said this feignedly or in truth of heart from fear of death* man's judgment cannot define with certainty. It was first put before her and explained that the time of grace was spent for her, and that she should think on the salvation of her

---

* *Sic:* such is the order in which the reporter writes all these words.

soul and reveal fully whatsoever she knew of the fact of heresy, whether in herself or in others. She promised to do and say thus, and that she would fain die in the faith of the Holy Roman Church." After long and solemn consultation with canonists and theologians, it was decided to stretch mercy so far as to give her a chance. She must abjure publicly, swear future fidelity and go straight to prison, in order that she might be prevented from infecting others, and that the judges might finally discover whether her penitence was feigned or sincere, "the sentence of her condemnation being in no other respect altered, unless it should appear clearly, by manifest evidence, that she was truly converted."

We may now go back again to the *Practica*, where the next section is headed *Concerning the Manner and Way of Life of these Manichæans*. This section is so important that I must give it here in full.

"It is expedient that I should say a little on this subject, whereby they may be easier known and caught.

"*First*, you must know that they swear in no case.

"*Item*, they fast thrice a year; from Nov. 13 to Christmas; and from Quinquagesima to Easter, and from Whit-Sunday to the Feast of St. Peter and St. Paul (June 29). They call the first and last week of each of these Lents *a strict week;* for then they fast with bread and water, and the other weeks they confine themselves to bread and water for only three days a week. Throughout the rest of the year, they fast on bread and water thrice weekly, unless they be sick or on a journey. *Item,* they never eat flesh, nor even touch it, nor cheese or eggs or aught that is born of the flesh by way of generation or coition.*

"*Item*, on no account would they kill any animal or fowl; for they say and believe that in beasts, and even in fowls, are those

---

* They did not here include fish, supposing it to be born of the water itself. Here again is a curious parallel to be found in monasticism. None of the Benedictine Orders were permitted by their Rule to eat "the flesh of four-footed beasts." It therefore became a moot question whether fowls were permitted; and some solved this by pleading that birds and fish were created on the same day: therefore, by implication, from the same elements: therefore, that fowls might count as fish.

spirits which quit human bodies, when they have not been received into the Manichæan sect by laying on of hands according to their rite, and that they pass from body to body.

"*Item*, they touch not any woman.

"*Item*, at the beginning of their repast, when they are among believers or among themselves, they bless a loaf or a piece thereof, holding it in their hands, with a napkin or other white cloth hanging from their neck, repeating a Pater Noster and breaking the bread into small pieces. Such bread they call Bread of Holy Prayer, and Bread of Breaking; and their believers call it Blessed Bread, or Signed Bread; and, by way of Communion, they eat thereof at the beginning of the meal and distribute it among their believers.

"*Item*, they teach their believers to show them reverence, which they call *melioramentum* but which we call *adoratio*: to wit, by bending the knees and inclining profoundly before them on some bench or even to the ground, with hands joined, inclining and rising thrice, and saying each time 'Benedicite,' and concluding at the end: 'Good Christians, God's blessing and yours! Pray the Lord for us, that God may keep us from evil death and may bring us to a good end, or to the hands of faithful Christians.' And the heretic [leader] answers: 'May you have that blessing from God and from us: may God bless you and snatch your soul from evil death and bring you to a good end.' By *evil death*, the heretics signify death in the faith of the Roman Church; by *good end* and *the hands of faithful Christians* they signify that they should be received at their latter end into that sect and order of theirs, according to their own rite, for that they call a good end. The aforesaid reverence, they say, is done not to themselves, but to the Holy Ghost, of whom they say that He is in them from the time when they were received into the sect and order which they profess to hold.

"*Item*, they teach their believers to make with them the pact which they call The Covenant: to wit, that at their latter end they will be received into their sect and order; and from thenceforth the heretics may receive such an one in his sickness, even though he have lost the power of speech or of orderly memory."

Gui goes on to describe how they preach their doctrines. First, they boast themselves as good folk "who neither swear nor lie nor curse any man, nor slay man or beast," yet whom the Roman Church persecutes, even as the Pharisees did with Christ and His apostles. "*Item*, for the most part they speak to the layfolk of the evil lives of clergy and prelates of the Roman Church. And they enter into details, and dwell upon their pride and greed and avarice and unclean lives, and whatsoever other evils they know.* And for this they quote authorities, according to their own exposition and understanding, from the Gospels and Epistles against the state of clergy and prelates and monks and friars and nuns, whom they call Pharisees and false prophets, such as say but do not. Then, little by little, they rend and vituperate all the Sacraments of the Church." The clergy (they say), in their greed, sell these empty things to the populace of dupes. "*Item*, they read from the Gospels and Epistles in the vulgar tongue, applying and expounding them in their own favour and against the state of the Roman Church, which it would be tedious to set forth here in full."

All these points are borne out more or less exactly by the confessions recorded in the voluminous documents which have come down to us. The questions of swearing and Bible-reading are so fundamental that I shall deal with them fully at a later point when we come to the Waldensians, in whose creed they played perhaps a yet more prominent part. One or two other points, however, shall be illustrated here before passing on farther.

The easiest practical test for an Inquisitor, next to that of the oath, was flesh-eating. In 1229 two Tuscan heretics abjured before Gregory IX. Two days later they proved the sincerity of their conversion by eating flesh publicly, in the presence of

---

* This last word is of extreme importance; Gui writes not *fingunt*, but *sciunt*; not "feign," but "know."

a number of prelates, with a notary to draw up an official record of the fact. Again, the Inquisitor Guillaume Pelisso tells a story from his own experience somewhere about 1230. A certain John Weaver, at Toulouse, "had as defenders many of the greatest folk of the city. For this accursed John would say publicly: 'Lords, hear me. I am no heretic; for I have a wife and lie with her, and have children; and I eat flesh and lie and swear, and am a faithful Christian.'" Yet in all this there was nothing different from the Fathers of the Desert, except that those earlier Christians fasted for different reasons, and that they would not always have been so obstinate in refusing flesh at another man's bidding. The tens of thousands of Benedictines, again, were strictly forbidden butchers' meat. Thus the chief difference is that which St. Bernard noted; these Cathari *abstinent, sed abstinent hæretice*: an accusation as unfair as to say that they "cast out devils by Beelzebub, prince of devils." Their personal objection to marriage was no greater than that of the Fathers of the Desert; and some of those latter went almost as far as the Catharists towards erecting Dualism into a principle for all mankind. As a matter of practical politics, the *Perfecti* were as little likely to convert the world, and bring about the extinction of the human race, as those extremist anchorites and monks whom the Church had revered among the greatest of spiritual heroes.* So, again, with that third long

AN ANCHORITE'S ANTIDOTE

and solemn fast which they added to the Lententide fast, obligatory upon all orthodox churchfolk, and to the further Advent fast adopted by cloisterers and the most strictly

---

* The secret abominations sometimes attributed to these Catharists by their enemies have no more foundation than those which were similarly attributed to the early Christians. Abbé Vacandard (p. 115) sums up the trustworthy evidence: "It must be admitted that, in general, they held out stiffly against temptation, and preferred death to impurity." No Catharist or Waldensian, I believe, is recorded to have confessed to such orgies, though, as we shall see, some Templars and Fraticelli did so under constraint of torture.

religious of other Catholics. That which would have been a
merit on the part of a monk becomes a sin on the part of a
Catharist. Their belief in transmigration might seem harmless
enough to all folk who do not cling to the crudest doctrines of
Heaven and Hell: and at least it impressed upon the believer
that his actions of to-day may have far-reaching consequences.
The heretics told a tale of a man who remembered having been

a horse in his former life, and how his
master had spurred him unmercifully
and caused him to wrench off a shoe
between two stones on the road. The
recollection was so clear, that he went
to the remembered spot, where he
found the shoe just as he had left it
in his equine days. On the other hand,
a certain woman thought she remembered that she had once been a queen.

ASCETICISM IN THE DESERT

Equally harmless was the objection to
shedding blood; the heretics who were hanged at Goslar in 1052
had steadfastly refused to defile their faith by killing a fowl and
eating it. Their ceremonies resembled very closely those of
Christianity at an earlier stage of development: it would be rash
to say that St. Peter would have found them more different from
his own than those of twelfth-century Catholicism. Even their
Dualism had, at bottom, much in common with the ordinary
orthodoxy of their day. Quite apart from the remnants of plain
heathenism which still lingered among popular superstitions, it
has often been remarked that medieval theologians lay almost as
much emphasis upon Satan as upon Jehovah: and monasticism
often tempted men to the false ideal of vicarious religion. Still,
between the Catholic pure and simple, and the Catharist pure
and simple, there was at this point the same impassable gulf as
in St. Augustine's time. To the latter, there were certain elements, regarded as essential to the former's creed, which seemed
not only reprehensible but damnable. At Toulouse, in 1247,
it was reported against Pierre Garcias that he had said, in

colloquy with a Franciscan friar: "If I could hold that God who, among a thousand men He hath created, saved one and damned all the rest, I would rend him and tear him, tooth and nail, as a traitor; I defy Him as a false traitor and would spit in His face." He added the further heresy that, even among the angels fallen from heaven, "not one in a thousand shall be damned . . . and, if a man is to be saved, the spirit which could not do [sufficient] penance in one body passeth into another, to do penance there." In spite of orthodox protests, it must be repeated that there was much in these heresies reminiscent of extreme Christian ascetics. Luchaire writes with little exaggeration: "Heresiarchs like Henry of Lausanne and Pierre de Bruys had exactly the same moral origins as the powerful founders of monastic Orders who were their contemporaries. They started from the same point: and, if they ended in dissimilar destinies, this was because their logic went to the very end, while the others stopped half-way. It was not always easy to fix the frontier of orthodoxy." One Catharist practice, however, the so-called *Endura*, does not come within this category. The most fervent believers had such horror of the flesh that they often escaped from it by religious suicide, especially on their deathbed. In that case the sick man was asked to choose between the death of a martyr or a confessor. If he chose the former, a pillow or a wet napkin was laid over his face while a prayer was recited. If the latter, he starved to death. His salvation was thus assured; whereas, if he had lived on, he might have lapsed and lost all virtue of that *consolamentum* which, to the Catharist, replaced the Extreme Unction and last rites of the Catholic Church. The *Perfecti*, naturally, pressed this suicide upon their dying *credentes*; and in a few cases they had even the cruelty to practise it upon children. Lea quotes two interesting cases where the Catharist vainly attempted to escape the stake by this method. "A certain Pierre Raymond, who as a Catharan '*credens*' had been led to abjure and seek reconciliation in The *auto* of 1310, and had been condemned to imprisonment, repented of his weakness in his solitary cell.

The mental tortures of the poor wretch grew so strong that at
last he defiantly proclaimed his relapse into heresy, in which
he declared he would live and die, only regretting that he could
not have access to some minister of his faith in order to be
'perfected' or 'hereticated.' He likewise placed himself in
endura, and after six days of starvation, as he was evidently
nearing the end he so resolutely sought, he was hurriedly
sentenced, and a small *auto* was arranged with a few other
culprits in order that the stake might not be cheated of its
prey."

On one point Abbé Vacandard, who is usually so fair and
judicial, fails to do justice to these innovators. He condemns
their creed as mainly negative, and their policy as wantonly
aggressive, writing: "The Church, after all, was only defending
herself. The Cathari sought to wound her mortally by attacking
her doctrine, her hierarchy and her apostolicity. She would
have been ruined if their perfidious insinuations, which brought
violent disturbance into men's minds, had prevailed in the
end" (p. 121). This would seen a strangely narrow view.
When once a Church has claimed for its exclusive province the
whole of human life, both on this earth and in eternity, then no
other creature can move without in some sense attacking this
position. It is one of the advantages of the Roman Church,
especially among those who are rather impulsive than reflective,
that she occupies a position from which she can complain of
every innovator as a trespasser, an interloper, a disturber of
settled peace. With more reflective minds, and in the long run,
this totalitarian claim is rather its weakness. Very seldom did
the Catholic clergy of the Middle Ages condescend to public
disputation with the heretics on anything like equal terms; nor,
on those occasions, did they gain any signal victory. On one
or two points the orthodoxy of that day was so obviously
vulnerable, especially in its encouragement of swearing and in
its discouragement of Bible reading, that its claim to infallibility, once shaken, was calculated rather to alienate than to
attract many of the most earnest minds. Thus, in the long run,

it proved a dialectical disadvantage. Bernard Gui himself, one of the ablest and most experienced, warns his fellow-Inquisitors that it is very hard to bring heretics to book. On the one hand, conscience bids us do our best not to punish the innocent; but "our minds are even more distressed" by the fear of letting the guilty loose upon society. Over-severity is regrettable, but over-laxity would be lamentable. Moreover, "faithful layfolk are scandalised when the business of the Inquisition, once set in motion against a man, is left in a sort of confusion. They are to some extent weakened in their faith, seeing that learned men are thus mocked by base and uncultured persons; for they believe us to have at our fingers' ends all the true reasons for faith, so clear and open that no man can stand up against us but that we know how to convict him forthwith, in such a fashion that layfolk themselves can clearly understand such reasons. Therefore, in such a case, it is not expedient to dispute concerning the faith against such astute heretics in the presence of layfolk."[2]

St. Louis, a little earlier, had given this same warning in a tone strangely discordant with his usual justice and charity. The layman (he says) must not argue with the unbeliever in such cases, but "thrust his sword into the man's belly as far as it will go."

CHAPTER VIII

The Lord's Vineyard

THUS, from the days of St. Louis's childhood and earlier still, these little foxes had steadily ravaged the Lord's vineyard in Provence, and no man had efficiently caught them. The bishops were sometimes too weak, sometimes too supine, to apply themselves seriously to the task. The heretics themselves were often quick-witted traders or artisans. As Luchaire says, "hawking their creed around at the same time as their wares, they converted lords and burghers and peasants." From the confessions and depositions of witnesses, we may gather a host of intimate details. We see them on the road with their pilgrim staff and, in one case, a barber's basin, the missionary thus gaining his livelihood. One *credens* will guide the missionary for part of the way through the hills or forests, and another will then take him in hand. Gifts are brought for his maintenance; some trout in one case, a gourd of wine in another, or "white wine boiled with rue"; or peas or corn. One female devotee makes a shirt for the wanderer. The preachers ingratiated themselves with women by presents of needles, just as Chaucer's friar, later on, did with knives. Naturally, great precautions are taken for secrecy. "When my husband lay on his deathbed, there came in the twilight two men with staves, while I was making his supper ready; and they entered in where he lay and spake with him while I tarried without, and then they departed. So I asked him who those men might be; and at last he told me that they were heretics, and bade me say no word of this to any man in the village."[1] David of Augsburg tells us how the German heretics had their passwords; and we may infer much the same concerning others. He relates this by way of appendix to his treatise against heresy, in a short

chapter headed *How do Heretics recognise each other?* "Note
that it hath been told me by a certain priest who heard this in
confession from a certain heretical woman, that, when heretics
first meet each other, and know not each other, then they do
and say as follows:

A. Take him by the ear.
B. Welcome! will you speak, or shall I?
A. Speak; for it is my pleasure that you should speak.
B. When we pray, we speak to God; when we meditate, God
   speaketh unto us.
A. Now speak again, for this pleaseth me well.
B. St. Paul saith, *Lie not.* St. James saith, *Swear not.* St.
   Peter saith, Render not evil for evil, but rather contrari-
   wise."[2]

The dialogue seems to bear rather a Waldensian than a Catharist
tinge; but by David's time (about 1275) the two had coalesced
to a considerable extent. Yet the general tenor of the earlier
evidence seems to make some such password system probable,
almost from the very first.

Here, again, is the story of a first acquaintance struck up.[3]
In this case also, the missionary seems probably a Waldensian.
Bernard Gui, in 1322, had before his Inquisitorial bench one
Gerald son of Fromond, who confessed as follows: "That once,
six years since, he found and saw on the market-place of
Miraud, where he then dwelt, a certain man who drew him
apart, asking whether he were Fromond's son. He answered
Yes; and then this man began to say to him that he should not
say or do evil, nor lie or swear, with certain words which
seemed good: and the man said that he should tell him his sins,
seeing that he knew not whether he would be alive on the
morrow. Then he answered that he had not taken ought from
any man, nor stolen; and thus he departed from this man, who
was Perrin Wudri, as his father told him afterwards, commend-
ing him as a good man who went about the land and taught

good doctrine. Again, another time, three months later, he met the said Perrin on the way, and there went with him one called Guillaume Motier, and he spake with them. Once again, in the town of Miraud where he then dwelt, a youth called Pierrot showed him a man, tall and corpulent, who (as he said) was a good man and preached excellently well and said good words and was named Cristin; and he adjured him* to say nothing of this Cristin. Again, in his father's house he saw as many as six strangers who came thither, not all at once but now these, now those, at divers times and seasons, concerning whom his father adjured him to tell no man that they were there. And these men in his father's house, before supper and after, would bend their knees and pray, leaning upon some bench, and he himself likewise prayed with them, saying there many Paternosters, and staying a long while there." He was compelled by his judges to name all these men, and to confess that "he believed those Waldensians to be good men because of what he heard from them, and because his father told him so; but then he knew not that they had been banished by the Inquisitor; and he was in that belief for about a year; then, hearing of their banishment by the Inquisitors, he no longer believed them to be good men." The Inquisitors find that "this Gerald is thought to have confessed with palliation and diminution [of his offence]. Moreover, after he had confessed and solemnly abjured all heresy, and had been penanced and marked with the Cross at the sermon of the Toulouse Inquisitor in 1319, after Michælmas, he is said afterwards to have laid aside his crosses and fled with his father." Therefore he was excommunicated at the "sermon" of 1322.

It was natural that these outlawed wanderers should pick up strange wander-fellows, and that heresy should become a sort of Cave of Adullam. On this point we have the evidence of a very remarkable document, the confession of one Raymond Dupuy in 1277.[4] He was a native of Sorrèze. At an earlier date he had been in the hands of the Inquisition and had solemnly sworn

---

* *Incantavit eum.*

never to practise sorcery again. He now confesses to have broken that oath. How often? He cannot remember. "Asked what persons he advised afterwards in that matter, he answered 'many clergy, and monks, and layfolk.' Asked for their names, he named the lord Guillaume, late Bishop of Carcassonne; P. Raymond, late lord abbot of Sorrèze; the late lord abbot of Alet, and many others, clerics and monks and layfolk, whose names he hath now forgotten. How often did he consult with the Lord Bishop? Once only. Concerning what matter? Concerning his sickness. Where did he speak with him? Between Saissac and Sorrèze, in the place called *al Jan de Portel*, whither the bishop had come from his castle of Louvière, sending as his messenger Peter of Puy Siuran, a man of Saissac, since dead. At what time? Some twelve years ago. As to the persons, many who were with the bishop saw them talk with each other at that place, but he thought they knew not of what they spake. How often did he counsel the abbot of Sorrèze? Four times or more. On what matter? On his election to the abbacy of Lagrasse; and he told him that he would obtain it, and so it was. The time? Ten years ago or more. The place? At Sorrèze. The persons? None other heard them. How often did he counsel the abbot of Alet? Twice. On what business? On the dispute which he had with the lord Olivier de Termes; and I counselled him to compromise in that dispute. Where? At Brugairdlas in Rodez: the time, some twelve years ago: no other person heard us. Asked whether he had any book of sorcery, he said he possessed one, beginning *si vols sabet que es cofres*.* The said book is clothed in a covering of red hairy calf-skin; and at the end it treateth of the observation of winds." On a later day, the Inquisitors extracted from him that "he wrought divinations sometimes for the lord Raymond, late bishop of Toulouse, concerning a business that he had at the Roman Court. *Item*, he wrought divinations for the lord Gui Fulcoy [archbishop of Narbonne and afterwards Pope Clement IV], first for the matter

* "If thou wouldst know that thou art a companion." *Cofres = confrère*, and apparently means "initiate" here.

of his cardinalate, and secondly for his papacy. But this Lord Gui never spake to me himself of those matters, but the said lord P. Raymond, afterwards abbot of Lagrasse, spake to me concerning them. The lord bishop of Toulouse spake in his own person concerning the divinations as to his own business . . . but twice or thrice there was an intermediary, Pierre Pottevin of Sorrèze."

One great interest of his story is that it records one of the earliest occasions on which the Inquisitors dealt with sorcery, on the principle which was afterwards so shamefully abused in the case of Joan of Arc. Even more important, however, is the sidelight which it casts upon ecclesiastical society in high life; the men who were arrayed against Catharism. If it seems frankly incredible to the modern reader that an archbishop, future cardinal and pope, should consult a common sorcerer, let me quote here what the orthodox Franciscan Salimbene tells us concerning Innocent III himself. Salimbene, it is true, writes some eighty years after the event; and, apart from details, we cannot lay stress even upon the general accuracy of this story, in spite of his customary care for truth. But, if it be only *ben trovato*, that scarcely diminishes its value for this particular case. The Inquisitors, evidently, did not reject Clement IV's dealings with this man Raymond Dupuy as inherently incredible. They tested him closely; but they give us no hint of final doubt as to the facts.

Salimbene's story runs as follows:[5] "One day, as he preached to the people, he saw how a certain scholar mocked at his words. So when his sermon was ended he called him apart into his chamber and asked him why he had laughed at the Word of God, which is profitable for salvation of souls. The scholar answered that the Pope's were mere words, but that he himself could show deeds, as for example raising of the dead and authority over demons. So the Pope learned from him that he was a necromancer who had studied at Toledo: wherefore he besought him to raise a certain dead friend of his own, with whom he would fain speak and hear of his soul's health. So they

chose a desert and secret spot in Rome, whereunto the Pope
went as though he walked abroad for air; and, when he was
come thither, he bade his attendants pass on and tarry until he
came again to them. They therefore did as he had bidden,
believing that he went down into this place at the call of
nature. So the scholar raised up before his eyes the Archbishop
of Besmantova, with the same pomp and vainglory with
which he was wont to come to Court. First came his servants
to make ready his lodging, then a great multitude of sumpter-
mules with his treasures, then his squires to wait on him,
and then his knights, and himself last of all with many chaplains
round him. The necromancer asked him whither he went:
and he made answer: 'To the Court, to my friend Pope Innocent,
who would fain see me.' Then said he: 'Here is thy friend
Innocent, who would fain know from thine own mouth how it
standeth with thee.' 'Ill indeed,' said the Archbishop, 'for I
am damned by reason of my pomp and vainglory and my
other sins: and I did no penitence: wherefore I am doomed
to dwell with devils and with those that go down to hell.'
When therefore these speeches were ended on either side,
the apparition vanished, and the Pope went back to his
attendants."

Another heretic's confession before the Inquisitors gives
us the story of a veritable Odyssey. His name was Arnaud
Cimordan, of the village of Gascogne. The year of this his
second trial was 1276. He had confessed earlier before the
late Inquisitor, Bernard de Caux, and had been sentenced
to prison, in all probability for life, at Toulouse. "Asked
why he had fled from prison, he said that there he had not
the necessaries of life; for no provision was made for him
from the King's goods, since his incarceration had not per-
tained to the King but to the bishop; nor was provision made
for him from the bishop's goods, because he had no messenger
whom he could send so frequently to the bishop's hall for
bread; and, when bread was sent him to prison from the
bishop's household, it was sent so hard that he could not

eat it. He also lacked garments and other necessaries.* . . .
He confessed that in those prison days he heard Raymond
Richard, of the honour† of Vaur, say that there were two gods,
fighting in heaven against each other, and that the blood had
mounted over the city wall, and other words which he hath now
forgotten." He threw himself now at the Inquisitor's mercy and
promised to perform any penance enjoined upon him, under
penalty of fifty *livres tournois* (about £400 modern value),
for which he pledged all his goods, present and future. He
was remanded to hear his final sentence a little later: "on
which day he came not; being in prison at Verfeil"; but on
the following Monday he appeared and told how the [royal]
seneschal and bailiff at Verfeil had kept his knife‡ and bound
him upon oath to pay 210 *livres tournois* before Palm Sunday,
and detained him in prison for a week after they learned
that he was bound by the Inquisitor to appear. The Inquisitor now insisted that he should reveal the names of
those who had assisted his escape from prison: he pleaded
forgetfulness. "It was enjoined upon him that he should
think it over again and come back and answer next morning." This was a hint which no prisoner could misunderstand;
and next morning he made a clean breast of it, giving names
at every point. He fled from Toulouse to his native Gascogne,
where one man harboured him in an outlying grange. Thence
he took refuge at a priory, where the prior, though not ignorant
of his condition as an escaped prisoner, kept him until November to labour in the harvest-field and the vintage, and for

---

* The rule was that whoever enjoyed the Inquisitorial confiscations was
responsible for the keep of the prisoners. The bishop in this case is described
by the Bishop of Beauvais as "a man of culture, very firm upon ecclesiastical
rights and ecclesiastical liberty, who consecrated his episcopate to the construction of his cathedral and spent his own fortune upon it," building the
fourteen apsidal chapels which are still to be seen.

† I.e., the estate appertaining to the barony of Lavaur.

‡ Medieval law, in the comparative scarcity of written documents, constantly used personal possessions in evidence; e.g., the casting down of a glove
or hood by way of solemn challenge. Benefactors would give lands or rents
to abbeys, laying their knife upon the altar in pledge. Arnaud's knife was
thus kept in testimony of his liabilities.

carrying wood;* "and he gave me no wages: nay, rather, I gave him, over and above my service, 10 *sols* (=£4 modern); and all this I did because the said prior had held out a hope of reconciliation with the grace of the lord bishop and the Inquisitor, or at least that he would do that which in him lay; whereof he did naught, in so far as I know." The abbot of another house, with the cellarer and three other of the monks, "knew me, and were aware that I had fled from prison, and nevertheless they kept me to serve their abbey for seven years or thereabouts. I promised and offered the abbot 15 *sols* if he would procure my reconciliation; he would not take anything, but answered me at last that he saw no remedy but that I should go back to prison. I gave 2 *sols* to one of the monks to beg the abbot that he would reconcile me with the Inquisitor." Thence Arnaud drifted to divers houses of refuge (*hospitiis*) in company with an outlawed homicide, who knew him for a fellow-jailbird. Then he settled down for two years, in a village where his story was not known. Then for six months at another village, where again he was unknown, and took a wife. Then six more, still incognito, at another village: here "Guillaume de Castelnau tried to take me: but I escaped." Then in another grange near Bagnères-de-Bigorre; thence to another, "and in many other places, unknown to all men except my wife Bernarde who is now dead, and my son Pierre. And at the procuration of my wife I went by night to Gascogne and to a garden which had once been mine own; and there I spake with Arnaud Escolan, then chaplain of the parish, who took 5 *sols* from me to reconcile me with the Inquisitors; and, if he succeeded, he was to have 10 *sols* more and 2 ells of linen for his shirts; but he did naught in the matter." The Inquisitors sent Arnaud back to prison, "reserving the power of imposing a heavier penalty by reason of his flight. . . . Afterwards they gave him back his knife and remitted the bond

---

* There is a similar case in 1252 of a heretic let out of prison to serve as mason for two years at the nunnery of Rieunette. Three sureties undertook for him, under pledge of 20 *livres*, that he would serve the nuns faithfully. (*Douais*, II, 197.)

under which he lay to the seneschal and bailiff, and another deposit he had made in sufficiency for the fine,* because they had kept him in prejudice of the Inquisition. And this was done in reverence for the lord bishop of Toulouse, and at the instance of his official, Master Bertrand de Ferrières."[6]

* That is, the fine to which he had bound himself in case of failure to appear on the appointed day before the Inquisitors.   The Bishop of Beauvais reads into this last sentence a proof of the bishop's kindness in taking Arnaud's part against the bailiff.   In fact it was only a matter of necessary justice involved in the bishop's assertion of his own rights.   The prisoner belonged to the Church, and she had the prior claim.   The royal officers had treated him as their own, and forced him by their detention to forfeit his pledge for appearance in due time in the Church court.   The bishop now protests against things done "in prejudice of the Inquisition"; and, out of reverence for him, the royal officers surrender their pledge taken from Arnaud.

CHAPTER IX

The Albigensian Crusade

WE have already seen how, before the middle of the twelfth century, St. Bernard described the prevalence of heresy in Southern France: "the churches are without people, the people without priests." Before 1200, on the testimony of other writers equally orthodox and trustworthy, things were far worse for the Church. When Innocent III came to the throne (1198), "[The Church] realised at last that there was one corner of Europe in which the Christian multitude, contrary to its usual habits, listened to the heretics instead of exterminating them."[1] This was Southern France, where Albi, though only one of the cities where heresy flourished, was so far the centre and focus that it gave its name to the whole party. As Lea says, "to the Church this state of things was unbearable. It has always held the toleration of others to be the persecution of itself."[2] And in this case it had more reason than usual. Innocent's own letters, and the chronicle of the monk Pierre des Vaux-de-Cernay, who wrote to Innocent of the things which he had himself seen and heard on the Crusade, are the first documents to which we turn when we wish to get at the real facts from the orthodox point of view. When we have made allowance for their natural bias, they are as trustworthy authorities as can be imagined. Pierre, in his first chapter, describes the state of things in 1203: "This city of Toulouse, steeped in guile [*Haec Tolosa, tota dolosa*], is asserted to have been seldom or never free, since its first foundation, from this detestable pest or pestilence of heretical pravity, seeing that the poison of superstitious infidelity has spread in succession from fathers to sons." It is a city "infected from of old," where heresy is "indigenous." The surrounding country followed the example of Toulouse its capital; it was "marvellously and miserably infected with this plague," and "almost all the barons of Provence had become harbourers and defenders of heretics." In Chapter III, again, Pierre tells us that the great city of Béziers contained "few Catholics" (*cf.* XVI). Moreover, Innocent recognised no less distinctly the chronic nature of the movement against which he fought. The heretics of Southern France (he writes in 1198) are "innumerable"; in 1200, the ecclesiastical province of Narbonne contains "more disciples of Manichæus [*sic*] than of Christ," while "the prelates are the laughing-stock of the layfolk"; in 1204 "the heretics are preaching their doctrines publicly everywhere." In other districts, also, a Waldensian memorial* represented the heretics as so strong that there was a fear "lest the simple, faithful folk that dwell among these heretics, and who do not receive the Eucharist, should grow hardened."[3] Luchaire points out how, from 1119 onwards, we have a series of papal and provincial councils testifying to the multitude of heretics in Southern France and to their steady progress (p. 40). Again, describing the state of things between 1167 and 1177, he writes: "It would seem that, at that time, the towns and country districts were peopled with sectaries"; and again: "The Albigensians were perhaps in a majority in certain small towns of maritime Languedoc, which was the headquarters of the sect" (pp. 7, 8). In 1178 the heretics were so numerous and influential at Toulouse that they "almost compelled the Catholics to conceal their own faith" (p. 42). And Havet, on pp. 148 ff, describes in considerable detail their steady and peaceable growth in Italy and Southern France about the same time. There were thousands, therefore, in 1204, who were born of heretical parents, and had sucked in heresy with their mothers' milk; in many families, heresy was probably a tradition of several generations. Moreover, we have the most definite factual corroboration of these literary judgments.[4] The foxes went openly abroad by

---

* Waldensians and Albigensians were originally inimical to each other; it was only persecution that drove them into each other's arms.

daylight. In 1167 they held a great Council near Toulouse, under their own "Pope" from Constantinople, and three "bishops"; three more "bishops" were presently consecrated. In 1178 the papal legate held a public discussion with two of these bishops at Toulouse. In 1196 one of their bitterest opponents, Bonacorso, wrote that "the cities and towns and castles are full of these false prophets."

Innocent acted at once: he sent a commissioner to deal with the matter on the spot. At the same time he commenced proceedings against two notoriously remiss and immoral prelates, the archbishops of Narbonne and Auch. It took him ten years to remove these; and meanwhile the still more serious matter of heresy promised no better. To the very end, the hierarchy never realised in practice what was so often confessed in words, that there was little hope so long as the clergy themselves were hated and despised. Gregory X, at the Ecumenical Council of 1274, confessed that the hierarchy was the ruin of the world—*quod prælati facerent ruere totum mundum*. At the next Ecumenical Council (1311) one of the best bishops was asked to send the pope a memorial of suggested reforms. He took this again as his first text: amendment must begin from the top: from the Roman Court itself, and then from the bishops in their sees. The same story will be told in every generation down to the sixteenth century and beyond, but with no better effect. Here, then, is the real tragedy of this Albigensian Crusade: that the people had moral reasons for listening to the heretics, and the barons had selfish reasons for envying their ecclesiastical fellow-barons. "The mistake of the promoters of this Crusade was to believe that these feudal lords, because they patronised the heretics, had embraced heresy."[5]

The greatest of these lords were the Counts of Toulouse, little kings in the south; they had fourteen counts among their vassals. In 1195 Raymond VI paid no attention to the Council of Montpellier, which anathematised all princes neglecting to enforce the papal decrees of that year against heretics. To have obeyed would have been to invite civil war against an enormous number of his subjects. It would have troubled the domestic peace of what was, at that moment, one of the happiest corners of Europe despite its anticlericalism; and the Count would have laid himself open also to watchful enemies on every side, who would catch eagerly at any opportunity for interference as a means of establishing their own influence in his devastated territories. All this he was asked to risk for the sake of a Church which he regarded as too rich and powerful already.

Innocent was not the man to accept defeat easily, and he now sent two Cistercian monks as legates. The Cistercians had been in the forefront of the latest wave of monastic and ecclesiastical reform; and they were still, after a century, stricter and more enthusiastic than the rest; for the Franciscans and Dominicans had not yet appeared. With great difficulty these legates half-commanded, half-bribed the magistrates of Toulouse to proceed against the heretics: but the concession was only in word, without fulfilment in deed. So was it, again, with a similar oath which they extorted from the Count. The Archbishop of Narbonne, with whom the matter essentially lay, refused to act with the legates. The bishop of Béziers even hindered their efforts for obtaining from the magistrates an oath to suppress heresy within their city. When the Bishop of Carcassonne threatened his flock for their heresy, they expelled him from the city. The sister of the Count of Foix, with five other ladies, was publicly "hereticated" by the Cathari amid an assembly of knights and nobles. Innocent now added a third legate, the head of the whole Cistercian Order. St. Bernard, five generations before, had been the one missionary who had met with some real success; and his Order were a natural papal militia for this coming struggle. They will fight now with other weapons than St. Bernard's, and their worldly success will be greater. France was governed by Philip Augustus, one of the best politicians she ever had; and to him Innocent turned for help in the extreme measures on which he was already resolved. He represented this as a Holy War, a conflict of Civilisation with Barbarism: moreover, as a profitable political speculation. For his soul, the King would earn plenary remission of all his sins; for his kingdom, he should enter into possession of the territories of recalcitrant Southern nobles. Similar bribes were offered to the King of Aragon, but in both cases without result. Politically, the game did not seem worth the candle; and, spiritually, there was not sufficient orthodox zeal among the sovereigns of Europe. The three legates, meanwhile, met with so little success that they had determined to give up the task, when new life was suddenly infused into the mission by an enthusiastic Spanish bishop, Diego of Osma. He persuaded the legates to go among the heretics not as ecclesiastical lords but as humble missionaries, setting the example himself. They and their companions wandered thus for three months among the people, finding the heretics in the majority almost everywhere; disputing with them, but converting few. It is most noteworthy, in the face of mutual barbarities and recriminations when once civil war had begun, that these missionaries suffered no more personal molestation than St. Bernard, though they travelled unguarded among this hostile population, against whom the pope all the time was invoking fire and sword. One legate, Pierre de Castelnau, who had made himself more unpopular than the rest, was indeed threatened at Béziers, but no more.

Pierre then went to Provence to muster the nobles against the heretics. Raymond gave him no active help. He was no heretic, and was willing that the legate should convert as many as he could; but he saw no sufficient reason for drenching his dominions in blood. Therefore, the legate excommunicated him; and Innocent sent him a letter (1207) confirming this sentence in the harshest terms. Unless he showed immediate obedience and satisfaction, the princes of Christendom would be called upon to seize his territories. Raymond paid little attention. Meanwhile the popular missionary effort of the legates and Diego had faded away. St. Dominic, it is true, was now beginning his life's work, the combination of learned preaching with apostolic poverty: but as yet he had only a handful of like-minded helpers. Innocent could only appeal again to Philip Augustus, adding this time a series of personal invitations to all the great nobles. There would be a Plenary Indulgence for all who came to fight against these heretics; and the victors should partition their confiscated lands. Philip's answer came practically to this, that nothing would induce him to move in the matter unless he could get even more favourable business terms.

Then came a thunderbolt. A sudden political murder set fire to this accumulated mass of rivalries and cupidity and hatred; and now that war, which the great pope had vainly tried for so many years to engineer, blazed up in a day. The unpopular legate, Pierre de Castelnau, was murdered at (or shortly after, for the accounts differ) an interview with Count Raymond. The Count's complicity is very probable, and certainly the murderer escaped unpunished; but there was never any trial in due form of justice. Innocent first excommunicated Raymond as a heretic, and then declared the forfeiture of his lands, though, in feudal law, the judgment of the King of France should have been required for that penalty. Thus, as Lea points out, a precedent was created for the introduction into European jurisprudence of the fatal principle that suspicion of heresy annuls all rights. Here stood the *fait accompli*, even if Raymond had been able later to prove his innocence of the murder.

Meanwhile the crime had played completely into Innocent's hands. These medieval populations, acting habitually upon impulse, looking always to the rites of the Church for their defence against plague and frost and hail and famine, were as easy to sway in one direction as in another. Those who could not join a Crusade to the Holy Land would sometimes scourge themselves, as penitents, half-naked through the streets. The Crusade of the Children, again, gives us in sober history what Hameln gives us in legend: thousands of children, without leader, marching out from their homes "to Jerusalem," and dying like flies by the way! To the criminal, again, a Crusade procured worldly pardon; and to all, if contrite and confessed, the certainty of a crown in heaven. Luchaire emphasises this

state of mind which characterised the Middle Ages (p. 36).
"The multitude, living under the perpetual terror of devastating
calamities, and convinced that pestilence, famine and war were
manifestations of God's anger, thought they could disarm that
wrath by exterminating His enemies. In the upper classes there
was less fanaticism, and it was not rare to find the priest more
tolerant than the layman, because he was more enlightened.
In fact, the higher we go up in the hierarchy, the less violent
we find religious passion." We find this to some extent in
Innocent himself: but only later, after more than one chastening
experience.

He was a man of great boldness, in full vigour of mind and
body, determined to make a clean sweep of many abuses in
Church and State, which he had watched with bitter regret
during an active political life. His personal influence was
enormous and well-deserved. He now proclaimed, for this
invasion of Languedoc, all the Indulgences that could be
earned by the far more difficult and dangerous campaigns in the
Holy Land; and his success was immediate and immense.
Philip Augustus now raised no opposition to the service of his
barons. Large contingents came also from Germany, others
from Italy, and some even from so far as Slavonia. It was easy,
as will be seen, to represent this Crusade as a decisive world-
conflict between civilisation and revolutionary barbarism.
Moreover, as the war went on, it became more and more
definitely national; for by this time the present European
nations were beginning to take shape, and there has never been
an age in which the formation of nations has not bred a
nationalism in rough proportion to the precision of national
frontiers. At contemporary Oxford, the students from North or
South of the Trent fought in the streets. As Rashdall has said,
there has perhaps been more blood shed in that High Street per
square yard than on many historic battlefields; and even at the
end of the Middle Ages, when St. John Fisher drew up the
statutes for St. John's College at Cambridge, he found it
necessary to insert a clause prohibiting quasi-national quarrels

between the Northern and Southern Fellows. So this Albigensian war developed into a struggle for the mastery between North and South. Thus it was that de Montfort finally conceived it; and in that spirit he won it. Tamizey de Larroque, in his apology for this Albigensian Crusade, emphasises "the implacable animosity which inflamed races of different origins separated by the Loire," and "the ardent covetousness excited by the riches of the South in the coarse minds of de Montfort's soldiers": in these two causes he finds the main explanation for "that character of ferocity which the Albigensian war kept from beginning to end."[6] In comparison with these he minimises the part played by religious prejudices: but we cannot go so far. Among populations in whom toleration has not become customary, at least to some extent, by a slow "broadening down from precedent to precedent," religious differences have immense power, if only as an excuse for personal hate and greed. In days when Jews were very commonly killed because they were Jews, it was natural enough for Christians to kill each other for religious differences. It was only too easy in this civil war for each side to regard the other as enemies of God and Society; and, as we shall see, blood-lust on one side bred horrible reprisals on the other. Nearly all our documentary evidence is from the Catholic side; Catharism, for the best of reasons, is almost voiceless. Yet, even from these scattered documents, the earliest responsibility for the worst barbarities seems to rest upon the ultimately victorious North. The learned Benedictine authors of the *Histoire de Languedoc* seem, on the whole, to incline definitely towards this view.

The first operation of primary importance was the storm of Béziers, one of the Albigensian headquarters (July, 1209). This hill-city had been thought almost impregnable; yet the papal legate reported to Innocent how, "while we were treating with the barons concerning the liberation of those who were reputed Catholics in the city, the rabble* and other vile and ill-armed

* *"Ribaldi et alii viles et inermes personæ."* The *ribaldi* were the lowest class of foot soldiers; the others were *inermes* only in the sense that they were not regularly armed.

folk, without awaiting their leaders' command, made an attack upon the city, and, to our amazement, while the cry was raised *To arms, to arms!* within the space of some two or three hours the moats and the wall were crossed and the city of Béziers was taken; and our men, sparing neither rank nor sex nor age, slew about 20,000 souls with the edge of the sword; and, making a huge slaughter, pillaged and burned the whole city, by reason of God's wrath wondrously kindled against it."[7] Tamizey de Larroque, who pushes his apology to the utmost limits compatible with recorded facts, dares not to put the hypothetical number of those who escaped this carnage, by fleeing from the city or otherwise, at more than 4,000 (pp. 187–9). Pierre des Vaux-de-Cernai says that "almost all were slaughtered"— *omnes fere necati.*[8]

The impression of these events was immense; more than one hundred strong and well-victualled castles were at once abandoned by the heretics. Carcassonne, perhaps the strongest city in France, was next attacked; the outworks were taken, and the legate writes to Innocent in a tone of apology for having allowed the citizens to surrender, on guarantee of their lives for a single day's march from the city. "Our leaders" (he writes) "were almost driven by necessity to this act of mercy," partly because the citadel might have held out so long, and partly for fear lest farther ravage like that of Béziers should render the district uninhabitable even for the conquerors,[9] "so they all went forth naked from the city, bearing with them naught but their own sins."[10] At Castres, Montfort acquiesced even in the burning of a heretic who had recanted and not relapsed.[11] When the castle of Brom was taken, "[the Crusaders] tore out the eyes of more than 100 of the defenders, and cut off their noses, leaving only one eye to a single one of the crew, that he might lead all the rest to Cabaret in mockery of our enemies. This the Count [of Montfort] did, not because such mutilation of men pleased him, but because his adversaries had done the same first, and these cruel butchers mutilated and slew whomsoever of our men they might find."[12] In June 1210, the Count laid siege to Minerve. The walls were battered, and the lord treated for surrender with Montfort, who referred him to the legate Arnaud. The legate (writes our Cistercian chronicler) "ordained that the lord of the castle and all who were with him, even those who were adherents of the heretics, should come out alive if they would be reconciled and obey the Church's commands; and that even the 'perfect' heretics, of whom there were a very great number, should yet escape if they would be converted to the Catholic faith. That noble and wholly faithful Catholic Robert Mauvoisin [Montfort's trusted lieutenant], who stood hard by, seeing that these heretics were to be freed, to destroy [*perdendos*] whom the Crusaders had come thither, and fearing lest, now that they were caught, they might perhaps be led by fear to promise fulfilment of all our demands—this Robert, I say, withstood the legate to his face, saying that our Crusaders would by no means suffer this. To whom the Legate made answer: 'Fear not; for I believe that very few will be converted.' " After the surrender, "hearing that a multitude of the heretics were gathered together in a certain building, the legate went to them bearing words of peace and warnings of salvation, desiring to convert them to better things; but they broke in upon his words, saying all with one voice: 'Wherefore do ye preach? we will have none of your faith; we abjure the Roman Church; ye labour in vain; neither life nor death shall separate us from the sect whereunto we hold.' Hearing this, he quitted that building, and went to preach to the women, who were assembled in another house; but if he had found the heretics hard and obstinate, still more obstinate did he find these heretickesses, and hardened through and through." The Count tried in turn: "but, finding that he produced no effect whatever, he caused them to be taken out of the town; for there were 140 or more of these 'perfect' heretics. So he prepared a plentiful fire, whereinto all were cast; yet there was no need for our men to cast them in; nay, all were so obstinate in their wickedness as to cast themselves in of their own accord. Yet three women escaped, whom a noble lady, mother to Burchard de Marly, snatched from the flames and reconciled to Holy Church."[13] At Lavaur there was a similar massacre. The prisoners included "Aimeri; late lord of Montreal, and eighty other knights; the noble Count [Montfort] purposed to hang them all. But when Aimeri, their leader, had been hanged, the hastily-made gallows collapsed; and the Count, seeing that this would cause great delay, ordered the rest to be slain; wherefore our Crusaders seized most greedily upon them and slew them forthwith on the spot. The lady of the castle, Aimeri's sister and an abominable heretic, was cast into a well, where the Count caused her to be buried in stones; moreover, our Crusaders burned innumerable heretics with prodigious joy"—*cum ingenti gaudio combusserunt*. So also, later, at Casses: "our Crusaders seized about 60 heretics, and burned them *cum ingenti gaudio*."[14] The author of the *Chanson de la Croisade* probably exaggerates no more than the orthodox have done on their side, when he makes the Count of Foix thus sum up the work of the Bishop of Toulouse in this war: "He hath destroyed more than 500,000 folk, great and small, in life and soul and body . . . he is more like Antichrist than a papal Legate."[15]

What, then, was Innocent's attitude towards these and other horrors which might be quoted? He was, it must be repeated, a really good man, with high ideals for which he was willing to make great personal sacrifices. At a later stage of the war he took the more merciful attitude towards the Count of Toulouse, and even risked considerable unpopularity by advocating comparative leniency at the Lateran Council in 1215.[16] This makes it more important to enquire how far he was aware of the atrocities of this war, and how far he approved the principle of religious massacre in the last resort, if not from the first.

There can be no doubt that Innocent heard these grisly details in due course, and knew them all before the Lateran Council met. Not only that, at this very Council, the Archdeacon of Lyons raised his voice boldly in favour of those multitudes whom the Bishop of Toulouse "was condemning to a life of misery, with weeping souls and bleeding bodies."[17]

From the first, Innocent had received authentic tidings straight
from the wars. We have seen how exultantly the legate sent him
official details of the massacre at Béziers; and, again, of the
sending forth of those multitudes from Carcassonne, naked but
for the clothes they stood up in, and with only one day's safe-
conduct. The fact that modern scholars would divide the
legate's figures for Béziers by four or five is here irrelevant:
"some 20,000" was what the legate reported, and what Innocent
believed and approved. A recent apologist has written (italics
mine): "There is *no evidence* that at the capture of Béziers the
papal legate gave the command 'Slay all, the Lord will know his
own.'" But when we read, in the legate's own solemn words,
that confession "sparing neither rank, nor sex, nor age," in
what is described by all the chroniclers as an orgy of victorious
soldiers, is it not almost certain that this massacre was almost
as promiscuous as any in history? Moreover, Cæsarius of
Heisterbach, who records that the legate is reported [*fertur*] to
have said: "The Lord will know his own," was a Cistercian
monk; the Cistercians were the most prominent Order in this
Crusade, and this legate himself was a Cistercian abbot. Professor Guiraud shows extraordinary ignorance when he pleads
that Cæsarius "wrote more than a hundred years after the
event"; and when he calls his book a "fourteenth-century prose
chronicle!"[18] Cæsarius, at the time of this massacre of 1209, had
in all probability been a Cistercian monk for some ten years;
and it is quite possible that he wrote those words as early as
1230. Though he is obviously wrong in some of his facts (as the
legate and Innocent III were, even at the time) yet he, like
them, may be trusted as reflecting the spirit of the Crusade.
Moreover, the Cistercian of Vaux-Cernay, upon whose bitterly
anti-heretical chronicle all apologists for the Inquisition
specially rely, gives a description which goes far to bear
Cæsarius out. He writes: "As soon as [the Crusaders] entered,
almost all were slain, and the city given to the flames." Soon
afterwards he relates that almost equally shocking incident of
Minerve without any qualifying *ut fertur*. That incident concerns

this same Cistercian papal legate concerning whom Cæsarius wrote; and it refers to the very next year, 1210. Innocent's answer to the Béziers report is not recorded in his Register; but we have his letter in response to Simon de Montfort, who had written about the same time. This (Ep. No. 123) begins with "praise and thanks to God for that which He hath mercifully and marvellously wrought through thee, and through others whom zeal for the orthodox faith hath kindled to this work, against His most pestilent enemies." The pope is glad to hear the land is being purged of heresy; he will do all he can to help Simon in "extirpating the remnants of heretical iniquity," and only regrets that the simultaneous Crusade against the East prevents him from doing more. There is not a word to hint that the Crusaders have exceeded their strict duty. This was on November 11th; as prompt a reply as could be expected from the papal chancery: "presque immédiatement Innocent sanctionne les faits accomplis," writes Luchaire (p. 145). At the same time he wrote urgent letters to the Emperor Otto, to the Kings of Aragon and of Castile, and to many abbots and other prelates, pressing them to help Montfort in this holy war (Epp. 124–128). These letters are noticeable for the first appearance of that word *exterminare* which, as we have seen, plays so important a part in papal policy. They are dated November 11th, the day of his approving letter to Montfort. He there reviews the summer's campaign, and enumerates the Church's religious and material gains (Ep. 136). He writes: "God hath mercifully purged His people's land; and the pest of heretical wickedness, which had grown like a cancer and infected almost the whole of Provence, is being deadened and driven away—*mortificata depellitur*. His mighty hand hath taken many towns and cities wherein the devil dwelt in the person of those whom he possessed; and a holy habitation is being prepared for the Holy Ghost, in the persons of those whom He hath filled, in place of the expelled heretics. Wherefore we give praise and thanks to God Almighty, because, in one and the same cause of His mercy, He hath deigned to work two works of justice, by bringing upon these faithless folk their merited destruction [*perniciem*], in such a fashion that as many as possible of the faithful should gain their well-earned reward by the 'extermination' of these folk. For, although He might at any moment have shattered them [*conterere*] by the mere breath of His mouth, yet He hath deigned, in their destruction [*contritione*], to grant a means of wealth—nay, more, of salvation —to the army of His Crusaders; which army hath lately triumphed marvellously over them under the command of our legates."

The rest of this sordid story must be abridged here; it is given in full by Lea (I. 129–208) and by A. Luchaire, one of the ablest French medievalists, in his *Innocent III et la Croisade des Albigeois*.

Raymond VI was no match for Simon de Montfort in war, or for Rome in diplomacy.* He was not a heretic, but neither was he more than an indifferent Churchman. His diplomacy was perhaps almost as crooked as that of his adversaries; certainly it was not always either straightforward or consistent. But in one essential matter he was never treated with ordinary justice. Even when the Pope granted that he should be no longer invaded unheard, but allowed a public trial by ordinary forms of Church law, the legates and bishops succeeded in frustrating this. Even when he came to Rome to plead his own cause, Innocent played fast and loose with him. The Pope did indeed rebuke his legates: how could the Count's lands be adjudged to Montfort, until a proper trial had been held according to the papal command? Yet when those legates, at the Council of Lavaur (1213), repeated that the Count was too notorious a perjurer to be listened to, Innocent ate his own words and gave way. The result was that this professedly religious war degenerated into perhaps the worst combination that can be conceived. We have here a fatal mixture of nationalism, race enmities and territorial greed, not only in the unhappy land given over to these battles and sieges, but in other States

* "[The monkish chronicler's] admiring ejaculations, 'O pious fraud of the legate! O fraudulent piety!' is the key which unlocks to us the secrets of Italian diplomacy with the Albigenses." (Lea, I, 179.)

glad to fish for themselves in the troubled waters. Thus, on all sides, selfishness utilises idealism. The parties bend to their own purposes, and thus intermingle inextricably in men's consciences, genuine religious enthusiasm with bitter religious rivalries, and with the hypocrisy of indifferentists who find the religious mask convenient. When Lea concludes that in 1226, after eighteen years of bloody warfare, "the question of religion had practically disappeared, except as an excuse for Indulgences and ecclesiastical subsidies and as a cloak for dynastic oppression," he is practically repeating the verdict of the Benedictines in their *Histoire de Languedoc*, and anticipating that of Luchaire, who writes: "with what prodigies of activity Simon de Montfort exploited his success [in war]! . . . Why should we now talk of Crusade, of heresy and orthodoxy, of religious interests? Here we have a political revolution at work: the systematic conquest of all Southern France, the formation of a dynasty! Innocent himself had been able only intermittently to react against the irresistible current. After [Montfort's crushing victory at] Muret, we find the Pope renouncing open opposition; but there was no abdication of diplomacy: that will continue its see-saw character." Of all these Crusaders, Montfort was perhaps the most truly religious, as he was certainly the greatest in other ways. Yet, shortly before his death, we find him quarrelling with the papal legate, Archbishop of Narbonne, for some of the worldly spoils of victory, and treating that prelate's repeated excommunications with contempt.[19] His priests sang Mass for him as usual in his chapel; and he answered the Archbishop's curse with derision. Finally his soldiers cast stones at the legate's palace in Narbonne. He apparently even died under this ban, and may thus have needed that exceptional indulgence which Dante grants to Manfred, the arch-rebel against the Church: *Per lor maledizion sì non si perde, Che non possa tornar l'eterno amore, Mentre che la speranza ha fior del verde.**

* *Purgatorio*, III, 133. "By curse of theirs man is not so lost, that eternal love may not return, so long as hope retaineth aught of green."

For, at the end of 1217, he began the second siege of Raymond's capital, Toulouse. The first had been memorable
enough. "All the old civic quarrels were forgotten, and as one
man they prepared for resistance. It is a noteworthy illustration
of the strength of the republican institution of the civic com-
mune, that the siege of Toulouse was the first considerable
check received by the Crusaders. The town was well fortified
and garrisoned; the Counts of Foix and Comminges had come at
the summons of their suzerain, and the citizens were earnest in
defence. They not only kept their gates open, but made
breaches in the walls to facilitate the furious sallies which cost
the besiegers heavily. The latter retired, June 29th, under
cover of the night, so hastily that they abandoned their sick and
wounded, having accomplished nothing except the complete
devastation of the land—dwellings, vineyards, orchards, women
and children were alike indiscriminately destroyed in their
wrath—and de Montfort turned from the scene of his defeat to
carry the same ravage into Foix. This final effort of self-defence
was naturally construed as 'fautorship of heresy,' and drew
from Innocent a fresh excommunication of Raymond and of the
city for 'persecuting' de Montfort and the Crusaders."[20]

The second siege was even more remarkable. "The burghers
displayed unflinching resolve to preserve themselves from the
yoke of the stranger—or perhaps, rather, the courage of despera-
tion, if the account is to be believed that the cardinal-legate
ordered the Crusaders to slay all the inhabitants, without
distinction of age or sex. In spite of the defenceless condition of
the town, which men and women unitedly worked night and day
to repair; in spite of the threatening and beseeching letters
which [Pope] Honorius wrote to the Kings of Aragon and
France, to the younger Raymond, the Count of Foix, the citizens
of Toulouse, Avignon, Marseilles, and all whom he thought to
deter or excite; in spite of heavy reinforcements brought by a
vigorous renewal of preaching the Crusade, for nine weary
months the siege dragged on, in furious assaults and yet more
furious sallies, with intervals of suspended operations as the

Crusading army swelled or decreased. De Montfort's brother Gui and his eldest son Amauri were seriously wounded. The baffled chieftain's troubles were rendered sorer by the legate, who taunted him with his ill-success and accused him of ignorance or slackness in his work. Sick at heart, and praying for death as a welcome release, on the morrow of St. John's Day, 1218, he was superintending the reconstruction of his machines, after repelling a sally, when a stone from a mangonel, worked, as Toulousain tradition says, by women, went straight to the right spot—'*E vene tot dret la peira lai ou era mestiers*'*—it crushed in his helmet and he never more spoke word."[21]

Miracles were wrought at his tomb.

---

* Literally: "And the stone went just straight to the spot where it was needed."

CHAPTER X

The Inquisition Founded

LET us go back for a moment to Innocent III, whose special creation this Crusade was, and one of the most remarkable incidents of his most remarkable reign. Luchaire emphasises justly the extent to which it brought him failure and disillusion. Already before this, his great Crusade of 1204, which should have freed Palestine from Muslim domination, had ended in what was practically a buccaneering expedition against the Greek Christians, from which by far the richest share of booty came to barons and merchants who had defied the Pope's most explicit prohibitions. This Albigensian Crusade was, in its final result, scarcely less disappointing. Innocent had hoped to clear Languedoc of heresy in a few months: but he had found civil war easier to kindle than to extinguish. In spite of his belief that he was the righteous champion of order against religious anarchy, he cannot have been indifferent to the horrible bloodshed, or the barbarous reprisals into which both sides gravitated so completely that they were soon taken for granted, or the debasement of religious ideals consequent upon those battles and diplomatic shifts by which his Church was attempting to realise them. Lea brings out another paradox almost as striking as that of de Montfort's last year. At the siege of the castle of Beaucaire, the excommunicated count's chaplain offered salvation to all who would work upon the ramparts; and this ecclesiastically valueless "indulgence" was almost as successful as when the Pope's legate, before the battle of Muret, had cried to his army: "Go forward in the name of Christ. I will be your witness and your warranty at the Day of Doom, that all who die in this glorious fight shall earn the everlasting reward and glory of martyrdom without any pains of purgatory, provided that he be confessed and contrite, or at least that he have a firm resolve of showing himself to a priest concerning such sins as he has not yet confessed."[1]

The last scene but one is at the great Lateran Council of 1215, in which Innocent made it a definite law for every orthodox Christian to seek out and "exterminate" heretics. In Languedoc, after more than twenty years of slaughter, they were still almost as numerous, if not as unconcealed and pushing, as ever. Not even open heresy, indeed, was altogether killed: in 1224 a public disputation took place between Catholics and Catharists, and a formal Council of Catharist clergy was held at Pieussan.

In some ways, this Lateran Council was the great glory of Innocent's reign. None such had ever been held in the West; those earlier Councils which equalled or surpassed it in importance had all been held in the East, under the actual or implied presidence of an Emperor. At Innocent's Council he published seventy decrees, drawn up by himself; the bishops had only the honour of assenting to them. They were mostly on matters of supreme importance for Church reform and education. Yet not a single contemporary chronicler took the pains to record these decrees in full. One, after recording No. 16, adds: "And many other decrees which are by no means well kept and obeyed."[2] The discussions on his Crusade must have brought home to Innocent, whose book *On the Contempt of the World* is his best-known literary work, the vanity of human wishes. His attempts to secure something like justice at this Council for Raymond VI and his son brought him unpopularity in the Church which he had laboured so hard to serve. Our Cistercian Pierre de Vaux-Cernay writes that the Party of Faith (i.e., Montfort and his friends) were opposed at the Council by some members—among whom, grievous to relate, were certain prelates—who laboured for the restoration to the two Counts of Toulouse of their patrimony. Fortunately this "counsel of Achitophel," writes Pierre, came to naught, and the hopes of the unrighteous were disappointed. But another contemporary tells us what Pierre omits, that Innocent was among those who favoured this counsel of Achitophel, and that he struggled vainly here against the overwhelming opposition of the prelates. "The scene changes. Innocent, in the garden of his Lateran palace, hides his affliction and seeks distraction. But the prelates of Languedoc, and other bishops of the majority, come to besiege him there and to force from him a pronouncement against the Counts." A few months later, the great Pope was dead; Montfort followed not long after; and, after twelve years more of bloodshed and crooked diplomacy, Languedoc finally fell into the pocket of the Kings of France. "It was for their benefit that everybody, beginning with Innocent III, had unwittingly laboured, suffered and struggled."[3]

Thus it became more and more evident that some further change of policy was required. Lynch-law and pogroms had failed to crush heresy; indeed, here and there populations had developed in which, if lynch-law was to be the rule, it was the Catholics who would suffer. The Crusade had only half succeeded; it had crushed Languedoc politically, but heresy still fermented under the surface. What has been called the Episcopal Inquisition had proved evidently insufficient. By this institution, first from 1184 onwards, and then with redoubled emphasis at the Lateran in 1215, it was made the Bishop's duty to enquire after heretics throughout his diocese, and for the faithful in each parish to report any suspect, even though it were his own parent or child. This, again, broke down through the remissness or incapacity or immorality of many prelates, with rivalries or jealousies between Church and State authorities. Evidently persecution must be further systematised and the edge of the law sharpened: there must no longer be this more or less ambiguous talk of "extermination," but the plainest insistence upon the sword or the stake. Innocent himself would probably have undertaken this if he had long outlived the Lateran Council; fourteen years later it was undertaken by Gregory IX, the friend and patron of St. Francis, who had been as distinguished a canon lawyer as Innocent himself.

During this interval the old policy of vague words and cruel acts was still maintained. It is often falsely imagined that the Roman creed of the Middle Ages was clear-cut and consistent, and that Canon Law formed a complete logical code. This is far from the truth. Orthodox medieval theologians fought then with each other, almost as Catholic and Protestant fight nowadays, about such questions as the Immaculate Conception and Papal Infallibility, both of which have been decided only within the time of thousands who are still alive. Canon Law, again, though more complete and perhaps less ambiguous than any State laws of that time, was a mass of inconsistencies and contradictions in comparison with any modern system. Thus, in our present subject, the vague phrase *animadversio debita* still reigned.* Louis VIII, in 1226, put it into the Laws of France; the magistrates, then, could either burn or not, according to their interpretation at any time or in any case. The Council of Toulouse (1229) uses it again, but with the significant addition that heretics who, henceforward, come back to the Church "not of their own accord but *from fear of death*" are so to be imprisoned that they may never again contaminate the flock. Vacandard, who would like to interpret Louis VIII's phrase as simple banishment, is compelled to admit that the Toulouse addition "would seem to prove the elasticity of the formula." In 1220 Frederick II followed a course which is only too common in religious politics, when the great man is willing to persecute others for crude and vulgar disbelief in things which he does not really believe himself. He brought the laws of the Empire into conformity with the Lateran decree of 1215. Heretics, ran his decree, "offend the Divine Majesty, which is far worse than to offend human majesty," and this argument, borrowed from Innocent III, will in future be fateful. As a natural corollary, in 1224, he condemned all future heretics to the stake. In 1231 he drew up a new code of laws for his favourite Kingdom of the Two Sicilies: it begins with death for

* For this phrase see Chap. VI, p. 65, where it will be seen that it, like *exterminare*, was perhaps designedly ambiguous.

heretics as guilty of High Treason against God, and commands the magistrates to seek them out. This may warn us against attaching exaggerated significance to the frequent (though by no means invariable) willingness of magistrates to burn those whom the Church bade them burn. Frederick was one of the most notorious free-thinkers of his day, at constant war with the Popes, and accused by Gregory IX of having said publicly that the world had been the victim of Three Impostors—Christ, Moses and Mahomet. Here, however, he was willing to make peace with the Papacy on the common ground of death for religious nonconformists. These two rivals for the domination of Europe—rivals all the more bitter because they were nominally equal partners—had one great common interest in this hatred and fear of popular independence. Therefore Frederick, between 1231 and 1238, published a series of persecuting edicts for separate regions of his empire. Gregory, meanwhile, did not lag behind. It is sometimes pleaded that he acted here only in self-defence: that the Church could not afford to let the State encroach upon her own province, thus diminishing her prestige and her ultimate influence. The theory is farfetched and gratuitous: nor does it help Gregory much even if we accept it. Politically, we must then regard it as an early precedent for "dishing the Whigs." From the religious and moral point of view, it would amount to a confession of weakness for so powerful a Pope to follow in the wake of such an emperor. Be that as it may, Gregory did in fact keep step with Frederick in severity. In 1231 he burned a group of heretics at Rome: it is significant that these were the descendants of those *Patarini* of Milan upon whose help Gregory VII had relied, a century and a half earlier, as a sort of papal militia in his campaign against clerical marriage. Gregory IX then circularised all the bishops, to press upon them the need of systematic and ubiquitous enquiry, *inquisitio*, into the beliefs of their flocks. In some of the Italian cities, again, the magistrates were burning heretics. From 1227 to 1233 he gave full support and encouragement to the fanatic Conrad of Marburg, whose

insane asceticism matched that of the Catharan "Perfecti."
This man (in the words of the papal commissioners themselves
later on) "gave implicit belief to the [accusing] witnesses, so
that the accused were given a bare option to choose spontaneous
confession and live, or to swear to their innocence and go
straight to death." In the words of a chronicler, "no chance of
defence was offered, no delay was granted for deliberation, but
the accused must either at once confess guilt and be brought to
penance, or deny it and be burned." Here Conrad had a rival in
the Dominican ex-Catharist Robert le Bougre, who discovered
a nest of heretics at Montwimer in Champagne. After a trial
lasting a week at most, he offered (to quote the Cistercian
chronicler) "a very great and acceptable holocaust to the Lord,
in the burning of Bougres: for 183 Bougres were burned in the
presence of the King of Navarre and the barons of Champagne
and many prelates." As Conrad's excesses finally caused his
murder, so Robert's also became too impossible; he was disgraced and ended his days in a monastic prison.

It was natural, then, that Gregory should take a further step
to put persecution upon a more regular and responsible
foundation. In 1233 he formally entrusted the work to the
recently formed and specially enthusiastic Dominican Order.
From among these he named certain Inquisitors, whom he sent
to different lands with powers to work with, and in many ways
to supersede, the diocesan bishops. It is from this year that we
must date, in so far as an exact date may be fixed, the full-
blown Inquisition: the *Monastic*, as some call it, in view of the
fact that it was mainly worked by Dominicans and Franciscans:
or the *Papal*, as it may be more exactly called in virtue of the
absolute papal responsibility for its creation.

The foregoing brief statements of fact in this chapter will show
clearly enough how gradually and slowly papal policy crystallised in this field. Vacandard writes truly: "In short,
Gregory IX only pressed upon Christendom the application of
already existing laws, and introduced, when no such existed, the
most rigorous legislation against heresy. But what belongs

specially to him is the procedure to which he had recourse for the prosecution of heretics: that is, his Inquisitorial system. The Inquisition proper, the *Monastic*, is in fact his work."

At this point we must pause to consider the plea that all this organised violence was only in self-defence against the initial violence of the heretics. A quite recent and able writer asserts: "There is ample evidence that, wherever they got the chance . . . they thought it their duty utterly to destroy every evidence of Catholic life and to murder those on whom they could lay their hands."[4] For this he claims the authority of that bulky and pretentious *Dictionnaire Apologétique* which is one of the ripest fruits of the Institut Catholique at Paris: let us therefore look at the evidence there offered. It begins with Abailard's complaint against the heretics of his day: "Civilibus bellis Ecclesiam inquietare non cessant"; "they cease not to trouble the Church with civil wars" (*Œuvres*, ed. Cousin, II, 83). But Abailard is there arguing on purely theological ground, quite apart from politics. He quotes, as specimens, the six most noxious of these heretics. One of them, Tanchelm, calls himself Son of God; another wishes to rebaptize the baptized, and preaches against the Cross and the Eucharist; the other four teach errors in Christology or concerning the mystery of the Trinity. Abailard does not breathe one word, throughout these two quarto pages, of physical violence or civil war in the literal sense. All that he is concerned to prove is that such doctrines introduce perpetual domestic dissension into the Church; they bring *civilia bella* into the *Ecclesia*. After all, we know a great deal about them from other sources; these represent them as relying mainly upon preaching, and as suffering more violence than they offered. The first, this Tanchelm, did indeed raise a force of 3,000 men and controlled Bruges and Antwerp for a while; but his real strength lay in the notorious immorality and neglect of the clergy, and in his refusal to pay tithes or to recognise the sacredness of the Eucharist when the minister's hands were polluted. The hostile chronicler who speaks of his 3,000 followers has nothing to say of actual bloodshed

or destruction of churches in the two great cities where he was
dictator for some time. He went to Rome with a few followers
on Church business: on his return in 1112 he and his friends were
imprisoned at Cologne by the Archbishop: three were burned,
others recanted or fled; Tanchelm himself was knocked on the
head by a priest three years later. Abailard, who names him
first among those six disturbers of the Church, alleges nothing
against him but false theology. The next criminal specified by
the *Dictionnaire Apologétique* is the Breton visionary Éon de
l'Étoile. We have seen in Chapter VI how, after many shifts,
Éon was at last "easily arrested by the Archbishop of Reims,"
condemned in full Council, and cast into a prison in which "he
lived but a short while longer." Next comes Pierre de Bruys, in
early twelfth-century Languedoc. He is indeed accused of
preaching the destruction of churches and crosses; but that he
had no body of followers capable of terrorising the general
population is proved by the ease with which he was captured
and burned. Then comes another in Southern France, the ex-
monk Henry. Of this man, again, no actual destruction of
churches seems to be recorded, though some nobles took up his
anticlericalism and would gladly, no doubt, have disendowed
the priests. St. Bernard was called down to preach against him
and his sect; the saint went about freely everywhere without the
least personal molestation, though he himself called upon the
orthodox to "follow and capture them, and desist not until they
perish altogether, and flee from your regions."

These are fair examples of the evidence upon which we are
asked to believe that the heretics thought it their duty to
murder those on whom they could lay their hands. The two
instances which come nearest to such an accusation—and even
these come definitely short of it—break down completely upon
examination. Count Raymond-Roger of Foix is accused of
bloodthirsty violence by a bitter personal enemy, whose
untrustworthiness in the face of documentary evidence is
emphasised both by the Benedictine authors of the *Histoire de
Languedoc* and by their learned editor, C. Molinier. Again, the

bloodthirsty mercenaries who ravaged many districts of
France are sometimes reckoned as formal heretics, in defiance of
the distinctions which both Pope and Canon Law draw between
them and the heretics proper, such as the Catharists. Those
mercenaries did indeed plunder everywhere, churches included,
and therefore Alexander III banned them at the same time as
the Catharists, and spoke of their conduct as "heretical." But
such miscreants were employed on both sides in these civil wars;
and they answered to those "ribaldi" who led the storm of
Béziers. As Luchaire puts it, they were "professionally impious"; they would have plundered a rich Catharist temple or a
wealthy Catharist prelate, if such had existed, with equal
gusto. The heretics proper were no more responsible for what
these men did on either side, than the Vatican was for poison-
gas in Ethiopia.

It is true that words and deeds are often inseparable in fact,
though separable in logic. However definitely a man's creed
may repudiate physical compulsion, few can altogether master
the temptation to employ it when opportunity plainly offers.
The Christian Church, as a whole, cannot escape from that
reproach; though a few small sections can, among whom the
Moravians and the Quakers are conspicuous. When Charles
Spurgeon boasted before an audience of thousands of Baptists
that they belonged to one of the few great religious organisations
which have never persecuted, he waited until the applause had
died down, and added "because we have never been able." So
far, medieval Catholicism had doubtless just cause to fear the
consequences if heresy should ever become supreme. Yet no
party, in strict justice, has a right to anticipate with actual
violence the merely potential violence of an adversary: the
onus probandi always lies heavily upon him who strikes the first
blow, as orthodoxy did in all or nearly all of these cases, by the
testimony of the orthodox themselves. Still less have men a
right to draw the sword first in what they claim as the cause of
pure religion. Yet, here again, it is the orthodox records which
tell us most plainly that the real excuse for violence was found

not in social but in religious nonconformity. The Church claimed the right of killing heretics as murderers not of the body but of the soul; and, from that point of view, the demurest and most virtuous heretic would be the most poisonous, since he would be most persuasive. He would not merely attract to his heresy, as any clumsy unbeliever might do, hundreds of those reckless souls which medieval eschatology consigned in any case to that overwhelming majority in hell; he would make some of his perverts, at least, among the very elect.

Nor, again, can the Inquisition fully justify itself on the plea that medieval religion was so inextricably interwoven with society that to touch the one meant inevitable ruin to the other. That plea is oftenest put forward in the matter of oaths: abolish swearing (we are told) and feudal society would have crumbled to pieces. Such an argument, on analysis, tells less in defence of the Church than in criticism of that social order which had so little cement beyond such oaths, the frequency of which, as contemporaries confess, led to common perjury and the debasement of moral standards in that field. Dr. Rashdall has pointed out how a man would sometimes be compelled to take an oath that he would actually keep his oath!

We must not be hypercritical; but, on the other hand, we must not attempt to justify the unjustifiable. It is possible in the same breath to confess that we ourselves might have done worse in the circumstances, and to point out that, in fact, the hierarchy was in this matter not only unfaithful to true Christian principles, but politically blundering. To have met the heretics with milder punishments than death—more especially, than burning alive—and to have approached them with cleaner hands and more Scriptural arguments before punishing at all, would have been more worldly-wise as well as more Christlike. We must cast the main blame not on individuals, but on the spirit of the age, newly emerged from barbarism and lacking that respect for toleration which, after all, has come more from the practical experience of the last four centuries than from any speculation or argument. To us, the historical effect of past religious wars has brought conclusive proof that neither orthodox nor unorthodox can in fact exterminate each other, and therefore that agreement to differ is happiest for both parties. The Middle Ages had not that experience, nor sufficient knowledge of history to make up for their disadvantage. They erred, we may say, in invincible ignorance, and the most self-righteous among us may well confess that he himself might have erred with them. But that is no excuse for setting ourselves, with history and experience before us, to justify their error. If indeed, as Lord Acton wrote: "the principle of the Inquisition is murderous," then no man in cold blood can justify what our forefathers did, without becoming an accomplice after the fact.

CHAPTER XI

Characteristics of the Inquisition

WE may now look into the constitution of this Inquisition. In Roman Imperial Law there were two widely different modes of procedure. The first was *accusatorial*, as in English Common Law: nothing was done unless somebody came forward as accuser, and the accused was presumed innocent until his guilt had been proved. The other procedure was by way of *inquisitio*, enquiry. If the man was branded as suspect by public report—*publica fama*, which legists often defined as a belief of half a dozen trustworthy persons—then he was, in legal language, *diffamatus* or *infamatus*, and the authorities might bring him into court. In this case his position was reversed; his guilt was assumed unless he could prove his innocence.

(1) Here, then, was an enormous disadvantage from the first: it goes far to explain why (as we shall see in due course) acquittal was almost unknown to the Inquisition.

(2) Again, the judges were purely ecclesiastical: that is, interested parties. The civil powers vainly attempted to assert the right of even consulting the documents. The Carcassonne Inquisition, in mid-thirteenth century, repeatedly compelled those from whom it took pledges to "renounce all [other] law, written or unwritten, and especially the court of the Lord King." On the other hand, the Inquisitors could excommunicate and finally hereticate any civil magistrate who refused to inflict the punishments which their own laws prescribed.

(3) The procedure was secret, and the Inquisitors jealously guarded their records from all outsiders.

(4) The names of the hostile witnesses were generally concealed, on the plea that this was necessary for their

protection. Even when the Inquisitors took assessors to assist
their judgment, no names were generally put before them,
whether of the accused or of the witnesses. These assessors thus
judged in the abstract, completely ignorant of those special
personal considerations which, in any difficult case, often prove
of extreme importance. Yet, as Vacandard pleads truly: "Law
courts ought to judge criminals, and not crimes; just as doctors
treat patients, and not diseases."[1] If the danger to witnesses
were really so great, this would reinforce our other evidence of
the widespread extension of heretical ideas, and the frequent
unpopularity of the Court. The injustice of this concealment
in the case of a possibly innocent prisoner seems to have
occurred to nobody in the hierarchy. The accused had indeed
the liberty of naming beforehand any enemies whose evidence
he would wish to discount as hostile; but if he named too
many, he exposed himself to the suspicion that, where there
was so much smoke, there was probably some fire. Sometimes
the accused answered that he would think it over and see
whether he could name probable false witnesses at a later
hearing: but in by far the most cases he seems to have made no
attempt whatever. The few recorded are sometimes very
significant.[2] At Carcassonne, in 1252, a man named as his
enemies "Bernard de Brom and his sisters, because he had
quarrelled with them about a certain hatchet. *Item*, Bernard
Séguin, because he slew some of the kindred of his wife. *Item*,
Saurina, because she alleged that he had seduced her daughter."
Again, in 1254, the Court has recorded "witnesses produced by
Bernard Pons to prove enmity between himself and his wife."
Here the "subchaplain" of the parish—in modern English,
curate—testified on oath "that he had heard say, and it is
public report in the neighbourhood, that Bernard's wife was
caught at Puy-Laurens by her husband with R. Gujeirat, who
was her adulterer, and she ceaseth not, but committeth adultery
still with many folk; and also a man of Monte Olivo keeps her as
his harlot, so it is said, and so the report goeth in his parish.
Asked whether he knew any other cause of enmity between

them, or could assign any such, he said *No*, only what had been rehearsed. The next witness corroborated: Bernard had beaten her for the offence, but she still continued in her adulteries. The third corroborated again, and added "that he had heard the woman say that she wished her husband was dead, in order that she might marry Pugoler of Monte Olivo, and that she would even wish to be leprous, so only she might have Pugoler for her husband. Asked at what time? He answered 'this year.' Where? 'In Bernard's house.' Who were present? 'A son of Bernard, who is a boy at school.' "

(5) Whereas, in all other courts, the evidence of infamous persons or heretics was ruled out, in this court they were welcomed, so long as their testimony was hostile. Pegna writes, in his great book published at Rome and dedicated to the Pope, "Eymeric's axiom concerning [the admission of] perjurers as witnesses in this matter [of heresy] is as follows: Since perjured witnesses are presumed to be about to tell the truth through zeal for the faith, therefore they must be heard. . . . Moreover, in causes of faith there is the special provision that we stand by the later words of the witnesses, as Eymeric teacheth truly, and his judgment is approved by common consent."

This last sentence marks another crying injustice. When a witness has obviously perjured himself, first swearing to one thing and then to its opposite, what is to be done with his evidence? Eymeric points out that common law required the first deposition to be counted, and the second set aside. Yet, on the contrary, perjurers may be admitted "where [the judge] presumes that they give their evidence through zeal for the Orthodox Faith. For, though [ordinarily] perjurers are repelled from the witness-box even after they have repented, yet if those who, swearing before the Inquisitors to tell the truth concerning the fact of heresy, conceal this in perjury, and afterwards wish to correct themselves by deposing both against themselves and against others their accomplices, concerning the fact of heresy, seeing that this crime is exceptional, therefore if it appear by manifest indications that such witnesses wish to correct their first words not from levity of mind or personal enmity or bribery, but from zeal for the Orthodox Faith, and that they now wish to reveal what they had not told before in favour of the Faith; then [unless there be some other obstacle] we must stand by their [second] evidence both against themselves and against others."[3]

On another most important point the Inquisition gave unique chances to the prosecution. It may be best stated in the words of Tanon, who agrees here with Lea: "If the witnesses were 'single,' that is, if their declarations did not agree with each other, no condemnation could be pronounced on their depositions alone. As to the question, in what conditions their depositions presented the degree of agreement necessary to constitute full proof, this was left essentially to the judge's discretion, in spite of all the distinctions suggested in this matter."[4] Yet the Inquisitor Carena points out that in Portugal his court regularly admitted condemnation on the strength of two "single witnesses," though not at Rome and elsewhere. But he adds that, even where this defect of evidence does not suffice for condemnation offhand, yet it is far from warranting the man's release. "For, albeit these *testes singulares*, even together with *publica fama*, are not conclusive for the punishment of a heretic by the ordinary penalty, yet they are conclusive enough for torturing him [to elicit confession], and for compelling him to abjure publicly, and for inflicting some punishment short of the ordinary penalty, as all the Doctors whom I have quoted allege." Lord Acton, in his copy of the book, has marked for special attention these last sentences, and that recording the greater severity of Portugal.[5]

While all this latitude was allowed for hostile evidence, on the other hand favourable witnesses were practically ruled out. Vacandard confesses frankly (p. 150): "Of all the legal objections in Common Law, which an accused person might make against the accusing witnesses, the Inquisition maintained one only, that of mortal enmity. As to witnesses in his favour, these seldom appeared; it is but rarely that we find them present. That is comprehensible enough; they themselves would almost inevitably have fallen under suspicion of complicity, as favourers of heresy." On the other hand, as against the prisoner, "if two witnesses whom the Inquisitor judged worthy of credit were in agreement in charging him, his fate was inevitably decided; whether he confessed guilt or not, he was declared a heretic."[6]

(6) In accordance with this same spirit, ordinary justice was no less grossly violated in the matter of advocacy. Innocent III, in a decree afterwards inserted in Canon Law, forbade advocates or scriveners to aid heretics. The effect of this, under a system of "justice" which assumed a man's heresy until he could prove the contrary, was almost inevitable. A prohibition nominally affecting only the hardened sinner was soon extended to an almost universal application. If an advocate were granted at all, it was rather to bring him to confession than to prove his innocence; so that, as Vacandard points out, "he was in some sort the Inquisition's advocate, not the accused person's." Any advocate who defended his client as they do in modern law courts would soon have found himself in the dock.

(7) A very small nonconformity might be magnified into a crime punishable by death. We shall see later on that it finally became a burning matter to possess a Bible in the mother-tongue, or to wear garments disapproved by the authorities. Bernard Gui's Register contains other cases like this following (p. 10): "Bernard of Bar, as we are certified by his lawful confession made in our court, saw heretics in his own house, to wit Jacques Autier and Peter his father; and once he heard the said Jacques read in a certain book of the Gospels and Epistles, as he said; after which the said heretic Jacques wished that he and others should do obeisance to him [*adorarent*]. And he himself, with the rest, did obeisance, bowing himself thrice upon a bench and saying, *Benedicite*! and the heretic answered: *God bless you*! Being examined concerning the belief of the heretics, he answered that he did not believe in them. He did not

confess these things until he was taken and put into prison." By such confession he escaped the stake and lifelong imprisonment, but was condemned to wear the cross of infamy.

(8) Beyond this, the theory of "constructive heresy" was pushed to its farthest limits. Any apparent want of respect for the Church might form a *prima facie* ground for suspicion.

(9) Whereas the persecutor Trajan had forbidden Pliny to seek out the concealed Christian, yet the Inquisition compelled every man to spy upon his neighbour's secrets. Neglect of tale-bearing was, in itself, constructive heresy. A heretic who abjured, and thus exchanged the stake for prison, was obliged first to promise that he "would prosecute the heretics, and inform against them, and reveal them wherever he knew them to be" (*ibid.*, p. 78). At Carcassonne (1254) "Ar Baud of Montreal is suspected of heresy because his mother was hereti-cated not long since; wherefore, seeing that he oftentimes visited her and sometimes supplied her with the necessities of life, he seemeth to have consented in her wickedness. Therefore he now swore to stand by all and every the commands of the Inquisitors, and pledged all his goods." The Inquisitors required six others to pledge for him, to the sum of 50 *livres* (£400 modern). Here, again, the commentators exerted their ingenuity to sharpen the rigour of their legal texts. Canon Law, since Innocent III, required that the bishop or archdeacon should get evidence as to heresy from "two or three persons of good fame" in each parish. The famous commentator Joannes Andreæ notes that some lawyers hold this to mean the requirement of more than the two witnesses ordinarily needed in law, since heresy is so grave a charge and witnesses' names are concealed. But he adds: "It seems truer to say that the text here mentions *three*, because, the greater the number to whom enquiry is committed, the easier it is to get a report: not that all three need to report, but one of the three; nor need the whole neighbour-hood, but one from the neighbourhood."[7] This insistence upon

the practice of delation must be weighed in connection with the fact that the law shielded all such accusers with a cloud of anonymity. The earliest Inquisitor's Manual, of about 1250, points out how the duty of tale-bearing against heretics is incumbent on every parishioner individually, provided that he be at least a boy of fourteen, or she a girl of twelve. This difference of calculation, according to sex, was a principle of Canon Law. The Cambridge canonist John of Ayton, writing about 1330, explains it by the ungallant proverb that "ill weeds grow apace." All this was in the regular routine; but, under fanatics like Conrad of Marburg, things might be far worse. The Pope's own official commissioners reported to their master that "brother accused brother, the wife the husband, and the master the servant. Others gave money to the shaven penitents in order to learn from them methods of evasion and escape, and there arose a confusion unknown for ages."[8]

(10) With all these dice loaded against the suspect, it is not surprising that acquittals pure and simple are almost unknown; the most that an accused could hope for was a verdict of "not proven." Tanon, a distinguished legal historian, here agrees with Lea. He writes (p. 433): "There is scarcely ever an acquittal pure and simple in the sentences of the Inquisition. We have two formulas for it in [the manuals of the Inquisitors] Bernard Gui and Zanchini. But Bernard Gui himself notes that this must be employed only in very rare cases, and by quite special favour. . . . Of the 200 accused or suspects who figure in the Register [of Carcassonne], we meet with no single case of acquittal. One woman, Alazais Debax, who seems for an instant to have been on the point of enjoying such a decision, is taken into custody again a little later, and condemned to wear the crosses." The usual cat-and-mouse procedure may be judged from a case which the Bishop of Beauvais quotes as typical (I. clxxxvii). A lawyer was accused. He had not taken advantage of a time of grace proclaimed, "first, because he knew himself to be convicted by witnesses; and secondly, because he had proposed to go to Rome and ask for penance there. He was

interrogated in the bishop's palace, like the rest of the accused;
then he was arrested and clapped into the bishop's prison,
whence he was brought on the following days for fresh examinations. He was examined six times; then again a month afterwards. Five months later, his judges communicated to him
his earlier depositions, and he had to declare whether he
recognised their truth or not. He is now awaiting his final
sentence, which hitherto has only been prepared, and which
will be pronounced at a later date. These examinations might
be repeated or resumed or continued, at the judge's discretion."
The fourteenth-century Inquisitor Eymeric gives a formula by
which the Inquisitor declares "that nothing hath been lawfully
proved against thee, before us, concerning those things whereof
thou hast been accused before us—to wit, that thou hast said
or done, &c.—on account whereof thou shouldest be reputed a
heretic or a suspect of heresy: wherefore we absolve thee by
this our present sentence from the present trial, and we release
thee by our judgment." But Eymeric adds: "Let him beware
of saying in his judgment that the man is innocent, or immune;
but only that nothing hath been lawfully proved against him.
Thus, if afterwards in process of time, he be again accused,
he may be condemned notwithstanding the sentence of
absolution."

Since, however, Lea's and Tanon's judgment on this question
has recently been ostentatiously repudiated in a bulky book of
considerable pretensions, it is necessary to give fuller evidence
here on this subject of crucial importance for the history of
civilisation. [9]

The two writers who have separately disputed this judgment
claim to do so on the strength of Bernard Gui's Register, which
records the 930 trials held during fifteen years. In these 930
trials (they claim) he records 139 acquittals. It may seem
almost incredible, but neither of them can possibly have read
even a single page of this all-important Register. This will
appear plainly if we take the first batch of these pretended
"acquittals," recorded on the very first page. The words run:

"Peter of St. Laurent-de-Garrigues.† Visitations of Toulouse twice a year; in the octaves of Easter to the church of St. Sernin; on the Invention of St. Stephen in August [i.e., August 2] at the church of St. Stephen. And the pilgrimages [enjoined] were remitted him by reason of his debility and old age. (2) Tholosana, wife of Bernard Hugues of Roche-Vidal.† The minor pilgrimages contained in the Inquisitor's letters and visitations of Toulouse as above. The Inquisitors reserve the power of increasing, diminishing and augmenting the aforesaid penance, and of bringing back the aforesaid persons to prison, without fresh cause (sine nova causa) if they judge it expedient."*
These two persons are not mentioned again; but we can trace some others of these so-called "acquittals" from stage to stage. In March 1311, one Raymonde, wife of Jacques Géraud, was condemned on a confession extorted from her in prison; but she retracted afterwards (p. 119). In September 1319, she was let out of prison on oath, to wear "two crosses of felt, of saffron colour, on all her garments except her shift; and let one arm be of the length of two palms and the other cross-piece one palm and a half, and each arm of three fingers' breadth; one on the breast in front and the other between her shoulders at the back; let her never go whether within or without her house without displaying these; let her repair or renew them if they are torn or worn out with age."† In addition to this, every prisoner normally suffered complete confiscation of property. There were also a series of penances and pilgrimages and compulsory attendances at church, and an oath to prosecute (persequantur) heretics, by whatever name they may be called, and those who believe or abet or harbour or defend them, and all who have fled for heresy's sake. There is the usual reservation for return to prison at the Inquisitor's pleasure sine nova causa (219). Either Raymonde did give fresh cause, or the Inquisitor was pleased to exercise his arbitrary powers; for in September 1322

* The two black crosses are the scribe's abbreviation for "condemned to wear the cross of infamy," as described here below.

† This condemnation to the sign of infamy is thus marked throughout the Register.

we find her let out again, among a batch which had been "many years in prison," with the same grievous penalties and on the same cat-and-mouse conditions as before (p. 338). These, then, are specimens of the 139 cases which are now described to British readers as "complete acquittals"! And the same story is told not only from beginning to end of the Register but also in Bernard's own manual of procedure, the *Practica*. No careful reader of either book could possibly have missed these things. The last batch in the Register differs from the first only in the slightly greater strictness of the formulas. Moreover, we have Gui's own warning in the *Practica*, where he gives a formula for acquittal, that it must scarcely ever be used—*de gratia speciali, quod nunquam aut rarissime fieri debet.* (Part II, c. 26.)

It is sometimes pleaded that, after all, there is no feature of Inquisitorial procedure of which examples cannot be found in one or other of contemporary law-courts. This would be at best a poor apology, to plead that this court, which was, above all others, the most characteristic creation of the Church, should adopt every fault of a comparatively cruel and lawless age. But it is not even strictly true. Eymeric notes explicitly that the Inquisition is peculiar in its principle of reckoning the *different* testimonies of two different witnesses as though they were *identical*. Bernard Gui, again, confesses plainly at the beginning of the fourth book of his *Practica* that *"multa sunt specialia"* in Inquisitorial procedure. His own analysis prefixed to that book fills page after page with headings of the points on which Inquisitors had a stronger position than ordinary judges. Moreover, even where the law itself did not grant exceptional privileges, yet casuistry enabled Inquisitors to stretch it, with little fear of consequences or even of opposition from a comparatively helpless public; except, indeed, in the cases in which their proceedings provoked counter-violence, or even sometimes open revolt in one district or another. Here, again, Vacandard puts the matter very frankly: "What the Inquisitors demanded was a perfectly free hand." A few extracts from the lengthy analysis with which Bernard Gui prefaces the fourth book of his *Practica* will give a sufficient, though still incomplete, idea of this. He first expatiates on "the height, length and depth of the Inquisitor's Office." Under this third heading comes: "The Inquisitors' excommunication is stronger than another man's in four respects. (*a*) They can compel *podestàs* or governors of cities to banish whomsoever they excommunicate; (*b*) they can likewise compel them to confiscate the goods of the excommunicate; (*c*) they can condemn as heretics all men who persist a whole year under their excommunication; (*d*) they can excommunicate all who participate or communicate with any whom they have excommunicated." Again: "The Inquisitors' power of punishment is mighty and excellent. (*a*) They can punish in person. (*b*) They can punish substantially in goods or possessions. (*c*) They can punish in reputation. (*d*) They can punish in honour. (*e*) The rigour of the power of the Office of the Inquisition, in those matters which are committed to the Inquisitors, must be executed according to their discretion and will." They can break through the ordinary clerical privileges and deal summarily with priests. "They can set up to auction the goods of heretics and their adherents after their death, in cases where the heirs are denied rights of succession by reason of the principal's heresy." "They can require the heads of any government—*presidentes alicui regimini*—to do justice upon heretics." And (most dangerous of all if we look into all its implications), "Inquisitors, in conjunction with the bishop of the diocese, or with his vicar, can interpret or declare whatsoever is doubtful or obscure in the statutes enacted against heretics." To this comparative irresponsibility of judgment is added equal freedom of action. "The execution of the Inquisitor's office is free and untrammelled, for all impediments are swept away. (*a*) The Inquisitors have no impediment from their superiors. (*b*) They have none from the inferiors against whom they proceed. (*c*) They have none from the officials or ministers through whose ministry they act. (*d*) They have none from the witnesses whom they hear. (*e*) They have none from contingent defects."

History affords few plainer examples of the demoralising

effects of absolute power upon fairly ordinary men. Not the least significant part of the whole story is the self-righteous complacency with which they looked down from this vertiginous height. To begin with, of course, they had priestly power. This included that power of absolution in the confessional, of which a fourteenth-century friar explains that it puts every priest, on this one point, on a level with the Pope himself: "moreover, in this power the priest is greater than John the Baptist: nay, greater than the angels, for they have no such power: nay, more, even greater than the Virgin Mary. For (as it is written in Canon Law) notwithstanding that the Blessed Virgin was more excellent than all the Apostles, yet it was not to her but to them that the Lord committed the keys of the Kingdom of Heaven."[10] From a later Inquisitor, Lea quotes an even stranger boast (I. 406). "Paramo, in the quaint pedantry with which he ingeniously proves that God was the first Inquisitor, and the condemnation of Adam and Eve the first model of the Inquisitorial process, triumphantly points out that He judged them in secret, thus setting the example which the Inquisition is bound to follow, and avoiding the subtleties which the criminals would have raised in their defence, especially at the suggestion of the crafty Serpent. That He called no witnesses is explained by the confession of the accused; and ample legal authority is cited to show that these confessions were sufficient to justify the conviction and punishment. If this blasphemous absurdity raises a smile, it has also its melancholy side; for it reveals to us the view which the Inquisitors themselves took of their functions, assimilating themselves to God and wielding an irresponsible power which nothing short of divine wisdom could prevent from being turned by human passions into an engine of the most deadly injustice. Released from all the restraint of publicity, and unrestricted by the formalities of law, the procedure of the Inquisition, as [the Inquisitor] Zanghino tells us, was purely arbitrary."

CHAPTER XII

The Minor Penalties

THESE were such as, in the case of any other tribunal, would be reckoned as severe. The most important was confiscation of the condemned man's whole property. Here, as in so many other matters, we go back to St. Augustine, who founds the principle on Roman Imperial Law, and from whom it passed into the *Codex Juris Canonici*. But Roman Law, except in cases of high treason, was merciful enough to reserve a certain proportion for the man's nearest heirs. Canon Law, assimilating heresy to high treason, and characterising it as the most intolerable of all high treasons, was able to refuse such merciful mitigations. Pope and Emperor in concert proclaimed the principle of confiscation in 1184; Innocent III repeated it twice, the second time at his Lateran Council; and all succeeding popes used it as one of their main weapons. It was held in threat not only against the culprits and their abettors, but over all princes or civil magistrates who might neglect to obey the Church's full behests in matters of heresy. Innocent pointed out that God punishes children for parental sins: it was by mercy that Roman Law left them their bare lives. However orthodox the children themselves might be, they went penniless henceforth, except in the sole case in which they had come forward primarily and spontaneously to denounce their heretical parent. This law of complete confiscation, like many others for good or evil, was not always strictly enforced in practice: unless the prisoner had been sentenced to death, or to imprisonment for life, it was ignored. Bernard Gui answers here the criticisms of others more bigoted than himself. By promising this mitigation (he writes) we secure many confessions from minor culprits, who therein reveal the names of the greater sinners. These greater men's goods are, of course, confiscated; and thus "that which seems to be lost in one case is recovered in many cases with interest"—*cum augmento*. If a man escaped the prison or the stake by death, his property did not escape with him. This explains the very large proportion of corpse-trials recorded in Inquisitorial documents. Out of 930 cases heard by Bernard Gui, 89 were against dead men. In many cases these sentences were followed by the destruction and solemn pollution of the house. In 1317 Gui learned by the confession of another heretic that the deceased Ricarda of Born had been "hereticated" on her deathbed by notorious Catharists, and that Guillaume Ysarn, with others, received "consolamentum" from the same two missionaries at his death. Therefore Gui's sentence runs: "We condemn them as heretics, commanding that, in token of their perdition, the bones of both be disinterred, in so far as they may be distinguished from those of faithful folk, and burned outside the graveyard. *Item*, that the houses wherein the said Ricarda and Guillaume were hereticated shall be torn down to the foundation, so that they be uninhabitable for evermore; and, as they have been dens of misbelievers, so let each become a place of filth, and take the place of a stinking dungheap." In England, by Article 21 of the Assize of Clarendon (1166), if any man received into his house any of the "exterminated" heretics of Oxford, "he shall be at the King's mercy; and that house wherein they were shall be carried out of the town and burned."* In those days, English houses were nearly always of timber; stone houses were rare, and brick practically unknown.

Popes sometimes denounced this multiplication of trials for the sake of the spoils; but they took no effective measures to cut the evil tree at the root. It may well be that the worst greed was shown by the civil magistrates who either shared with the Inquisition or, as generally in France, took all the spoils on

---

* We see here how *exterminare*, from its original milder meaning of *banish*, acquired in effect its modern meaning. Those who were "banished" from Oxford in winter, with royal prohibition against their reception by any of the King's subjects, might as well have been killed outright.

condition of bearing all the expenses. But, in any case, this
financial nexus was very prejudicial to religion, and to the
character of the Inquisition as a court of pure justice. For we
must remember, to begin with, the notorious venality of
medieval courts, by the general testimony of the most orthodox
contemporaries. All were swayed by pecuniary considerations,
especially the Church courts, and most especially the centre of
all at Rome. It was regarded as one of St. Bernard's great
claims to sanctity that, though his pupil Eugenius III could tell
him "men say that you are Pope, not I," yet in all his visits to
the Roman Court he never took a penny of bribe. So again of
St. Thomas More: the cleanness of his hands as judge was noted
among his saintly characteristics. For all medieval courts
reposed, to a considerable extent, upon the basis of pecuniary
penalties, so that *magnum emolumentum est justicia*—"justice
is a very profitable job"—became a legal proverb. Abbots and
barons would dispute the right of hanging felons for the sake
of their "spoils"; undignified fights between clerics over a putre-
fying corpse were common enough. In 1270 the lord of Mire-
poix, who was the King's Marshal in Albigensian lands,
demanded and obtained possession of the bones of certain
heretics burned by the riverside at Carcassonne, in virtue of his
"peaceful possession of the right of burning heretics on his
lands, when condemned to the fire by the Inquisitors of
Carcassonne, and of taking their movable goods if they were on
the King's demesne."* The Inquisitors' arbitrary powers gave
terrible temptations to injustice. As Lea points out (I. 517),
"so assured were the officials that condemnation would follow
trial, that they frequently did not await the result, but carried
out the confiscation in advance. . . . The Inquisition so
habituated men's minds to the belief that no one escaped
who had once fallen into his hands, that the officials

---

* Douais, I, 226: *in possessione pacifica comburendi hereticos.* Compare
Lea, I, 529: "As late as 1337 the office of [royal] bailli of the confiscations for
heresy in Toulouse was sufficiently lucrative to be worth purchasing under
the prevailing custom of selling such positions; and the collections for the
preceding fiscal year amounted to 640 *livres 6 sols*," i.e., about the equivalent
of £5,000 sterling to-day. In 1317 the result had been much less.

considered themselves safe in acting upon the presumption."

A further source of Inquisitorial income was soon discovered in the system of fines for offences and of payment for special mitigations. This system had, for centuries, been consecrated by the Penitential Books and by papal and episcopal Indulgences. Attempts were made at first to keep it out of the Inquisition, as lending itself to suspicion of baser motives, and as incompatible with the Inquisitorial profession of poverty; for nearly all were friars. The Dominican General Chapter forbade it in 1242, and the Council of Narbonne in 1244. But these prohibitions seem to have been little respected; and in 1251 Innocent IV explicitly authorised fines in cases where they seemed the only convenient penance.

A similar practice was that of commuting for money the penance named in the Inquisitor's sentence. This practice had long been in vogue for the Crusades; immense sums were raised all through the Middle Ages by redemptions of Crusaders' vows. In all these cases the monetary contributions were supposed to be applied to defray the working expenses of the Inquisition, or to other pious purposes: but in fact there was much peculation. Innocent IV, in 1249, had rebuked Inquisitors for levying extortionate fines, to the disgrace of the Holy See and the scandal of the faithful. Boniface VIII, in 1302, publicly rebuked the Franciscan Inquisitors of Padua and Vicenza for exacting immense sums, which they expended not even for the benefit of the Ecclesia Romana or of their own Order: his own commissioner had verified the truth of these complaints. In 1304 they were renewed in a different form; about the same time, the Dominicans of Languedoc were arraigned for similar excesses; and in 1311, at the Ecumenical Council of Vienne, Clement V based his reforming statutes partly upon his conviction that the Inquisitors frequently extorted money from the innocent, and accepted bribes from the guilty. In 1346 the Republic of Florence rose against their Inquisitor, who fled and refused a safe-conduct for his appearance before the investigators. One witness swore to 66 cases of extortion; in one case the sum was 1,700 gold florins. We have emphatic evidence on this subject from a particularly well-informed witness and a champion of orthodoxy, the Spaniard Alvarus Pelagius, Franciscan friar and Papal Penitentiary, who gives a gloomy picture of medieval society as it appeared to an ardent papalist a few years before the Black Death fell upon Europe. Whatever allowance we make for his indignant exaggerations (and it is probable that he generalises too freely here from the cases known to him) yet he and his readers were sufficiently well-informed to give us no excuse for complete scepticism. He tells us that his fellow-friars, when they are employed against heretics, regularly pocket the spoils of their victims: "wherein these Inquisitors commit two mortal sins; for whereas, by papal privilege, this money [earned by the Inquisitor] ought to be divided into three parts, one for the government of the land wherein the heretic dwelt, another to the officials of the Holy Office, and the third for the diocesan bishop for necessary expenses of the Inquisition, yet these Inquisitors, though no share has [thus] been assigned to any one of them, usurp the whole for themselves, even though the Roman Church assigns to them no part for their expenses; and thus they are truly thieves and robbers of the Inquisition money, usurping it beside and contrary to the will of the Roman Pontiffs, and spending it abusively at their own pleasure upon their brethren and their kinsfolk. Their second sin is that, whereas they ought to be Friars Minor and touch no money, yet they spend it as they please, and think themselves to be making a holy offering to God when they give alms of this money to their friaries or their brethren—alms, literally, of the mammon of unrighteousness— that is, of other men's money. And a third sin also, that they scarce punish any man accused of heresy except by condemning him to lose his money, in order that they may put it into their own purses [*ut eam imbursent*]. Therefore, I can scarce believe that any one of them escapeth that papal excommunication which is rehearsed in Canon Law."[1]

All this is rendered credible by that which his younger

contemporary Eymeric tells us, from a different angle. He is speaking of the system which attributed the confiscations to the civil powers and charged these with the Inquisitors' expenses; and he continues: "Now, however, since heresy has in most cases been so far extirpated that pertinacious heretics are rare, and relapsed heretics still rarer, and rich heretics rarest of all, but they are [nowadays] poor folk such as the Fraticelli, or Béguins, or Waldensians, therefore the temporal lords have not the frequent confiscations of property which they had of old; and on that account they are unwilling so to provide for the Inquisitors that Inquisitions may be carried out at their expense."[2]   The Bishop of Beauvais notes how, before 1350, the records show that "the Inquisition is declining for lack of cases." We shall see later how far this may be attributed to the real decline of heresy, and how far to the fundamental weakness of the Inquisitorial system. Meanwhile, on this point of confiscation (as, indeed, on most others), Abbé Vacandard agrees with the Quaker-bred Lea, that this system inflicted poverty upon thousands of innocent women and children, paralysed ordinary social relations to a degree hard for us to realise, and broke down business guarantees, since no bargain made by a heretic was good in law, and the man might be hereticated and all his affairs cast into the melting-pot even after his death (p. 246). And he ends approvingly with a quotation from Lea (I. 480): "While the horrors of the crowded dungeon can scarcely be exaggerated, yet more effective for evil and more widely exasperating was the sleepless watchfulness which was ever on the alert to plunder the rich and to wrench from the poor the hard-earned gains on which a family depended for support."

Many other penalties followed automatically from condemnation for heresy, including loss of civic rights. Even the mildest judgment nearly always involved a succession of burdensome pilgrimages, with yearly visits to a cathedral for public penance and the cross of infamy. This last is indicated nearly always in Bernard Gui's *Register*, with grim brevity, by the simple sign ✝. What this cross of infamy meant we have already seen in the case quoted in Chapter XI, where the phraseology agrees almost word for word with the formula which Gui gives in his *Practica*. On this, Mgr. Vidal remarks (p. 241): "The multitude spared neither insults nor mockery to those who bore this token of salvation as a sign of infamy. They were pointed at with the finger of scorn; men avoided their company and refused all alliance with them and their children. In spite of the remonstrances of prelates and Inquisitors pleading on their behalf, they were treated as pariahs. The Inquisition often consented to remit or commute this penance." This, however, as we have seen, often involved a money payment; and, where the remission was gratuitous, either it was after the punishment had already been borne for some time, or it was in the face of very strong reasons. In 1309 Gui allowed Raymonde Got to drop the crosses which she had worn for nearly forty years. He tells us in his *Practica* that girls were often excused, lest they should find it impossible to get husbands; and the formula he gives assigns other possible reasons, such as a man's age or infirmities, or the impossibility of his supporting his children or marrying his daughters under so great a burden. There is multiple evidence for the insults and injuries to which this badge of infamy might expose the wearer. At Carcassonne, in 1252, Riccarda Manifaceria, "marked with the cross for the crime of heresy, appeared without crosses before the Inquisitor; and, when asked why she wore no crosses, in violation of her own oath, she said that she wore none on her tunic because she had no money to buy one, and the first crosses were in rags (*ruptæ*). She said also that she wore crosses on her cloak; but her mistress, with whom she dwelt as nurse, forbade her wearing the said cloak with the crosses, and gave her to wear a certain other cloak without crosses."[3] Another, Arnaud Isarn, pleaded that a year's experience had shown him the impossibility of earning a living under this disability. Bernard Gu remitted the cross to one Matthew Aycard at the price of thirty *livres*; say, £240 at the present day.[4] At Carcassonne, if a culprit neglected to wear his, as he had sworn to do, his two sureties were to pay a fine of fifty *livres*.[5]

The last minor penalties we may notice are the compulsory pilgrimages and public penances.

The heaviest pilgrimage was that to Palestine: in 1252 we twice find remission of this tax at ten *livres* (say, £80) and once at twenty, probably in accordance with the culprit's means.[6] The earlier Inquisitors frequently imposed this penalty: once we find twelve citizens of Albi sent in a single batch. But this had its inconveniences. In 1244 the Council of Narbonne, under papal orders, decreed the suspension of this system, lest the Holy Land should become so strongly leavened with half-converted heretics as to endanger rather than promote the Faith. Two years later, the Council of Béziers removed this embargo; and the *Register* of Carcassonne contains numerous examples of this sentence. Thenceforward it became less frequent, and with the failure of St. Louis's Crusade it ceased almost altogether. The caravans started twice a year from Marseilles or Aigues-Mortes, in March and August. The sentence ran usually for three years: sometimes a man was condemned to as many as eight or as few as one.

Other penal pilgrimages for Provençal offenders are grouped by Gui as *major* and *minor*. The former were Rome, Compostela, Canterbury and the Three Kings at Cologne. The latter were twenty-four in number, including some as distant as Paris, Pontoise and Boulogne, and others as celebrated as Le Puy, Rocamadour, St. Antony of Vienne (whose pigs ran free in all lands), Chartres, Conques and St. Denis. In some cases, Gui possibly imposed all, both major and minor; but generally only a selection. The pilgrim received an official note naming his destined shrines, which formed at the same time a letter of safe-conduct. He was bound to bring back certificates from each of them.

Again, public penances were practically universal, even in the mildest sentences. Gui usually sent his penitents, for life, twice a year to Toulouse, and once yearly to the cathedrals of

Pamiers, Albi and Auch. At each of these they were to be publicly flogged. The Council of Narbonne added severer prescriptions which, however, were probably too extreme ever to find fulfilment in practice. The condemned heretic was to receive flagellation from his parish priest every Sunday at Mass, and on solemn procession days; again, on the first Sunday of every month, he was to be beaten in the street before the door of every house in which he had communicated with a heretic. At all these penitential visits which were actually carried out the ceremony was solemn and uniform. "The penitent came to church barefooted, in his shirt and drawers, with a taper in one hand and the executioner's rods in the other. Then he stood or knelt during Mass in a conspicuous place. After the gospel or offertory, or the sermon if there was one, he laid his taper upon the altar and offered the rods to the priest: then he knelt down to be scourged. At time of procession, he followed in the same guise after the priests and clerks, and was scourged at the last halting-place. As soon as he had received this penance, he proclaimed aloud that this was in reward for the faults that he had committed against the Inquisitors and the Inquisition."[7]

CHAPTER XIII

Prison

THE main penalties wielded by the Inquisition were three: imprisonment, torture and death. In all three of these fields it justified Gui's boast of exceptional powers; those of summary judgment and comparatively irresponsible action. The two first of these penalties, as will be seen, were not quite clearly distinguished from each other.

For a heretic actually convicted, the normal punishment was at least imprisonment for life: but confession before actual conviction might shorten his term. Here, as often elsewhere, the strict rigour of the law was not always enforced. Motives of pity come in sometimes; but economic causes were also strong: for prisoners were always an expense, and at times it was complained that strict enforcement of the law would entail the building of new gaols. Of the 149 prisoners condemned at Toulouse from 1246 to 1248, sixteen were sentenced for an indefinite period, six for ten years, and the remaining 127 for life. The Inquisitorial prisons themselves were apparently not more loathsome, as a rule, than was ordinary in the Middle Ages. It was an ordinary lay prison in England from which, at the end of the thirteenth century, one felon could not be brought for trial at the next assize, because his feet had rotted in the dungeon. But English law, according to Bracton, forbade the abuse of keeping a prisoner constantly in chains; yet we shall see that there was no such provision in Canon Law in favour of prisoners under the Inquisition. The fate of the heretic depended enormously upon chance. Sometimes we find him with a surprising amount of freedom in prison; at other times he is evidently dying by slow torture. A few extracts from official documents will best show these contrasts.

In 1286 the consuls of Carcassonne sent a formal complaint against their local Inquisitor to the Pope, the King of France, and the bishop's vicars. We must discount this by medieval violence of language; but these officials pleading for full enquiry, in the face of other powerful officials, must needs have had some serious ground for their assertions. They accused the Inquisitor of indiscriminate torture; he had fitted up cells "for torturing and racking men with divers kinds of torments." Among his victims, "very many, through the severity of these torments, lose the use of their limbs and are rendered utterly impotent. Some also, by reason of impatience and excessive pain, end their days by the cruellest death."* The same document proceeds: "Some of those cells are so dark and airless that the prisoners cannot discern night from day; and thus they are in continual and complete lack of air or light. In other cells there are poor wretches, in wooden stocks or iron chains, who cannot move even for the necessities of nature, nor can they lie except on their backs and on the cold earth; and in such torments, by night and day, they remain daily for long times. The prisoners in other parts of these prisons are deprived not only of light and air but of food also, except the bread of affliction and water, which itself is most grudgingly administered." The towers of Carcassonne still survive in marvellous completeness, and among them the "Tour de l'Inquisition." In the embrasure of a window in the upper storey is an inscription wrung from a prisoner, *æscam!* "[give me] food!" The lower dungeon is approached by a trap-door and lighted by three deep loopholes; the stone pillar is worn by prisoners' backs and the chains are still riveted to it. There seem to have been two iron cages in the upper prison. It forms a living commentary upon one sentence from the Inquisitors' Register at Carcassonne—"[the woman], after long detention in prison, added to her testimony . . ." Again, an accused person complained afterwards of the threats of a priest, "that he would

* Compare the concrete case cited by Tanon (p. 362, A.D. 1273). The prisoner "had smitten and wounded himself in the head, desiring to die and willing to slay himself."

make him (the present deponent) and his father and brother and all of his house, to rot in the prison of Carcassonne, and that he would so deal with them that they should never come again to Montaillou."[1]

The next King, Philip the Fair, sent to his seneschal at Toulouse a letter evidently referring to these or similar complaints. It runs: "We have been informed by trustworthy persons . . . that the Inquisitors punish innocent folk, imprison them, and inflict many vexations, and, by means of certain newly-invented torments, extort from them many falsehoods concerning many law-abiding and trustworthy persons, living or dead." A few years later, he addressed a similar letter to his seneschal at Toulouse and to the bishop there.

Meanwhile, a still stronger movement of protest had been started at Albi by a Spiritual Franciscan named Bernard Délicieux, whom we shall meet again later on. It began with something like a personal quarrel between the Franciscans and the Dominicans, who controlled the Inquisition at Albi, as in most other places. It attained such proportions that, in 1304, Benedict XI issued an order for Bernard's arrest; but he died before this order was executed. During the interregnum of nearly a year which followed his death, a very remarkable petition was presented to the College of Cardinals at Rome, beseeching it to judge between the Inquisitors and the whole countryside of Albi. The suppliants represented the capitular bodies of Albi cathedral and the great collegiate church of St. Salvi, and the abbey of Gaillac: sixteen official seals are solemnly appended to it. It rehearses how "He from whom nothing is hid knoweth to what disasters and ruins our country is exposed by reason of the questions and discussions whereby the county and the Inquisitors are brought into conflict with each other; and the trouble hath grown to such a pitch that the people, stirred to wrath, seem to gape after nothing less than that they should commit themselves to violence, and liquidate [deducat] with the edge of the sword not only those whom they count as their adversaries, but others also, thus turning to courses which could never be made straight." They protest the sincere Catholic orthodoxy of the district as a whole, and beseech that something may be done to restore the countryside to due peace and tranquillity. This appeal was apparently fruitless; for Clement V, on his accession, found a very serious state of affairs. His letter of March 13th, 1306, rehearses how he has been besieged by piteous complaints not only from Albi but from two other important cities, Carcassonne and Cordes. It is represented to him that the Bishop of Albi and the Inquisitor "had adjudged many men to perpetual imprisonment for heresy, and had confiscated all their possessions, iniquitously, against God and justice, seeing that these men had hitherto been commonly esteemed in those parts as Catholics, true and good Christians, as we the complainants offer to prove." They asserted that the reigning terrorism rendered it unsafe for witnesses to come forward, fearing "that, if they appeared, the Inquisitors would rage against them, and that those whose cause they are pleading would be still worse vexed; men who are detained in the prisons or dungeons of the bishop and In- quisitors, and are so grieved, and have been grieved hitherto, with the narrowness of prison and beds, with lack of victuals and fierceness of torments, that they are compelled to give up the ghost." We must doubtless make allowance here for the coloured language of medieval documents; but Clement saw that the matter demanded very serious consideration, far beyond what his predecessor had vouchsafed to it. He recognised that "it is to the public profit that we should know the truth, whether the Inquisitors have acted well." Therefore, to give the witnesses freedom of speech, he ordained that no Inquisitor in those parts shall hand over to hard or strict prison, nor expose to torture, any man arrested or to be arrested for heresy, "pending final judgment of this case." That judgment he committed to two local bishops, cardinals both. The Bishop of Albi, as defendant, cannot properly sit as judge; therefore he is to be represented by the abbot of the irreproachable orthodox

Cistercians of Fontfroide, one of whose monks at this very moment is the future Benedict XII. The first step of the Cardinals was to grant a safe-conduct to the two Dominican friars and the twelve citizens who came as representatives of three aggrieved cities, and to proclaim that neither the Inquisitors nor the Bishop of Albi shall employ torture or grievous prison till the cause is settled. Going here beyond the Pope's words, they set forth that each party complains of the other's terrorism: therefore they solemnly excommunicate all who, in virtue of conspiracy or oaths of secrecy, shall impede the Inquisition on the one hand, or, on the other, hinder free speech on the part of the accused. The next two documents set forth, with imposing solemnity, the powers granted by Carcassonne and Albi to their plenipotentiaries. It is impossible to doubt the strength of the feeling behind them; at Albi even the King's lieutenant, as keeper of the royal seal, affixed it to the document "for the greater confirmation of all the aforesaid." About April 20th, the two Cardinals came themselves to Albi, and found forty prisoners there, including one professor of law, two other doctors of law, a notary in the court of the bishop's own official, a notary in the King's court, a friar, and the wife of a merchant at Albi, with three other women. The status of the others is unfortunately not recorded, except that nearly all were citizens of Albi: that is, were more probably of the upper than of the lower middle class. These (says their official report) the cardinals "caused to be brought before them; and, having inspected them—because they found some infirm and broken down by age, tearfully and almost unanimously complaining of the malice of certain persons who supplied their bedding and victuals and who open and shut the prisons, bringing them in and out—therefore, to quiet all suspicion, the cardinals ordained that the aforesaid gaolers should be removed and others set in their places; also, that the chief gaoler, who was set there as the Inquisitor's servant, should have as coadjutor another head gaoler, who should act in the meanwhile, by papal authority, in the name of the Bishop of Carcassonne"—not, it will be noted, of the incriminated Bishop of Albi. Moreover, "that the said gaolers, whether the Inquisitor's or the bishop's, shall swear upon God's four Holy Gospels that they will faithfully employ all possible diligence in guard of the said prisoners; and that no one gaoler shall say anything to any prisoner secretly and without the hearing of another gaoler; and that whatsoever the King may provide for these prisoners, and that which their friends and kinsfolk or others may offer them, shall be given them faithfully and without any diminution. Again, in the case of certain sick persons, and those broken with age and otherwise feeble, the cardinals commanded that, for just and reasonable causes, such folk should have a change of dungeon, and should be raised up from the deeper cells unto those which are higher, so soon as these have been repaired; and let these repairs be carried out at earliest convenience by the lord Bishop of Carcassonne, present upon the spot: or again, if it seem expedient to the said bishop and Inquisitor, let them be free to walk and stand inside, by the cart-ways (*carrerias*) of the broad wall. With regard to those who, at the time of the cardinals' coming, had obtained this said liberty of release from the strict dungeons and of walking inside by the galleries of the broad wall, the cardinals decide that these shall remain in such release and liberty pending the present trial, or until the Lord Pope shall vouchsafe to ordain otherwise."

A few weeks later (May 4), one of the cardinals being ill, his colleague inspected officially the other prison complained of, that of the Bishop of Albi. He reported that he had found "some of the prisoners in fetters, and all imprisoned or confined in strict and very dark dungeons. He decided and ordained that none of them, pending this trial or until the Pope should otherwise decide, is to be detained in irons or in chains, but that they should be kept in other good and secure custody. He further ordained that the said dark dungeons should be made lighter and that, in addition, three or four other chambers or prisons should be made, within one month at furthest, in the upper storey or below it, better and lighter than the prisons in

which they are now detained; into which chambers those may
be transferred whom the Inquisitor and the Abbot of Fontfroide
or his substitute may choose: more especially because the said
prisoners have not yet been condemned, and they have been
kept in these dungeons for five years or more, as they themselves
have said. . . . And, that this be done without suspicion, he
hath added to Ponce Texier and Bertrand Austort, gaolers of
this prison, against whom the prisoners had no complaint—nay,
rather, they commended them very much—brother Isar de
Sales, monk of Candeil, a Cistercian of the diocese of Albi, fit
and faithful by the testimony of the claustral prior and convent
of that place."

A week later, the citizens of Cordes put in an equally piteous
complaint. They protested the orthodoxy of their city and its
loyalty to the Roman Church, and disavowed any intention of
personal animus: but they besought the cardinal's attention to
the case of their fellow-citizen Guillaume Cavalier, "who lieth
bound in prison at Toulouse, in those most grievous and painful
dungeons of the Inquisitor. We pray you so to proceed in
accordance with the form committed to you in this business,
that he be not unjustly vexed with insufficiency of bedding or
lack of victuals or fierce torments." Again, let them have some
assurance that their witnesses be not subjected to such direct or
indirect torments, so long as this case is being tried. "*Item*,
seeing that the processes and books of the said Inquisitors are
deservedly suspected by us, both by reason of change or
burning or cancellation of writing in the said books, and also by
reason of confessions extorted by the Inquisitors from the
prisoners, uncanonically and by force of torture, and written
down (as it is said) otherwise than the matter stands in truth,
and seeing also that this is reported and noised abroad in the
district of Albi and in the regions round, therefore, we, the
Consuls of the city of Cordes, beseech and require you to
vouchsafe to inform yourself on this matter, according to the
form delivered unto you. Moreover, since it is publicly reported
that certain witnesses, through whom ye may gain clearer

information concerning the alterations and burning and cancellation and injustice of the said records and processes, have at the command of those Inquisitors sworn certain pre-judicial oaths, to wit, that they will not reveal that which they know of these matters, under pain of being condemned as relapsed heretics and burned—by which oaths, if they were kept, the truth might be concealed—therefore the said consuls beseech and require that, by authority of your commission, you will absolve from the bond of such oaths and other obligations, if they are under any such bond, all witnesses from whom you desire information on these matters, that they may give their testimony safely and fully as to the truth of this business. Also that you will grant your letters [of guarantee] to all whom you may judge needful, while the proctor of the Bishop of Albi and the Inquisitor demand copies thereof, since he protesteth that he doth not admit this consul [as representative of the city of Cordes], nor doth he consent unto the protests contained in this schedule, except so far as he be constrained by legal necessity: nay, he contradicteth, in so far as they make against his party." That same day, the cardinals recognised the four delegates from Cordes as legal representatives of that community, and decreed that, pending the trial, no man in the dioceses of Albi or Carcassonne was to be severely imprisoned or tortured by the bishop or Inquisitors; nor might they proceed against any suspect except in co-operation with the Abbot of Fontfroide, as substitute for the Bishop of Albi in this particular case. The cardinals also appointed new gaolers at Albi and at Toulouse, making them swear to faithful distribution of the prisoners' allowances, and the other matters prescribed on April 20th.

It was in such conditions as these that a suspect might find himself kept indefinitely, without full trial. Clement V, in 1310, wrote to the Bishop of Albi and the Inquisitor to cut this proceeding short in the case of certain prisoners who appealed to him from Albi, pleading that they had been eight years in prison without trial. He ordered that they should now be tried

without further delay, and the judgments sent for confirmation
to the two cardinals to whom he had entrusted the reform of the
prisons in 1306. The bishop and Inquisitor, catching at the fact
that some of the prisoners named were already dead, argued
that the letter must have been obtained on false pretences, and
contemptuously disregarded it. Some time later Clement
learned this and wrote peremptorily that all, whether living or
dead,* must be tried at once. This, again, was disobeyed.
"After Clement and his cardinals had passed away, and no
further interference was to be dreaded (by the Inquisition), in
1319 two surviving ones, Guillem Salavert and Isarn Colli, were
brought out for further examination, when the former confirmed his confession and the latter retracted it as extorted
under torture. Six months later, Guillem Calvarie of Cordes,
who had been imprisoned in 1301, was abandoned to the
secular arm for retracting his confession (probably before
Clement's cardinals) and Guillem Salavert was allowed to
escape with wearing crosses, in consideration of his nineteen
years' imprisonment without conviction."² For, all this time,
the Inquisitorial archives contained a bull of Innocent IV
authorising indefinite delay so long as this might seem profitable to secure confession and conviction; and, in the tangle
of medieval Church law, it was always possible for so powerful
an institution as this to defy even a stronger pope than Clement.
Bernard Gui looked upon this man, his own sovereign pontiff,
as a bungling meddler in the business; he quotes only the bare
title of Clement's decree, and treats it as negligible because
earlier popes had decided otherwise. Eymeric, a generation
later, omits all Clement's decrees from his *Inquisitorial Manual*,
because (as he pleads) they are nowhere observed. This prison
system, a system of torture in all but name, was far too convenient to be abandoned. Pegna writes in the sixteenth
century, in that commentary on Eymeric which he dedicated to
Gregory XIII, that the Inquisitor should not hastily torture: it

---

* It was frequent, as we have seen, to try and condemn the dead. Thus,
apart from the effect of example, the Inquisition acquired the right of con-
fiscating all the dead man's property.

is better to prolong the suspense.[3] "For frequent meditation, and the frequent instruction of honest folk, dispose towards the elicitation of the truth."[*] In this he was but echoing the sentiments of the Archbishop of Narbonne's instructions to Inquisitors in about 1250. "In the case of those who are suspected and *infamati* of heresy, confession should be extorted from them, according to their quality, by hard prison and scanty diet"—*per durum carcerem et vitam artam.*[†] A generation later, David of Augusburg gives similar advice: "If the man refuse to confess, let him be shut up in prison, and let fear be instilled into him that we have witnesses against him, and that, if he is convicted by witness, he will be sent to death without mercy, and let him be kept on scanty diet; for such fear will humble him; and let none of his accomplices be suffered to come unto him, lest they encourage him." Of this we have a concrete example in the *Register* of Jacques Fournier, Bishop of Pamiers and afterwards Pope Benedict XII, of honourable memory for his monastic reforms. The bishop's secretary records how, "wishing to know the truth and extract it from the said Bernard and Bernarda, he ordered and decreed that both should be sent to the prison or dungeon of the Tour des Allemands, which is assigned for such persons, there to be kept in strict confinement until they confess the truth."[4] We may compare this with Philip the Fair's words in his plea to Clement V for more decent prisons at Toulouse. "Prisons are for custody, not for pains"—*ad custodiam, non ad pœnam.*[5] Monsignor Vidal, in his study of Fournier's *Register*, adds reflections of his own (p. 167). "For some of these poor wretches, preventive prison is a lengthy affair. Raymond de la Côte languished in the Tour des Allemands [at Pamiers] for nearly nine months, from August 9th, 1319, to May 1st, 1320, when he died. Agnes Frane, his fellow-believer, remained there for the same period. Jean de

---

[*] Occasionally, however, there was another side to this. Bernard Gui complains that prisoners, thus herded together, sometimes grew not more pliable but stubborn and rebellious. (Vidal, 164.)

[†] Upon this Monsignor Vidal comments (p. 171, *note*): "If this passage does not speak of torture, it implies proceedings which are very like it."

Vienne and his wife Huguette, imprisoned in August 1319, came out only to be burned (August 2nd, 1321) after two years' detention. Master Arnaud Tisseyre, of Lordat, entered in January 1321 and died there in May 1323, after two and a half years. Raymonde Guillo of Vernaux, imprisoned November 20th, 1321, left her dungeon on June 19th, 1323, only to hear herself condemned to spend her life there. These were the specially obstinate cases. Others, bending more easily, regained their liberty sooner. Grazida Lizier, after "seven weeks and more," made up her mind to speak out; she was at once released. He adds: "It depended only on the accused to shorten their term of imprisonment." In a sense, yes: but at what cost?

Lea (I. 494–5) deals with the cases when imprisonment was used not as a means of conviction but as a punishment. He points out that, of the 930 suspects heard by Bernard Gui, forty (in fact, forty-two) were burned and 300 condemned to prison. He writes: "No records remain, if any were kept, to show the average term of those condemned to lifelong penance; but in the *autos de fe* there occur sentences pronounced upon prisoners who

had died before their cases were ended, which show how large was the death-rate. These cases were despatched in batches. In the *auto* of 1310, at Toulouse, there are ten who had died after confessing their heresy and before receiving sentence; in that of 1319 there are eight. The prison of Carcassonne seems to have been almost as deadly. In the *auto* of 1325 we find a lot of four similar

GRAFFITO FROM DUNGEON AT CARCASSONNE

cases, and in that of 1328 there are five." "There is one case in which a woman was graciously discharged with crosses, in view of her having been for thirty-three years in the prison of Toulouse."

The deepest shame of the Inquisitorial system in this matter of prisons, if not the very worst plight of the prisoners, is recorded in a bull of Gregory XI in 1376. He instituted a fresh campaign against the Waldensians of Dauphiné, with the help of a specially energetic Inquisitor and Charles V of France. The result of this drive was to rope in such a host of accused and suspects that, even when the obstinate had been burned, the prisons were utterly insufficient to contain them. Men calculated that it would cost 4,000 florins to build the necessary new prisons, and 800 a year to maintain them. The Pope permitted the bishops to direct funds to this from other pious uses: but, after three months, it was again reported that the prisoners were starving: he answered that their maintenance was the bishops' duty, and that those who failed to fulfil this should be excommunicated. He tried to get Charles to bear his own legal share in the business, and to devote to the prisoners some portion of the money brought in by confiscations of their property: but in vain. Finally he appealed to the faithful at large by offering an Indulgence for all who shall help to feed these "many heretics and those defamed for heresy, who in consequence of their poverty cannot be sustained in prison unless the pious liberality of the faithful shall assist them as a work of charity. . . . We wish that these prisoners shall not starve, but shall have time for repentance in the said prisons." Yet, at the same time, he pressed the royal officials on two separate occasions to do their duty more zealously and bring in more abundant victims. Upon this Lea comments (II, 155): "There is something so appallingly grotesque in tearing honest, industrious folk from their homes by the thousand, in thrusting them into dungeons to rot and starve, and then evading the cost of feeding them by presenting them to the faithful as objects of charity, that the proclamation which Gregory issued August 15th, 1376, is perhaps the most shameless monument of a shameless age."

CHAPTER XIV

Torture

WE come now to what, on the whole, is perhaps the blackest chapter in this story, for it shows the Church adding hypocrisy to exceptional cruelty. An able and enthusiastic modern apologist frankly stops short of his fellow-apologists at this point. He speaks of the episode as one which detracts heavily from the claims often made for the thirteenth century as the high-water mark of Catholic civilisation, however true those claims might be for the intellectual, artistic and material fields. He points out that, in this matter, the Church showed herself false to that early maxim which is enshrined in the first volume of the *Codex Juris Canonici*, "confession should not be extorted, but rather be brought forth of the man's own accord." "It was not" (he writes) "that the thirteenth century had not yet risen to the standards of the twentieth; it was rather that she had fallen enormously below those of the eleventh." And, after enumerating all that can be said to render the Inquisitors' practice in this matter less odious than it might seem, he adds: "Yet, in face of the appalling truth that the popes sanctioned its employment at all, such petty details are of little importance."[1]

The Dark Ages had no place for formal torture in their laws, except those of the Visigoths. They had, however, a proceeding almost as patently unjust, the ordeal, or Judgment of God. Even St. Bernard seems plainly to admit this barbarous custom; he speaks of a heretic as having been "justly" condemned by the ordeal of water. The Council of Reims, in 1157, prescribed it for all suspected heretics. Peter the Precentor, a little before 1200, marks the dawn of reason here; he condemns such judgments as absurd and wicked, and quotes two concrete

cases of gross injustice under the system. About the same time a
bishop of Besançon actually employed a clerical necromancer to
consult the devil as to a batch of suspects: the devil betrayed
them, and they were burned. It was not until the Lateran
Council of 1215 that Innocent III formally forbade to all
clerics the use of the ordeal. Then the Church, in her terror of
heresy, drifted into panic-legislation, and dug up from pagan
Roman law the practice of formal torture, not only for the
accused but for witnesses. Here, again, the unorthodox emperor Frederick II had set a precedent. The Italian cities also
adopted the practice not infrequently; and at last, in 1252,
Innocent IV published a bull authorising it for heresy cases.

This was not so sweeping a change as it might seem to those
who believe that Canon Law always means what it seems to say.
Not only is it probable that torture, in disguised forms, had
survived to some extent in the civil courts, but there are plain
indications of its employment by ecclesiastical judges, whether
directly or indirectly, in the eleventh and twelfth centuries.
That sentence "confession should not be extorted" must not be
taken too literally; it did not express a final and absolute
judgment any more than St. Bernard's famous "Faith should
not be compelled." Upon the three passages which mention the
subject in early Canon Law, the commentators decided that
physical compulsion had a proper place in the Church courts,
though only in the form authorised by a text from St. Augustine,
which commended flogging to elicit the truth. As one of the
early commentators puts it, the bishop is permitted to extract
the truth by judicial torments, so long as he does so indirectly
through the lay magistrate. Moreover, even in his own court, in
certain cases, men "are subjected to torture (cruciatibus); not
indeed to those fiercer torments whereby, in the civil courts,
they are submitted to question by the judges' attendants (to
wit, the rack or thumbscrew or cord and so forth) . . . but with
lighter fustigation, with birch rods and the like; for this
method of flogging is customarily used by teachers of the
liberal arts, and by parents upon their children. Schoolmasters

and parents had a heavy hand in those days, and Tanon quotes a MS. in the Bibliothèque Mazarine which contains a miniature illustrating this chapter of the Decretum. "We see a cleric, kneeling and naked to the waist, with a suppliant turn of the head towards the executioner, who stands bending over the patient and pressing one hand hard upon his shoulder, while the other brandishes a great whip with many thongs." A thorough flagellation, as he points out, is "a real application of torture." Indeed, we have conclusive proof here from a concrete case recorded in the trial of Dame Alice Kyteler for sorcery by the Bishop of Ossory, a Franciscan friar, in 1325. One of her waiting-women, after six separate scourgings, broke down and confessed all that was required of her, that she had acted as go-between betwixt her mistress and the devil. The medieval commentators show clearly that they understand this flagellation in its most serious sense. One of them sums up the paragraph from Canon Law in a marginal note: "The truth should be sought out by tortures—*tormentis*." Others set themselves to reconcile this passage with the other passage in a letter of Alexander III, prescribing that confession must *not* be elicited by torture. The Pope (they say) does not here intend a *general* prohibition; he is referring only to "certain lay tyrants who compelled bishops and clerics, by torments, to make public confession of things profitable to themselves."[2] That is, clerics may rightly employ torture, but it is wrong for lay folk to employ it against clerics. Thus the principle had been recognised very early in Church law; only in practice considerable mitigation was introduced, especially under the influence of that maxim "the Church abhorreth blood," which long restrained the clergy from harking back openly to all the severities of pagan Rome. Now, however, in 1252, Innocent IV finally and formally adopted what the civil courts in Italy had been gradually accepting, only with the mitigating clause that such legal torture should stop short of "loss of life or limb." Thenceforward, the application of torture in heresy cases was a principle of Church law not only for the whole Middle Ages but also far beyond; it probably held good, in strict law, until the promulgation of the new *Codex Juris Canonici in* 1917. Innocent IV impressed his command upon all the lay magistrates of Italy; and his bull was renewed with slight variations by Alexander IV and Clement V before the end of the century. The only obstacle yet remaining was the canonical prohibition against clerics pronouncing any sentence involving bloodshed—*Ecclesia abhorret a sanguine*. This, strictly taken, compelled the bishop or Inquisitor to do his torturing indirectly through the civil magistrates: otherwise he became "irregularis," and was cut off from saying Mass until he had procured papal absolution. But that last obstacle was removed in 1262 by Urban IV, who gave the Inquisitors and their assistants authority to absolve each other quietly from "irregularitas." The gate thenceforth was open: the clerics X, Y and Z had assisted at the torture of a heretic, but X by papal powers absolved Y and Z, and Z rewarded this good turn by absolving X, and the time-honoured principle became a legal farce. It can scarcely be a mere chance that, soon after this, violent protests arose from many quarters against the excesses of the Inquisition. For now there was no bar, even in law, beyond the farcical appeal to a far-distant pope, against such a proceeding as is described briefly in the *Register* of John XXII and more minutely by the later Italian Inquisitor Masini.* The Pope writes to an official at Poitiers, who had "examined" a woman accused of witchcraft, "On the counsel of certain honest folk (*proborum*) who said that they had seen heretics examined by tortures in the parts of Toulouse, thou didst cause the feet of the said woman to be set near the burning coals." Masini [in his *Holy Arsenal*] and the no less orthodox Marsollier in his *Histoire des Inquisitions*, describe this in detail. "A fierce fire is lit; the patient is laid with his feet shackled and turned towards the fire; they are rubbed with lard or grease or any other penetrating and combustible matter. He is thus burned horribly. From time to

* Vidal, p. 182, and Vacandard, p. 182. They give a reference to the MS. register of John XXII; *Regest. Vac.* LXIX, f. 452.

time a screen is set between his feet and the brazier: this is a moment of respite which enables the Inquisitor to resume his examination."

There were at least two other flagrant legal fictions in this matter of torture. It was usual, in registering the accused man's confession, to make him add that this was proffered "without torment or fear of torments." But certainly sometimes—how often, the scattered documents and their usual brevity do not enable us to judge—this was done with the most cynical disregard of truth. At Pamiers, the episcopal scribe writes in one breath that the man confessed "of his own accord" and, in the next, "after he was taken down from the torture"—*confessus fuit sponte . . . postquam depositus fuit de tormento*. So, again, another's confession is recorded as *non factam vi tormentorum*, though we know from elsewhere that he had been tortured in fact. Tanon, the juristic historian, characterises this as it deserves (p. 380):

"According to a constant rule, confessions made under torture had to be renewed after the accused person had been released from it; and, by a fiction worthy of this barbarous procedure, such confessions were then counted as having been made freely and without any constraint."[3] In fact, if the victim had denied outside the torture-chamber that which had been confessed within, this might quasi-legally have led to fresh tortures. We must say *quasi-legally*, because Canon Law nominally disallowed any repetition of torture. But, here again, the casuist came in to find a way for the Inquisitor, whose main object was to elicit a confession. A second visit to the rack was called not *repetition* but *continuation*, even if it took place on another day. No mere summary can give a just idea of these cold-blooded Inquisitorial prevarications and subtleties: therefore I must here cite as much as space will permit from Eymeric, the Spanish Inquisitor who wrote in Chaucer's day, and from Pegna, who printed him two centuries later in Rome, with his own comments, under the patronage of Pope Gregory XIII. The quotations here following range between pp. 516 and 522 in the edition of 1585. They begin auspiciously. Those modern apologists who seek to justify the Inquisition by blackening the Catharists will be found to quote very little evidence beyond what is to be found in the writings of their enemies; or, again, in their own confessions which were made either under actual torture, or within mental or physical sight of it. Here, then, we find an Inquisitor beginning with concessions which would seem logically to minimise the value of torture; or indeed, more logically still, to deny it any place whatever in a court of real justice. If the prisoner (writes Eymeric) denies the truth, then "let them torture him moderately, without effusion of blood, knowing that tortures are fallacious and inefficacious. For some men are so soft-hearted and crazy that under slight torture they would grant everything, however false; while others are so obstinate that, however they be racked, the truth cannot be extracted from them. . . . Some, also, are charmed, and use witchcraft under torture: these would die rather than confess anything, for they are rendered, as it were, insensible." Yet those reasonable words are (as Pegna duly notes) borrowed almost verbally from the pagan-jurist Ulpian! Our man of God may unctuously quote such reasonable maxims; but he is no more fettered in action by them than by his own catchwords "The Church abhorreth bloodshed," or "Faith must be persuaded, not forced," or "Confession should not be extorted." We have here a study of great psychological interest; and those who find it difficult to grasp the Inquisitor's mentality in this matter should read Bishop Butler's sermon on Balaam, with his pious prayer "May I die the death of the righteous, and let my last end be like his!" Turning to the next page, we find our Inquisitor Eymeric writing: "If, when he has been decently tortured (*quæstionatus decenter*), he will not confess the truth, let other kinds of torture be laid before him, and let him be told that he must go through all these. If, even so, he will not, then a second or third day may be fixed to terrify him, or even in truth, as a *continuation* of his torture, but not a *repetition*; for tortures may not be repeated unless fresh evidence comes in against him; then indeed they may be repeated. But there is no prohibition against the *continuation.*" A little further, again, "If, having been tortured, he reveals the truth, let it all be written in the *procès-verbal*; and, after the torture, let him be brought to another place where the tortures are out of sight; then let his confession made under torment be read to him and let him be again questioned more diligently, once and again, until the truth be obtained. But, if he persists not in his first confession—nay, still denies the truth —and has not been decently tortured, then (as aforesaid) he may be submitted again to questions and torments, not by way of repetition but of continuation. If, however, he hath been decently tormented, as aforesaid, then let him be dismissed freely, and if he demand insistently to be expedited by sentence, let it be done unto him as hath been said immediately.* . . . If he confess nothing by reason of the torments, he must not be acquitted (*non est absolvendus*), but let him be proceeded against according to the proofs; and he shall abjure either as a suspect or as one caught [in the offence], according as the merits of the process exact and require."

Upon this section Pegna comments: "At first sight that which Eymeric saith here seemeth absurd. For he saith that the man who hath been decently tortured should be thoroughly frightened (*perterrefieri*) by setting new tortures before him; nay, even that he may lawfully be tortured. But this is unjust; for, when a man hath been decently tortured, he hath already conquered and overcome the torments; and therefore he should be freed and not further terrified or tormented. Wherefore from the words which follow, and the whole of this context, we gather that Eymeric intended thus: When the accused hath been decently tortured on the first day, according to that degree of torment which hath originally been judged sufficient to force the truth from him—even though this may not have been given

---

* In a later paragraph Pegna quotes three authorities who hold that, when a man has been frequently (*pluries*) tortured and still denies, the case must yet be left undecided. Eymeric and Pegna take the more merciful view, that in this case the prosecution has failed and the man must be released.

with due severity, as is customarily done, for we must always begin with the milder torments—and when he has not confessed the truth, then, although he has been decently tortured for that day and that time, yet his torment has not been sufficient. Then they may show him new torments, whereby he may be further tortured in the sequel unless he shall confess: and this counsel is laudable and safe; for Eymeric speaketh not of a man who hath already overcome all torments according to the severity of the judgments, but of one who, even though he has been tortured sufficiently for that one time, yet still remains a subject for torture according to the law; and this he plainly indicates by those words of his, *For the continuation, not repetition, of torture.*"

Later on, Pegna recurs to the subject: "Eymeric's judgment seems to be that, if he who revokes his confession hath not been sufficiently tortured, then he may be tortured again, not with repetition, but with continuation of his torments; but if, having been sufficiently tortured, he revokes his confession, then he should be dismissed. . . . But the greater difficulty is this: When the accused revokes his confession, how often may he or should he be brought back to torture?" Pegna then names five legists whose opinion seems to be as follows: "When the accused, twice tortured, twice confesses and revokes, then he may be tortured a third time and the whole examination reopened. But this decision, to many folk, seemeth too cruel, and may be rebutted by many reasons."

Yet torture must not be without natural respect for persons and circumstances. "Concerning those who are not tortured either by reason of unripe age and bodily debility (as, for instance, children below the age of puberty) or else by reason of old age, the doubt is whether they may at least be terrified. The truer decision is that they may, but slightly and moderately. . . . If, however, law forbids the use of torture for some other cause, as in the case of a woman great with child, for peril of her delivery, then she may not even be terrified, since from such terror and menaces abortion might follow. Therefore we must wait until she hath brought forth, if truth cannot be obtained but by torture or by terror." "It is hopeless, however, to attempt prescribing for every possible contingency. Much depends on the Inquisitor's intelligence, and especially on his experience. The judges will be able to employ many lawful stratagems (*cautelæ*) both in words and in deeds; but these will rather be taught by use and experience and by the variety of affairs, than by any art or teaching."

We come back, then, to the point from which this chapter started. These things had been among the worst injustices permitted in pagan Roman Law; yet they were gradually and deliberately revived by the Inquisition. Not only would the earliest Christians have rejected any such idea with horror, but even the theologians of the Dark Ages. Nicholas I wrote in a solemn public letter that legal torture is a thing "utterly inadmissible in law, either divine or human." "If" (he adds) "the accused, under such sufferings, is no longer able to hold out, but confesses to have done what he never did, upon whose head, pray, does this load of impiety fall, except upon that man's who compelleth him to make such lying confessions?"[4] Yet the Church gradually entered upon the slippery slope. Abbé Vacandard shows plainly how, "as a matter of course, the severest penalties of Inquisitorial rule received the approval of canon lawyers and theologians. . . . St. Thomas Aquinas, writing in days when the Inquisition was in full swing, found himself in a manner compelled to justify the penalty of death for heretics and for those who had relapsed."[5] In his next few pages, this orthodox modern theologian goes on to analyse the historical and logical errors into which St. Thomas falls in this attempt. But the Church, which claimed inerrancy, had set her seal upon these horrors almost before St. Thomas was born, and he was faced with the *fait accompli*: therefore he must either find some philosophy to justify them, or quit that Church which was far dearer to him than life. Yet, while the philosopher-theologian thus quieted his conscience, one mere lawyer, at any rate, recorded in his native French a protest such as the oppressed have voiced in all ages: "In the case of the judges who torment a man unjustly, the torment of him who is given over to torture is soon past, but the torment of him who tortureth him endureth for ever."*

* "Cil juige qui martirent aucun à tort, li martires de celui qui est livres à martyre est tost passez, mais li martyres de celui qui le martyre dure tozorz." (Quoted by Tanon, p. 364, from the *Livre de Justice et de Plet*.)

CHAPTER XV

The Stake

MUCH has been said already on this subject in earlier chapters: here it only remains to expose briefly the death-penalty as it was in theory and practice when once the Inquisition was fully formed. When the code is once fixed on this point, we shall find it reposing upon a legal fiction as outrageous as any of those in the matter of torture. We shall find the Church adopting, deliberately and finally, the cruellest prescriptions of the ancient Imperial code, and adding insult to injury by shifting the responsibility to other shoulders.

It was not only that her whole conception was based upon theories of heaven and hell which, in their medieval crudity, the most orthodox theologian of to-day would not dare publicly to support. That was natural and inevitable; since, in the Middle Ages, these theories were accepted whole-heartedly by enthusiastic Churchmen, whose minds were sometimes haunted and tormented by such thoughts to an extent which no later Calvinism has surpassed. By ordinary unenthusiastic folk they were accepted with different degrees of passive acquiescence; and the small minority which actively disbelieved was either prudently silent or pitilessly silenced.

On those medieval eschatological grounds, then, the death-penalty was perfectly logical. If an eternity of ineffable bliss or unspeakable misery does in fact depend upon man's attitude towards God at the moment when the breath leaves his body, and if, again, the only right attitude is that of the Catholic Church, and the *Ecclesia Romana* is the only true Catholic Church, then all sincere and devoted churchmen, from St. Thomas Aquinas down to St. Thomas More, were right in accounting heresy the worst of crimes, worse even than what we call murder; for that can only destroy the body, while the other destroys the soul. Worse, again (as Innocent III points out and others obediently in his wake), than high treason; for that repudiates only an earthly sovereign, while this disowns the King of Kings. So plain do all these consequences seem in logic, that the real difficulty lies with those who undertake nowadays to deny St. Thomas Aquinas's cruel conclusion in favour of the death-penalty, while they dare not repudiate his premisses.

Again, although he and his fellow-schoolmen make allowance for the exception of invincible ignorance, the practical consequence of that is very small indeed from their point of view. The wide extension given to this exception by modern apologists would have brought them to the stake in the thirteenth century, if by ill-fortune they had lived then and had refused to recant. St. Bernardino of Siena devotes the greater part of a sermon to refutation of the idea that a man will be saved by living truly according to the false creed in which he has been born and passed his whole life. Innocent III and Aquinas knew perfectly well that there were whole populations which had sucked heresy in with their mother's milk; yet neither in their elaborate arguments is any explicit allowance made for this, nor in their actions; though, as the pithy canon law maxim points out, actions are the best interpreters of the law—*consuetudo est optima legum interpres*. Ignorance was indeed allowed for to some extent: a man might flatly deny an indubitable dogma and yet be hitherto only a "material" heretic, deserving rather of pity. If, however, after the truth had been explained to him, he still retained his false opinion, then it depended only on the churchman's discretion at what point his *ignorantia* should be condemned as no longer *invincibilis*, but merely *affectata*. At that point he passes from "material" to "formal" heresy, and must recant or be burned. In short (apart from mental defectives), the invincibly ignorant is only he who has had no fair opportunity of hearing and considering the Catholic Faith.

A plain and decisive test-case here is that of the Greeks:

we see how empty the plea of invincible ignorance was in their case. Rome condemned the Greek Church as schismatic; and Catholic theologians are pretty unanimous in pointing out that the difference between schism and heresy is little more than one of words: that they may be considered apart in logic, but in fact they are generally inseparable. Aquinas argues, therefore, that the schismatic, like the heretic, may be punished not only with excommunication but also with the secular arm.[1] Here, as usual, he justifies by philosophy what was already a *fait accompli*; he is hypnotised by ecclesiastical actions which he could scarcely have repudiated publicly without falling himself under suspicion of heresy. For Innocent III had already twice treated the Greeks almost as he would have treated open heretics. He conceived them much as modern Rome conceives modern Protestantism. Here were Christians, not of his fold, and yet his subjects: for it is a Roman dogma that all baptized Christians are in reality subjects of Rome and amenable to her authority, whatever they may think of themselves. The Greeks, in this matter, had an even stronger position than modern Protestantism; during forty generations they had not acknowledged Roman primacy: it was in their blood. Yet Innocent gave them, in effect, no benefit of "invincible ignorance." He laid his commands upon them, and was ready to punish them to the utmost with very little further discussion. His Crusaders at Constantinople, in 1204 (to quote his own words), "imbued in Christian blood those swords which they ought to have wielded against the pagans; spared neither age nor sex; practised incest, adultery and fornication before men's eyes; and exposed to the filthy embraces of their grooms not only matrons but even virgins dedicated to God." They had stormed the city in defiance of his own orders; yet Innocent accepted the practical fruits of this crime and justified it to the Greek Emperor. To him he wrote, in answer to his expostulations: "Although these men are not altogether guiltless, yet we believe that the Greeks have been punished through their hands by the just judgment of God: these Greeks who have striven to rend the Seamless

Robe of Jesus Christ. . . . Those who would not join Noah in his ark perished justly in the deluge; and these have justly suffered famine and hunger who would not receive as their shepherd the blessed Peter, Prince of the Apostles. . . . Evil men have been evilly destroyed in order that the land itself might be let to such husbandmen as will render fruit in due season." Moreover, his legate inaugurated a reign of terror over the Greek Church: "he wished" (writes a Greek chronicler) "to compel us to recognise the Pope's primacy among all prelates, and to commemorate his name in public prayers, under pain of death against those who refuse." In answer to these things, the Greeks sent a remarkable protest. It ran: "Thou knowest, honourable Lord, what a mind God hath given to man, and how the mystery of piety pertaineth to willing folk, unoppressed by violence. If this were otherwise, we should even baptize the Jews against their will. Seeing, then, that the proclamation of penalties and the employment of violence in matters of dogma is absurd—for it is the easiest course and that which lies ready to every powerful man's hand—while the part of the good man who reverences truth is to persuade by the employment of those reasons which lie at the root of dogma—wilt thou, then, O Lord [Pope], choose to use force against us without discussion, as against brute beasts, for our conversion? or wilt thou rather receive our reasons and exchange reasons with us, in order that the truth of divine things may be discovered and known? For know that we ourselves commend and seek after the second of these courses, in obedience to that divine precept which saith: 'Search ye the Scriptures.' For none of us can be caught by force; nay, rather we will all suffer peril as for Christ's sake." Temperate as this was, it is impossible to trace any effect that it had upon Innocent's further words or actions. They vainly appealed for judgment before a General Council of all Christendom.[2]

In the face of these facts, and many more which might be produced, we need not wonder that no instance has been found of an accused person absolved by the Inquisition on the score of invincible ignorance. The utmost granted to the most ignorant person was that, if he conformed now at once to what the priests taught, then his "material" heresy would be forgiven. No ignorance was so great (thought the Middle Ages) but that it was vincible by torture or the stake. This, again, was perfectly logical, on these presuppositions from which the hierarchy started. If the heretic was a deadly germ-carrier for scores of souls—or perhaps even for thousands—how could any other human quality redeem him? The man to whom no arguments could bring conviction of ecclesiastical infallibility was dangerous to society in direct proportion to his good faith and his other excellent qualities. On the stock argument that the scabby sheep must be removed from the world lest he infect the whole flock, there should be most pitiless elimination for him whom the rest were least likely to avoid as a dangerous associate. Everything spoke in favour of death or perpetual imprisonment; and the former solution was by far the easier. Not only might the culprit escape from prison, but the Church treasury could ill afford to maintain so many captives as the other policy would necessitate. Moreover, death at the stake was far more impressive; and we have the clearest evidence that Inquisitors, naturally enough, hoped to work even more effectually by general terrorism than by actual elimination. Lea has brought out very clearly that for them the stake was the last resort, and actual burnings were far fewer than has often been supposed. In Spain (to which we shall come in a later chapter) things were much worse. But in early fourteenth-century Languedoc, which we have every reason to take as typical, Bernard Gui in fifteen years condemned 930 heretics and burned only forty-two of them. By Church law, the "relapsed" heretic was unpardonable. When once he had solemnly abjured his unfaith before the judges, the first subsequent lapse entailed death: this was so from at least 1258 onwards. If this second time he again recanted and accepted the true Faith, then he was allowed to receive the Eucharist, but he must die: thenceforward, therefore, relapse was the main cause of capital punishment.

Even then, however, the Inquisitors are often found stretching their powers in the direction not of severity but of mercy. For one thing, when the Count of Toulouse finally submitted in 1229, the Treaty of Paris stipulated that an oath of abjuration should be taken every two years by all males over fourteen and girls over twelve, after which any act of heresy would be technically a relapse; but it would have been materially impossible to burn wholesale like this. Moreover, the ordinary Inquisitor had his decent human feelings; he was in most cases a respectable and earnest churchman; even the most active persecutor was seldom sadistic. He was convinced in his own mind that the prisoner was guilty—as, in the very large majority of cases, the man certainly was—of what, to him, was the worst crime possible. He would have wished to convert the man, and did in fact attempt this: it is implied in his instructions, and we have convincing concrete instances on record. But it comes out plainly from those same records that, in each particular case that came before him, his fear of letting a soul-murderer loose upon society overpowered his fear of committing an injustice. We may apply to the Inquisitorial Society those words which were written of the Society of Jesus by Lord Acton, by far the greatest of English-speaking Roman Catholic historians. They "existed in order to sustain the credit of the Popes. . . . It is the combination of an eager sense of duty, zeal for sacrifice, and love of virtue, with the deadly taint of a conscience perverted by authority, which makes them so odious to touch and so curious to study."[3]

For, in this matter of the death-penalty, it was the Inquisitor's studied policy never to say plainly the thing that was in his heart. Once, indeed, in the fifteenth century, Sprenger may be caught writing of "those [witches] whom *we* caused to be reduced to ashes"—*quas incinerari fecimus*: and a century later, when the Venetians in their revolt against Roman despotism tried to assert State control of the machine, Cardinal Albizio asserted against them that the Inquisitors "regularly came to the sentence and, if it was one of death, it was immediately and necessarily put into execution by the Doge and the Senate." But, all through the earlier centuries, pains were taken to disguise this unbreakable chain. The cleric who pronounced a sentence of death became automatically "*irregularis*" thereby: and, in deference to this, although all the rest of the trial might take place in a church, the sentence of "releasing the culprit to the secular arm" was performed in a public square. The friar who accompanied the victim to the scaffold was warned against exhorting him to step up the ladder and meet his fate promptly, lest he should thus hasten a human being's death and become "*irregularis*." Again, though the executioner's work was left to the civil powers, the bill of costs came in to the Inquisition. This "Holy Office," however, avoided public responsibility by always adding a merciful formula to what was in fact a death sentence. It regularly besought the State officials to act with moderation and avoid "all bloodshed and all danger of death." Upon this Abbé Vacandard comments (p. 241): "This was, unfortunately, an empty formula which deceived no one. It was intended to safeguard the principle which the Church had taken for her motto: *Ecclesia abhorret a sanguine*. In strongly asserting this traditional law, the Inquisitors imagined that they thereby freed themselves from all responsibility, and kept from imbruing their hands in bloodshed. We must take this for what it is worth. It has been styled 'cunning' and 'hypocrisy'; let us call it simply a legal fiction." Mgr. Vidal, again, speaks no less unhesitatingly from his study of original sources (p. 236): "The Inquisition did not herself light the faggots; that job was reserved for the secular arm. But everybody knew that the dreadful euphemism, 'we abandon thee to the secular court,' was equivalent to a death sentence. Nobody, again, was deceived by the platonic formula behind which the judge strove to shelter his dignity: 'We abandon thee to the secular arm, beseeching it affectionately, as Canon Law requires, that the sentence of the civil judges may spare you death or mutilation.' Let us for a moment suppose that the civil magistrate had taken this recommendation literally, what penalty would he have pronounced against the poor wretches who were handed over to him? No doubt he could have condemned them to prison for life; but for that job the Inquisition had no need of him, and she was not accustomed to confide the custody of her prisoners to other folk than her own. She had her own dungeons and was very jealous of them. The clause which we are discussing, therefore, was merely illusory; the impenitent heretic was always put to death." As Peter the Precentor had written in protest, while his Church was as yet only feeling her way towards his system, it is the man in authority who is responsible for the actual deed: *Illud ab eo fit, cujus auctoritate fit.* A century ago, when the study of these historical sources was yet in its infancy, it was possible for a distinguished layman, more clerical than the clerics, to count "among the innumerable errors propagated by the eighteenth century" "the belief of the ignorant multitude that priests could condemn a man to death!" "Never did the priest raise a scaffold; he mounts the scaffold only as a martyr or a consoler." So wrote Count Joseph de Maistre; and even nowadays, as Vacandard complains, there are apologists who timidly plead something of the kind, in face of the notorious fact that any magistrate, if he refused or pertinaciously neglected to burn a heretic delivered to him with this formula, would find himself condemned for heresy and given his choice between abject amendment and the stake. Sometimes, it is true, the lay magistrate was even more merciless than the Inquisition. In 1249 Raymond of Toulouse attempted to atone for his feud with the Church by burning eighty heretics in a batch. In 1352 the Inquisitor at Toulouse found that, when "relapsed" heretics had been sentenced only to life-prison, the secular authority had burned them; he appealed to the Pope. The answer has not been recorded; but it was probably on the stricter side; for this was just about the time when Rome finally decided that all relapsed heretics should be unconditionally handed over to the secular arm. Henceforth, the main doubt was as to the amount of guilt which constituted "relapse" in this technical sense.

The execution itself can best be judged by an eyewitness's account of John Hus's death at Constance in 1415. We see here not quite the elaborate pageantry of ignominy adopted later in Spain, but sufficient cruelty and elaboration to support the deliberate policy of terrorism. "He was made to stand upon a couple of faggots and tightly bound to a thick post with ropes, around the ankles, below the knee, above the knee, at the groin, the waist, and under the arms. A chain was also secured around the neck. Then it was observed that he faced the east, which was not fitting for a heretic, and he was shifted to the west; faggots mixed with straw were piled around him to the chin. Then the Count Palatine Louis, who superintended the execution, approached with the Marshal of Constance, and asked him for the last time to recant. On his refusal they withdrew and clapped their hands, which was the signal for the executioners to light the pile. After it had burned away there followed the revolting process requisite to utterly destroy the half-burned body—separating it in pieces, breaking up the bones, and throwing the fragments and the viscera on a fresh fire of logs. When (as in the cases of Arnaldo of Brescia, some of the Spiritual Franciscans, Hus, Savonarola, and others, it was feared that relics of the martyr would be preserved) especial care was taken, after the fire was extinguished, to gather up the ashes and cast them in a running stream."[4] Thus it was with Wyclif's bones, by decree of that same Council of Constance. From Carcassonne, we have a surviving statement of the expenses for burning four heretics in 1323. It runs thus:

"For large wood	55 sols	6 deniers
For vine-branches . . .	21 sols	3 deniers
For straw	2 sols	6 deniers
For four stakes	10 sols	9 deniers
For ropes to tie the convicts . .	4 sols	7 deniers
For the executioner, each 20 sols .	80 sols	
In all	8 livres	14 sols 7 deniers

or a little more than two livres apiece."

The *livre* most usual in Southern France may be taken as roughly equivalent at that time to £8 sterling at the present day.[5]

CHAPTER XVI

The Vaudois

IN this, as in the next two chapters, it will be necessary to give as much as possible in the Inquisitors' own words, in order that readers may realise for themselves the actual working of the machine.

The Inquisition, as a final crown to victory in civil war, did succeed in destroying Catharism as a serious and open rival to the Roman Church. The two creeds differed too widely in essentials to breathe openly the same air; one or the other must perish, in an age in which the experiment of general tolerance had never been tried. Such an idea then seemed visionary to almost all men—Utopian, we may say, in the most literal sense, since St. Thomas More, in his imaginary republic, was the first orthodox Catholic to popularise any such idea, and even he himself could not put it into practice.[1]

In the thirteenth century, public heresy, mass-heresy, involved almost necessarily a series of pitched battles; and for such great-scale battles the Inquisition enabled existing society to mobilise overwhelming forces. The massacre of two Inquisitors with their nine clerical escorts at Avignonnet, in 1242, did no more than to show the extent of popular hatred for the Inquisitors, and especially for the Dominicans. Two years later, all the usual melancholy features of civil war were displayed at the siege of Montségur, the last stronghold of Catharism. The heretics attracted from outside a famous maker of military machines; sympathisers brought them money and munitions and food through the imperfect ring of blockade; they held out to the last in hope of a relieving army to come from the Emperor Frederick II. But the odds were too great: a traitor finally guided the Crusaders by secret paths along the cliffs, and

the castle was surrendered on promise of life to all but the
heretic "bishop" and his "perfecti." A huge fire was lit at the
bottom of the cliff; each "perfectus" was offered death or
recantation; 205 men and women chose death and were cast into
the flames. The other captives were utilised as informers
against the heresy of the district. The Council of Narbonne
asked Inquisitors to postpone sentences for a while, since it was
impossible to build prisons fast enough for the crowds who
came to confess heresy before the time of grace should expire.
Catharism did indeed linger on for three generations longer:
but Montségur was its last effort as an open and organised
institution.

Meanwhile, however, other heresies rose which troubled the
Inquisitors almost as much, and which are entitled to far more
sympathy from the modern world. These are the Vaudois and
the Fraticelli or Béguins.

Of the Vaudois we know a good deal from their own writings,
of which the principal is called "Noble Lesson"—*Nobla Leyçon*.[2]
This shows a simple evangelical rule of faith and morals; and
contemporary records give exactly the same impression. The
pages which here follow will be translated from two of their
most determined opponents—Riniero Sacconi, converted heretic
and Inquisitor in the district of Passau, and Peter v. Pilichdorf,
an anti-heretical missionary of a little later. We can fix
Sacconi down to about 1254 and Pilichdorf to shortly after 1300.
Both authors, together with an anonymous contemporary who
wrote a sort of appendix to Sacconi, were printed by M. de la
Bigne in Vol. XXV of his *Maxima Bibliotheca Patrum*. It will
be seen that all three, while perfectly willing to force these men
to recantation or the stake, testify honestly to qualities which,
at an earlier or a later period of European civilisation, would be
held far to outweigh all theological differences, at any rate in the
eye of the law.

Sacconi's account of their origin is brief and simple. It was
towards the end of the twelfth century that a rich citizen of
Lyons, startled at the sudden and public death of a comrade,

gave all his treasures at once to the poor.* "Hence there flowed unto him a very great multitude of poor folk, whom he taught to practise voluntary poverty and to become imitators of Christ and His Apostles. Having some little knowledge of Latin, he taught them the text of the New Testament in the vulgar tongue; and, being rebuked for this temerity, he contemned the rebuke and began to insist upon his own doctrine, saying to his disciples that the clergy, since they were evil livers, envied their holy life and doctrine. When the Pope had pronounced ex- communication against them, they pertinaciously contemned this; and thus even to the present day their rancorous teaching makes progress in all regions."

From other exactly contemporary sources we can fill in this picture. Waldo made this French translation of the New Testament not himself, but through a priest whom he hired; and to this he added a selection of "Sentences" from the Fathers. Though the archbishop of Lyons forbade their preaching, the Pope at first allowed it, whenever they could get permission from the priests. This compromise naturally broke down; its practical impossibility is shown in the experience of St. Francis a generation later. Francis himself was willing to kiss the very footprints of the priests; he protested on his death-bed: "If I had the wisdom of a Solomon, and found paltry secular priests, I would not preach against their will in the churches wherein they reside." But St. Bonaventura, who had actually seen the Saint in his childhood, wrote very differently when he was Minister General of the Order: "If we were never to abide in parishes but by the priests' will, then we should scarce ever be able to stay long; since, whether of their own motion or at others' instigation, they would eject us from their parishes sooner than heretics or Jews."[3] This contrast records the actual experience of forty years: but in Waldo's case the breach came earlier and was more complete. True, at the Third Lateran Council (1179) these Poor men of Lyons came before Alexander

* According to another account his conversion was brought about by hearing a *jongleur* recite the Life of St. Alexis.

III and were benevolently treated by him, though a learned cleric like Walter Map naturally found them mainly ridiculous. Lucius III objected to their wearing sandals and a quasi-monastic garb, and to their going about with women; the admission of women-preachers was one of their tenets. He anathematised them in 1184 at that Council of Verona which marked a stage further in the death-penalty for heretics; and from that time forward they gave far more trouble than the now moribund Catharism. They called themselves "Christ's Poor Men," or "Poor Men of Lyons," others called them "Leonistae," "Waldenses," or "Insabbatati" from the rough sandals—*savates*—which they wore in pursuance of their claim to imitate the Apostles. They multiplied with a rapidity which testifies to the need that they met. Sacconi reads in this a plain token of the imminence of the world's end, just as St. Thomas More suspected the Last Judgment when Lutheranism came in like a flood. Sacconi quotes, I. John II. 18: "as ye have heard that Antichrist shall come, even now there are many Anti-christs, whereby we know that it is the last time;" and he adds: "upon this text the gloss saith: 'All heretics are Antichrists.'" Almost at this very moment, again, in 1250, Bishop Grosseteste was formally laying before the Pope and three of his greatest cardinals a memorial upon the then state of the Church. He pointed out how a considerable part—the Greeks—are separated altogether: moreover, even among those who remain nominally under the Roman obedience, "no small fraction is separated from Christ by heretical pravity:" and finally, even among the orthodox remnant, "almost all is separated from Christ and incorporated with the devil by the seven deadly sins."[4]

The immense advantage that this gave to heresy is confessed by practically all orthodox missionaries. Sacconi shows it even in that section where he attributes the main stream of non-conformity to a far less laudable source. He writes: "The first cause of heresy is vainglory. The second is that all [heretics] men and women, great and small, night and day, cease not to teach and learn. For the workman, labouring by day, learns

or teaches by night; and therefore for the sake of study they
spend little time in prayer. They teach and learn without
books; even in leper-houses they teach and learn. Again, for
introductions, they teach men to avoid the seven mortal sins,
and three [others], to wit, lying and backbiting and swearing.
This they prove by many authorities, and call those the Ten
Commandments. Moreover, a convert of ten days' standing will
seek another and teach him, so that curtain draweth curtain.*
If they excuse themselves, saying 'I cannot learn,' then they
say unto them, 'Learn only one word a day; and by the end of
a year thou shalt know three hundred; and thus shalt thou
progress.' This is true that I say; a certain heretic, for the sole
purpose of turning a man from our faith, swam to him one
winter night through the river Ibs. Wherein we may blame the
negligence of Catholic teachers, who are not so zealous for the
truth of their faith as these faithless heretics are for their false
misbelief. The third cause of heresy is that they have translated
the Old and New Testament into the vulgar tongue, and thus
they teach and learn it. I have heard and seen a certain ignorant
rustic who recited Job, word for word; and many who knew
perfectly the whole New Testament. And, seeing that they are
unlearned layfolk, they expound the Scriptures falsely and
corruptly. For instance, that text of John (i. 11) *in propria
venit, et sui eum non receperunt*; here they say 'sui, to wit,
swine,' saying *sui* for *sues*. And those words of the psalm
(lxvii, 30) *increpa feras harundinis*, they interpret 'rebuke
the beasts of the swallows,' mistaking *harundinis* for *hirundinis*.†
Moreover, they give titles to the psalms; they thus call *Eructavit*
'The Maiden's Psalm' and *Exurgat* 'The Psalm of Vengeance,'
and *De Profundis* 'The Psalm of Repentance,' and so with the
rest. They teach and learn in secret places and times, admitting
none but of their own faith. At their assembling, they say first:
'Beware lest there be among us any crooked wood'; to wit, any

* Allusion to Exodus xxxvi, 10.

† The commoner form is not *harundinis* but *arundinis*. These blunders, it
will be noted, are not comparable in gravity to those which are recorded in
Chapter V from orthodox clergy against their own priests.

stranger. Also they prescribe that their doctrine be hidden from the clergy. Even as some men converse by signs known only to themselves, so the heretics twist words into significations understood by no others. They call a church *stone-house*; an altar *stone-heap*; the clergy, Scribes, the monks and friars, Pharisees, and thus with many other things. They never give direct answers.

"The fourth cause of heresies is the scandal from some men's evil example. Thus, when they see a man of evil life, they say: 'Thus did not the Apostles live; nor do we, who are their imitators.'

"The fifth cause is the insufficiency of the teaching of some [Catholics], who preach sometimes frivolities and sometimes falsehoods. Wherefore, whensoever a doctor of the Church teacheth anything which he proveth not by a text of the New Testament, they hold this (in contradiction to the Church) for a mere fable.

"The sixth cause is the irreverence with which certain ministers of the Church treat the Sacraments.

"The seventh is the hatred which they have towards the Church. I have heard from the mouths of heretics that they purposed to reduce the clergy and cloister-folk to the state of diggers, by taking from them their tithes and possessions, and through the power and multitude of their own believers and abettors. A certain heresiarch named Henry, a glover in Cheron,* was led to his death; he cried in the hearing of all men: 'Ye do justly condemn us; for, if our state had not been lessened, we should have used against you all—clergy and cloister-folk and layfolk—that power which ye now use against us.' But in all the cities of Lombardy and in Provence and other realms and lands, there were more schools of heretics than of theologians, and more orators disputing publicly and challenging the people to formal disputations. They preached in the market and in the fields and in houses, and no man durst hinder them, by reason of the power and multitude of their abettors. I have

---

* Or, by another reading, in Xeroin.

oftentimes been present at the Inquisition and examination of heretics; and we counted fifty-one schools of heretics in the diocese of Passau."[5]

Pilichdorf puts it even more plainly. "And, because those who believe in [these Vaudois] saw, and do daily see, that these men are strong in outward holiness, and that very many (quamplurimos) priests of the Church, alas! follow after vices, and especially after those of the flesh, therefore they believe that they can better be absolved from their sins by these [Waldensians] than by the Church priests. And, unless God's mercy vouchsafe to inspire the prelates of the Church with greater vigilance, it is to be feared that perchance these men will draw even greater power to themselves."[6]

The gravity of the moral question comes out, again, even in his attempts to confute these unauthorised critics. "Thou barkest also against the priests of the Church, saying: 'They are fornicators, tavern-haunters, dicers, forgers; and thou castest in their teeth (conjectas in eos) many other vices.' What then? Are they on that account not priests? God forbid! For even as a man's goodness doth not confer priesthood, so also doth his wickedness not take it away. . . . Therefore the worst man, if he be a priest, is more worthy than the holiest layman. Where is the layman so holy that he would dare to handle with his hands the venerable Body of Christ? I say boldly, if he dared to handle it, he would then be no holy man." And finally (Ch. XVIII): "Dost thou think that all priests of the Catholic Church are evil? Thou errest; if thou wouldst look closely, thou shouldst find that the good, by God's grace, are very many. And, if thou confessest the truth, thou knowest that many criminous have been found among thy Waldensian fellow-heresiarchs, and not few also among the believers."

Again, he cannot help granting them some points on one of the most keenly disputed questions. "The reason why not only Waldensian heretics, but even many Catholics, are sometimes wavering in faith (titubant) concerning Indulgences, is in the indiscreet pronunciations of covetous (quæstuosorum) priests, who promise Indulgences promiscuously to all folk who do this or that. This is not the intention of the Lord Pope or of other prelates, who give no Indulgences but to such as are truly penitent and confessed."[7] His next chapter, *De Anno Jubilæo*, shows that he wrote after that first Papal Jubilee of 1300 which did so much to quicken discussion as to the theory of Indulgences and Works of Supererogation.

Moreover, when it comes to a description of these heretics' behaviour, by which they may be suspected or identified, the modern reader's sympathies will be even more strongly enlisted. "Heretics are known by their manners and their words. For in their manners they are composed and moderate; they have no pride in dress, for they wear neither precious garments, nor very vile. They use no trade, for avoidance of lies and oaths and fraud, living only by labour as artisans; and for doctors [i.e., learned teachers] they have cobblers. They multiply no riches, but are content with necessaries. Moreover, they are chaste, especially the Waldensians: also they are temperate in food and drink. They go not to taverns or to dances or other vanities.* They restrain themselves from wrath; they are always either working or learning or teaching; and therefore they pray little. Again, they go feignedly to church and confess and communicate and attend sermons, but this in order that they may catch the preacher in his speech. They are known also by their precise and moderate words. They beware of scurrility and backbiting and loose speech and lies and oaths. They do not even say *In truth*, or *Certainly*, and so forth; for they regard those as oaths. Moreover, they seldom answer questions directly: for example, if they are asked, 'Knowest thou a Gospel, or Epistles?', the man will answer, 'Who should have taught me those things?' or, again, 'It is men of great or deep understanding who ought to know such things, or for those who have leisure or opportunity' . . . Heretics study cunningly how they may creep into familiarity with nobles and

---

* Franciscan Tertiaries were similarly forbidden to attend dances or weddings.

great folk. This they do thus. Some carry tempting wares, such as rings and garments, for lords and ladies to buy. When these have been sold, if one ask, 'Hast thou more to sell?' the man will answer: 'I have more precious jewels than these; I would give them to you if you would assure me that you would not betray me to the clergy.' Then, when assurance is given: 'I have a gem so luminous that therethrough a man knoweth God. Another I have, so resplendent that it kindleth in its possessor's heart the love of God'; and so forth, speaking of gems metaphorically. Then he will recite to the other some devout chapter, as for instance in Luke (i. 26), *The angel Gabriel was sent*, etc.; or our Lord's speech in John (xiii. 1), *Now before the feast of Passover*, etc. When therefore he hath begun to please his hearer, then he addeth such a chapter as Matthew (xxiii. 2), *The Scribes and the Pharisees sit in Moses' seat*, etc., or Luke (xi. 52), *Woe unto you! for ye have taken away the key of knowledge; ye enter not in yourselves, and them that were entering ye hindered.* Or again (Mark xii. 40), *Woe unto you who devour widows' houses!*' Then, when his hearer asketh: 'Of whom are these curses to be understood?', he will answer: 'Of the clergy and the cloisterers.' "

Our Inquisitor then describes the sort of sermon which the heretics preach from those texts. They compare the "Roman Church" (for Pilichdorf uses the term commonly applied both by orthodox and by unorthodox to the Church of that day) with their own. "The doctors of the Roman Church are pompous in their garments and in their manners." "*Item*, they are incontinent; yet among us each hath his own wife, with whom he liveth chastely." "*Item*, they are rich and avaricious . . . *item*, they love pleasure. . . . *Item*, they fight themselves and lead others into war . . . whereas it is written *He who taketh the sword shall perish by the sword*. . . . *Item*, they eat the bread of idleness, doing no work, whereas we work with our hands. . . . *Item*, they would have all teaching reserved for themselves; while among us both women and men are teachers, and the disciple of seven days old teacheth some other. *Item*, there are few doctors among them who know by heart, in the original Latin, three continuous chapters of the New Testament; while among us there are few men or women who cannot recite the text in the vulgar tongue. And it is because we all hold the true faith of Christ, and teach His true doctrine, that the Scribes and Pharisees persecute us causelessly to death, as they did with Christ." "The clergy now, as then, lay burdens on men which they do not touch with their own little finger. They compel men to obey the traditions of men rather than God's commandments. They lay upon the sinner grievous penances; whereas we follow Christ's example, and say unto him *Go, and sin no more,* loosing him from all his sins by the laying on of hands. In the hour of death, we send souls to heaven, while they transmit almost all souls to hell.* . . . By this and other propositions, the heretic saith: 'Consider which state of life and which faith is the more perfect, ours or that of the Roman Church, and choose that one.' And thus the man is perverted by their errors and seduced from the Catholic faith. And so he becometh their believer and receiver, abettor and defender; and, hiding him for months under his roof, he learns the tenets of his sect."[8]

Again, our Inquisitor gives a description of the behaviour of a "Bishop," or "Perfectus," and his converts. When the faithful find themselves in his presence, "they fall on their knees, adoring him, and each saith 'Spare us, O Lord!' Then each saith in the German tongue, 'Never may I die without obtaining from you that I may make a good end!' Then he, laying his hands on each, says thrice in German over each adorer, 'And thou becomest a good man.' They give their disciples no hope of salvation unless they forsake all and join their sect, or at least accept from them the imposition of hands at their last gasp." This is from Sacconi, ex-heretic and present Inquisitor, by way of a practical clue to all who would follow the heretical scent and join in the chase of these Little Foxes.

---

* It must be remembered that, by orthodox medieval belief, the majority of mankind would find their way to hell.

Pilichdorf corroborates the generally humble origin of these men. He casts it in their teeth that their "doctors" are mere tailors, smiths, cobblers, husbandmen, millers, or other artisans. Bernard Gui, in his *Practica*,[9] gives a description less strikingly favourable, but recognisable as essentially the same, except that he suggests occasional secret abominations. Here, however, he does not profess anything but hearsay—*ut dicunt*—and the passage is, in fact, borrowed from David of Augsburg, a Franciscan who wrote about 1270 and who believed that, in fact, these stories were falsely transferred to the Vaudois from other heretics. On this whole subject of the Vaudois we have a most important original source in Mollat's Latin edition of part of Gui's *Practica* with French translation. The book is cheap, and thus accessible to any non-specialist reader with ordinary command of French.

CHAPTER XVII

Bible-Christians?

WE must face now, what these quotations have shown hitherto only incidentally, the Bible-confidence of the Vaudois, the horror of oaths which they drew from this, and the extent to which Inquisitors treated both those tenets as heretical.

When Johannes Textor protested before the assembled citizens at Toulouse, "I lie, and swear, and am a faithful Christian," he spoke not as a theologian but as a politician, concerned to warn the burghers that the Inquisitors were encroaching upon civic liberties, and would reduce Toulouse to servitude. But it must not be forgotten that in all this audience, not always excepting even the clergy, there was probably not one soul who, in knowledge of Bible text, had even the fragmentary smattering of an average Sunday-school child of to-day. The church walls, we are often told, were then the Bible of the poor: but how could any man there read Christ's words: "Swear not at all"? Lying, it may be pleaded, is very plainly condemned in the scene of Ananias and Sapphira. That scene we ourselves know well from Rafael's cartoon; but who has ever discovered, among the tens of thousands of figures on wall or window of the medieval churches, one single representation of that tragedy? Even of Christ's own parables it is extremely rare to find any pictorial representation. Nor were the ordinary well-to-do citizens much wiser here than the illiterate: we may even say, not much less illiterate than the illiterate. The Knight of La Tour-Landry's book for the education of his daughters, the most famous of its kind in the Middle Ages, was compiled by him with the aid of two priests and two other clerics, but it contains the grossest Biblical errors.[1] There is no papal or conciliar decree concerning vernacular translations of the Bible, in the whole Middle Ages, which is not either restrictive or flatly prohibitive. Although Waldo may have been far from the first to attempt giving a real Bible to the unlettered of the Western Church, he was certainly the first to popularise it on this scale, and to put it in the forefront of his creed. Here was one of those new ideas which are stronger than dynamite. Here was the fulfilment of that prophecy in the Apocalypse, the opening of the Book sealed with Seven Seals, with all its consequences of conflict and final triumph. Therefore, as early as 1199, Innocent III was compelled to step in. Common folk in Metz, one of the most civilised districts in Europe, were found possessing and discussing French translations of the New Testament, the Psalter, Job and other portions of Scripture. Innocent decreed no hard-and-fast prohibition; but he pointed out that the Bible is too profound for the comprehension of simple folk: therefore the people must abandon this attempt and return to a proper degree of respect for their pastors. Yet at Trier, hard by, in 1231, heretics were found in possession of German versions. The Council of Béziers, in 1233–4, forbade not only vernacular versions but, for layfolk, the possession even of Latin Bibles! In 1234 King Jaymé I of Aragon decreed that all who possessed books of the Old or New Testament in the vulgar tongue must deliver them within eight days to the bishops for burning, under pain of suspicion or heresy. All the rest of the long story will be found in Miss M. Deanesly's *Lollard Bible*, but this may suffice to show the importance attached to the question by both sides. All men agreed (except the Cathari and a few other heretics) that Old and New Testament are the inerrant word of God. Beyond this, all recognised the frequent difficulties of exposition, with the apparent inconsistencies and even contradictions. The priest claimed a monopoly of interpretation; upon that monopoly his whole position was founded. These heretics here suspected a complete sacerdotal bankruptcy. Testing the priest by the Bible, which he professed to follow, they seemed

to find him not only a mistaken interpreter again and again,
but even ignorant of the text itself. Here, therefore, was an
obvious battleground: battle to the death, in the most literal
sense.

What Sacconi tells us concerning Vaudois Bible-knowledge
is corroborated by others, and especially by one of their ablest,
frankest and most determined persecutors, the Dominican
Étienne de Bourbon, a few years later. He writes: "They know
the Apostles' Creed excellently in the vulgar tongue: they learn
by heart the Gospels of the New Testament in the vulgar
tongue, and repeat them aloud to each other. . . . I have seen
a young cowherd who had dwelt but one year in the house of
a Waldensian heretic, yet had attended so diligently and
repeated so carefully all that he heard, as to have learned by
heart within that year forty Sunday gospels, not counting those
for feast-days . . . and other extracts from sermons and
prayers. I have also seen some layfolk who were so steeped in
their doctrine that they could even repeat by heart a great part
of the Evangelists, as Matthew or Luke, and especially all that
is said therein of our Lord's teaching and sayings; so that they
could repeat them continuously with scarce one wrong word
here and there. This I say on account of their diligence in evil
and the negligence of the Catholics in good; for many (*plures*)
of these latter are so negligent of their own and their families'
salvation as scarce to know their Pater or their Creed, or to
teach the same to their servants."[2] Berthold of Regensburg,
at about the same time, says the same of the Jews, that they
knew their Bible better than Christian laymen, and were therefore dangerous adversaries. Yet the Church blindly attempted
to right herself by suppressing these "heretical" Scripture
studies, instead of rivalling them by the thoroughness of her
own instruction in orthodoxy. Thus, in the fifteenth century,
even the enlightened Johann Busch, who would allow the laity
some religious books in their mother tongue, disapproved of
"such lofty or divine books" as a translation of the Communion
Service: indeed, finding one in the hands of some nuns, he

committed it to the flames. Pilichdorf is doubtless right in his complaint that these Vaudois often stumbled badly over the more difficult Bible passages, though he gives no instances so ludicrous as Giraldus Cambrensis and Erasmus give from their own experience of the orthodox clergy. He attacks them for despising University studies as mere vanities: so, however, did Richard Rolle, our greatest English mystic of that same early fourteenth century. He reminds them that they know no Greek or Hebrew: yet that was the most notorious defect of orthodox medieval University education, complained of as bitterly by Roger Bacon in the thirteenth century as by Erasmus in the sixteenth. Moreover, on several of the most important questions for true religion and moral conduct, later ages (and sometimes earlier ages also) agree far more nearly with the heretic than with the Inquisitor.

The clearest test case is that with which this chapter has begun: the heretical horror of oaths. Modern apologists plead that oaths were the very cement of the whole feudal fabric. There was the regular oath of fealty to one's lord—or, if it comes to that, to many lords, whose divergent claims might render it almost impossible to keep one's faith on one side without perjury on the other. There were oaths at every step in the King's court, in the Church courts, in the Manor courts. No efficient substitute (it is argued) could have been found for these oaths; and therefore the heretic was pulling down the whole social fabric round men's ears. There is, of course, much truth in this; but, in proportion as it is true, in that same proportion it emphasises the rudimentary character of that civilisation with which we are here dealing. Moreover, the plea, in its modern form, is so exaggerated as to be seriously misleading; and for this we have one piece, at least, of conclusive evidence. Petrus Cantor, Peter the Precentor of Notre-Dame-de-Paris, is in the first rank of medieval theologians. His orthodoxy was unquestioned; he was almost an exact contemporary of Waldo; and he knew the world of 1200 very well. Swearing, he argues, is forbidden in the Old Testament except in exceptional cases: *Thou shalt not take the name of the Lord thy God in vain.* Yet, "on the other hand, for our imperfection, nowadays under the Gospel men swear far more frequently, and in cases of less importance, than under the [Mosaic] Law. If we ought to swear for the utility of the hearer, because an oath hath authority, since men are slow to believe, then it is lawful to support with an oath whatsoever is profitably persuaded; but for the profit of what sort of matter? Not for temporal profit, but for that of the Faith, for spiritual profit. In such a cause it is lawful to swear as St. Paul did;* but not for a worldly and perishable matter.... Also the Lord saith: 'Let your communication be Yea, yea; Nay, nay; for whatsoever is more than those cometh of evil' (Matt. v. 37)—evil on the part not of him that sweareth but of him that maketh [another] to swear. Therefore it is of evil on the part of the [chapter of] Canon [Law] which compelleth the oath, since it compelleth a man to bear witness, and all witnesses are sworn. Therefore, again, it is of evil whensoever any prelate compelleth men to swear; and it seemeth that to be thus compelled is to transgress the Lord's precept. Again, if I may, by my own vow, undertake and fulfil all other evangelical perfections, why may I not also, likewise, follow this counsel of perfection? Or why do we forthwith proclaim that the man who keeps this [command of Christ] is a Catharist? Now, some oaths are spoken in careless haste, and others deliberately. Men plead that the first is a jesting word; yet it would seem to be a crime. For a plain word, spoken by itself, would [suffice to] convey the jest; therefore the addition of an oath maketh it something more than jest. Moreover, the oath hath three concomitants; truth, judgment and justice; yet this [hasty oath] hath not such concomitants; wherefore it is perjury. Further, at the courts of certain princes it is forbidden, under a standing penalty of five *sols*, to swear by

---

* The supporters of swearing were accustomed to appeal to I. Cor. xv, 31, where St. Paul writes: "I protest, *by your rejoicings which I have in Christ Jesus our Lord*, I die daily." As Peter points out, they also adduced Heb. vi, 16.

the Lord's limbs.* Yet some men are distinguished from their fellows and characterised, as it were, by their own particular and execrable oath."†

Thus the judicial oath and what we may call the sporting oath reacted upon each other, to the general debasement of the moral currency. One decree of the Council of Albi has special significance here, in view of the place and the time (A.D. 1254). The assembled fathers "considering that the religious nature of the oath (*religio juramenti*) is now set at nought more than usual," enjoin that perjurers be sent by their parish priests to the bishop for due penance (Labbe, 1671, XI. i. 736).

It would have been well if the Inquisitors could have approached the question in Petrus Cantor's spirit; but their actual manner of approach is fairly represented by the Appendix to Sacconi's treatise.³ The author there treats his opponents as an ignorant herd. "These wretches, illiterate, ignorant asses, not knowing the construction of the words [in Matt. v. 34], understand not that there is a great difference between 'not swearing at all' (*omnino non jurare*), as the heretic saith, and 'not swearing altogether' (*non jurare omnino*), as Christ saith . . . In three ways may we expound that saying of Christ in the Gospel, *nolite jurare omnino*. First, we may understand it as 'Swear not in every word' (*in omni verbo*); secondly, 'Swear not for every matter' (*pro omni facto*); thirdly (and this is more plainly to the point in the Gospel), 'Swear not altogether'—that is, not by all things; not by aught created, but only by the Creator, and His creation as sanctified by Him."

It need scarcely be said that here it is not the heretic but the Inquisitor who misconstrues the plain Latin of the Gospel, and the equally plain Greek original from which it is translated. Here we need only appeal to the modern Roman Catholic

---

* Thus *'Zounds!* is a corruption of *God's wounds; Ventrebleu* of *Ventre Dieu;* Chaucer's *Cokkës Bones* of *God's Bones*, etc. St. Bernardino of Siena puts the case picturesquely: when a gambler loses his money and his temper, then he eases himself by "rending Christ limb from limb."

† *Verb. Abbrev.*: Ch. CXXVII (Migne, *P.L.*, CCV. 322). William Rufus had his favourite oath: "By the Holy Face of Lucca," i.e., the wonder-working Crucifix of that city.

version, in the so-called Douay Bible. The words run there
(practically as in the Anglican Authorised Version): "But I say
to you not to swear at all"; and the authorised footnote attacks
the difficulty in a very different spirit from our Inquisitor's!
It runs: "*Not to swear at all:* 'tis not forbid to swear in truth,
justice and judgment; to the honour of God, or our own or
neighbour's just defence; but only to swear rashly, or profanely,
in common discourse, and without necessity."

Our Inquisitor himself seems to feel that his philological
argument needs reinforcement from theology. He puts it to the
Waldensian that there are other Gospel precepts no less plain,
on the face of them, than this: is he prepared, then, to follow
them in the same uncompromisingly literal spirit? Does he turn
the other cheek to the smiter, give his coat to him that taketh
his cloak, tear out the offending eye or amputate the foot or
hand? As an argument in modern life, this has considerable
cogency, but the thirteenth century Vaudois to whom it was
addressed might have answered most pertinently: "I do not
complain of your arguments, but of your practice. Would you
have burned St. Francis for persistently turning his other cheek
or giving his coat away? And, if not, why do you burn me for
this matter of oaths?" For by this time the Church had fixed
that penalty in Canon Law; and Bernard Gui, for instance,
asserted this most definitely in his sentences of condemnation.
He argues: not only do the Doctors of the Church, and Catholic
tradition, affirm the lawfulness of oaths, but "by the statute
long since decreed against this error, all those who, with damnable superstition, repudiate oaths and refuse to swear, are *ipso
facto* condemned as heretics."[4] Again, the prisoners' confession
repeatedly records against him such a sentence as this: that he
had met two men who "warned him not to do or say evil, nor
do unto any man as he would not have done to himself, and
that he should not lie or swear, since it is a mortal sin to swear
in any case."[5] He confesses it as a sin that he listened to any
such teacher. This is explicitly connected by contemporaries
with the habit of Bible reading. For instance: "The said

Waldensian, after his prayers, sat and preached unto them many words from the Gospels and Epistles, and among other things he said that a man must not do or say evil, nor lie nor swear." "*Item*, they preach from the Gospels and Epistles and other Holy Scriptures, which they corrupt with their expositions, as masters of error who know not to sit at the feet of truth, whereas preaching and the expounding of Holy Scripture are altogether forbidden to layfolk."[6]

The sympathy with which the Dominican ex-heretic Sacconi describes the manners of the Vaudois lends the greater significance to his description of their theological errors.[7] We may take these in order.

The Waldensians claim that their own is the true Church, and "the Roman Church is no Church of Christ, but a Church of Malignants." They reprobate Church wealth, and the "regalia," or high feudal privileges, of bishops and abbots: they would abolish all ecclesiastical privileges, and maintain that no man should be compelled to believe—*quod nullus sit cogendus ad fidem*.

"Secondly, they condemn all the Sacraments of the Church." They maintain that "priests in mortal sin cannot make [the Body of Christ]; Transubstantiation takes place not in the hands of a priest who celebrates unworthily, but in the mind of him who receiveth it worthily." "They disapprove of the fact that the faithful communicate once a year; for they themselves communicate daily." The priest of evil life has no power of remitting sins. "They condemn the Sacrament of Matrimony, saying that married folk sin mortally if they come together without hope of offspring." "Whatsoever is preached, and is not proved by the Bible text, they hold for fables. They assert that Holy Scripture hath the same effect in the vulgar tongue as in Latin: wherefore they even celebrate [the Eucharist] in the vulgar tongue, and give the Sacraments. They know by heart, in the vernacular, the text of the New Testament, and a great part of the Old. They repudiate the Decretals and Decrees [i.e., Canon Law] and the sayings and expositions of the Saints, and cleave to the [Bible] text alone. . . . They deride the lay-folk who choose by lot their [patron] saints at the altar. . . . They deny the mystical sense in Holy Scripture, especially in sayings and acts handed down by the Church: for instance, that the weathercock on the steeple signifies a Doctor (of the Church)." "Thirdly, note that they hold the following errors concerning approved Church customs. They scorn all whereof they read not in the Gospel, as Candlemas, Palm Sunday, the Reconciliation of Penitents, the Adoration of the Cross on Good Friday. They contemn the feasts of Easter, Corpus Christi and the Saints, because of the multiplication of feasts; and they say that one day is like unto another: therefore on holy-days they work secretly. *Item*, they take no heed of Church fasts [quoting Isaiah lviii. 5]: '*Is it such a fast that I have chosen?*' *Item* [they reject], all dedications, blessings and consecrations of candles, of flesh, of palms, of chrism-oil, of fire, of tapers, of the Paschal Lamb, of women after childbirth, of pilgrims, of holy places or persons, of garments or salt or water. They scoff at the church of masonry, looking upon it as a barn, and calling it in their vernacular *Stone-House:* nor will they allow that God dwelleth therein, or that prayers there are more meritorious than in a chamber, according to Matthew vi. 6: *But thou, when thou prayest, enter into thy closet,* and so forth. *Item*, they take no heed of the dedication of a church or altar. *Item*, they say that church ornaments are sinful, and that it would be better to clothe the poor than to adorn walls. Of the altar, again, they say that it is a pity for the cloth to rot upon a stone; and that Christ gave His Apostles neither stole nor chasuble nor mitre. Again, they celebrate with a mug instead of chalice, and com-pare the *corporas* to a breech-cloth* . . . They say that men are compelled to go to church for the sake of gain: yet they themselves go thither in pretence, and offer and communicate, but all this feignedly. . . . Again, they dissuade men from those confraternities of layfolk and clergy which they call *Zeche*

---

* The *corporas* or *corporal* is a linen cloth upon which the Host is laid after consecration.

('drinking-bouts'); and they say that all these things are done for the sake of gain. . . . They say that one Paternoster availeth more than the sound of ten bells, and more than a Mass. . . . They say that every oath is a mortal sin, according to Matthew v. 34–7. *Swear not at all . . . but let your communication be Yea, yea, Nay, nay.* When a man saith *in truth*, or *certainly*, they count that for an oath. . . . Again, they say that these Church courts which the priests hold are not for correction's sake, but for gain."

CHAPTER XVIII

The Heretic in Court

To get a glimpse of the practical working of the Inquisition in the face of this kind of heretic, let us take three typical cases out of the 930 recorded more or less fully in Bernard Gui's *Register*. The culprits in all cases are from Languedoc.

In 1321 Guillaume de Bayssans confessed how, "some 18 years ago, one night when his father and Perronne his mother and John his brother sat by the fire, his father asked him whether he would see the good men. He asked what sort of men these were; and his mother buffeted him on the cheek, and then his father and he and his brother went up into an upper storey of his house, where they found two men, whose names his father gave him afterwards as Pierre Auter and Amelius. They sat down with them; and Pierre said: 'Welcome, fear not, for we will do you no ill'; and he said some words which this deponent remembereth not. Afterwards, he and his father came down from the loft and left them there. He himself was then, as he said, some eight or nine years old. Again, the third night after, while he and others whom he nameth* sat at home by the fire, the aforesaid two came down from the loft and sat there with them; and one of them said: 'Maynada, we are good men, of those whom folk call heretics, yet we are no heretics': and he began to read certain words from a certain book, what words the deponent remembereth not, as he saith. Again, the night after, he and his father went up to the said loft and found there the said Pierre and Amelius; and, while they were there, two men came in (whom he nameth), and then his father bade

* To refuse the names of others who might be implicated was, in itself, a crime which might be punished with death.

him go to bed, and he left them there. Again the next night or some other following, as he and his father and mother and brother sat at home by the fire, the aforesaid two came from without, and Guillaume Mercadier of Born with them. Then, when they had entered, Guillaume Mercadier bent his knees twice or thrice before the said heretics, saying some words which he understood not; and then he departed and the heretics remained; and then his father and mother and brother, one after the other, adored the said heretics, bending their knees thrice to the earth, and doffing their hoods and laying their hands on the bench, saying certain words which he understood not; and then he himself, Guillaume de Bayssans, adored the said heretics after heretical fashion. Questioned as to the belief of the heretics, he said that he was eight or nine years old and knew not well how he should believe of them, nor had he faith in their sect, and he acted as aforesaid by the inducement of his father and mother. Questioned why he deferred so long coming to confession of the said matters, he answered that when his father was summoned by the Inquisitor to come to the sermon at which he was imprisoned,* he said to him: 'Son, I know not if I shall see thee again; but beware, while I or your mother are alive, of telling any man those things which thou hast seen or learnt concerning the matter of the heretics': and this (said Guillaume) is why I deferred confession so long."

He was sentenced, with six others, to the following punishments. He was to wear the cross of infamy, swearing on the Gospels that he would never quit it, within or without his house. He must undertake twenty-one solemn pilgrimages, including shrines so distant as Chartres and Paris, "bringing back letters testimonial from the authorities at each of those places, to the effect that ye have fulfilled the said pilgrimages; and ye must begin them within three months of this present day, and strive for their completion in virtue of the oath that ye have sworn." They must fulfil their Church duties busily, fasting through Advent in addition to the general Lent; and

* The Inquisitors' sentences were preceded by a solemn public sermon.

become talebearers, prosecuting or denouncing heretics of all descriptions. "All this we enjoin upon you, reserving to ourselves and our successors in the office of the Inquisition full powers of adding, diminishing, and also remitting in the matter of the said penance, if and whensoever it may seem good to us or to them."[1]

In that same year, Bernard dealt with Hugh of Vienne. "He refused to swear, pretending the feigned reason that he dared not, because, having sworn on another occasion, he had incurred the falling sickness. . . . Therefore we, Bishop of Pamiers, intimated and explained to him the written law, that any man suspected in matters of faith, and brought before the judge, and required to swear as to the truth, must be judged a heretic if he refuse to swear; yet he would on no account swear; nay, he said that it repented him to have sworn elsewhere before the said bishop and the Inquisitor of Carcassonne, saying that he had thus sinned grievously and believed that it would be a sin to swear again; nor, though oftentimes required, would he thenceforth swear to tell the truth in court in a case of faith. . . . Item, he said that that man sinneth who compelleth another to swear, for the Lord hath commanded us not to swear. Item, that he believed his soul would be saved if he were judged to death for the said cause [of refusing to swear]. Item, asked whether the secular powers can without sin condemn to death men guilty of mortal crimes, as homicides and other felons, he answered that he knew not what to believe in this matter, for the Lord commanded Thou shalt not kill.* Item, he said and affirmed that he would persist and live and die in the aforesaid faith, though often questioned [on that point]; nor would he swear in any manner. Item, he said and affirmed that he would not believe or obey the Lord Pope, if he told him that it is lawful to swear to the truth, and that Purgatory existed, and that the prayers of the Church availed dead men. Item, that he did not believe himself subject to the Lord Pope, but to

* Non occides, the Vulgate rendering of the Hebrew, where both Deut. v. 17, and Mark x. 19, have φονεύω, more exactly rendered in the Anglican Catechism and Communion Service as "do murder."

God alone. Afterwards it was said and expounded to him that, unless he revoked and abandoned these errors, he would be proceeded against as an impenitent and obstinate heretic; yet he answered that he would stand by them in life and death; nor would he in any way abandon them; to wit, that swearing is sinful, for the truth or for other causes; that there is no Purgatory after this life; that prayers for the dead avail them not; that excommunication, however rightly and canonically pronounced, did not shut him out from the Kingdom of God or from spiritual benefits; and that the secular powers which possess jurisdiction sin when they slay malefactors: also, that he held himself not subject to the Pontiff of Rome except when he commandeth the same as God doth." He and his wife were handed over to the secular arm, "beseeching it, as Canon Law prescribeth, that it will moderate its judgment upon them short of death and mutilation"—*citra mortem et membrorum mutilationem.*[2]

Here is another death sentence, from 1319: "Thou, Perrin de Vincendat . . . didst long since confess to Brother Gui de Reims, Inquisitor for heretical pravity in Burgundy, that thou wert implicated in the fact and crime of the Waldensian sect; and in the presence of that Inquisitor thou didst promise on solemn oath that thou wouldst never return to the said crime or participate with the Waldensians; and thus the said Inquisitor absolved thee from whatsoever thou hadst committed in the same crime, which thou hadst confessed to him. Afterwards, however, like a dog returned to his vomit, fearing not to add fresh guilt to the old, thou hast relapsed in manifold fashion into that sect and heresy which thou hadst already abjured before the judgment-seat, participating with many Waldensians in meat and drink, listening to the monitions or exhortations and sermons which they make to believers in their assemblies, and praying according to their manner and rite, bowed on bent knees with them. *Item,* confessing thy sins to certain Waldensians, one by one, and receiving penance and absolution from the same, and believing that sect (formerly abjured) to be good, and persevering many years in that belief. *Item,* after that thou

hadst confessed the aforesaid things before the judgment-seat
of the Inquisitor of Toulouse, and hadst there once again (that
is, for the second time) abjured the said sect and heresy, then,
while thou wert in prison, thou didst receive a certain super-
tunic and a sum of money through some person who passed it
to thee, saying that Huguenin Pisaud, a Waldensian whom
thou hadst formerly known and believed to be such, sent the
aforesaid gifts to another prisoner who was a Waldensian
Perfect, and thou didst pass that super-tunic and money to him
to whom the said Waldensian sent it: nor didst thou reveal
aught of this to the Inquisitor or his lieutenant or any other
man who might have revealed it unto them, nor to any other
man through whom it might come to the notice of the Inquisitor
or his lieutenant, in order that the bringer might be caught, and
the said Waldensian might be sought after and, if possible,
taken. Finally, again, showing more evidently thy faithlessness
and thy faithless creed, when brought to judgment to tell the
truth of the fact and crime of the Waldensians, concerning
thyself and others, and required repeatedly to swear according
to Canon Law, thou didst refuse, alleging that swearing is a
sin, and that thou wouldst believe thyself to sin in swearing,
and that thou hadst sinned formerly when thou hadst sworn
elsewhere before the judge; nor wouldst thou now swear, but
didst pertinaciously refuse; and it cannot be doubted that thou
hast acted thus through following of the error of that Waldensian sect, formerly approved by thee, which doth refuse altogether to swear. Nor, again, when the Inquisitor assigned unto
thee a peremptory term for receding from the said error and
acquiescing in judicial swearing within a fixed term of days,
thou wouldst not return from the said error, nor swear in court,
though repeatedly summoned to do so in canonical form. Nay
further, when the said Inquisitor examined thee and asked
whether thou didst believe that the Waldensians are good men,
and that they hold and keep good faith and a good sect—*item*,
that the Roman Church sinned in persecuting and condemning
the Waldensians; *item*, that those of the Roman Church held and

kept true faith; *item*, that confession of sins made to the Waldensians and penance received from them profited to the salvation of those who confessed; *item*, if thou believedst that there is a Purgatory for souls after this life—thou wouldst not answer the Inquisitor's judicial questions on these matters, neither then nor after some days when thou wert re-examined and frequently required again to answer, under pain of excommunication pronounced canonically and in writing against thee unless thou shouldst have answered by the day following; whereby thou hast incurred *ipso facto* the sentence of excommunication. Nay, thou maintainest this still with pertinacious mind, and perseverest therein with hardened heart, despising and scorning, after Waldensian fashion, this sentence of excommunication pronounced upon and against thee. Therefore since thou Jean Chaucoat [another prisoner] and thou Perrin de Vincendat after abjuring judicially the said sect and heresy, have been since convicted of having relapsed, by approving it and its followers, and refusing utterly to swear judicially in consequence of that error which was formerly approved by you. *Item*, seeing that ye will not be converted from the aforesaid sect and heresy, nor return to Catholic unity, though long awaited and often invited and required in due canonical form, but rather persist with hardened mind in your faithlessness: We the said Inquisitors and Commissaries Delegate, having taken counsel of many religious men, wise and learned in Canon and Civil Law, lest, as a scabby sheep in the Lord's flock, ye should further infect those that are whole, having God before our eyes and the purity of the orthodox faith, with the Holy Gospels of God laid here before us, in order that our sentence may come forth from God's presence, and our eyes may behold the thing that is equal [Ps. xvii. 2], sitting in judgment, by definite sentence in these present writings, do pronounce you and each of you (present in court before us on this day and place which have been peremptorily assigned for the hearing of a definite sentence) as having relapsed into the sect and heresy of the Waldensians, or Poor Men of Lyons, which ye had aforetime solemnly abjured, and as being heretics of the aforesaid sect; and we leave you to the secular arm as men relapsed into your formerly abjured heresy and as impenitent and obstinate heretics. Yet we affectionately beseech the said secular court, as Canon Law prescribes, that it may keep you unimpaired in life and limb—*ut vobis vitam et membra illibata conservet.*"[3]

Pilichdorf, with this sort of machinery at the disposal of his party, was able to reproach the Waldensians for their numerical inferiority and their unwillingness to court a certain death. To their missionaries he writes: "Of the Apostles it is written: *Their sound is gone out throughout all the earth;* therefore thou art not that good shepherd of whom the Lord saith [John x. 11]: *The good shepherd giveth his life for the sheep.* Why didst thou not persist with thy sheep in Thuringia, the Mark, Bohemia and Moravia, where (by God's grace) within the space of the last two years some thousand Waldensian heretics have been converted to the Catholic faith? Why comest thou not into Austria and Hungary, where the Inquisitors of heretical pravity hope that even more than a thousand of thy believers will be torn from the jaws of Leviathan? Thou appearest nowhere; thou fleest ever, and leavest the simple poor in their tribulation. I say boldly: If thy doctrine were true, it would be easy for thee to preach it in every place. Now, forger, thou must needs hide thy false coin with greater caution!"

Yet time had shown here, as in so many other questions, the hollowness of what may be called the majoritarian argument. Bulk counts far less than vitality; and, after the lapse of six centuries, the doctrines of this handful of sufferers, with all their obvious shortcomings, command far wider sympathy than those of their persecutors. In spite of slaughter in detail and slaughter in the mass, generation after generation, there were more Vaudois in Luther's time than in Pilichdorf's. It was impossible to root them out from the wild valleys of Dauphiné and Piedmont; they went to church with the Catholics; not only the nobles often protected them, but the Eldest Daughter of the Church; French kings sometimes refused to march with the

Inquisitors. When a specially vigorous Inquisitorial effort was made in 1376, the prisons (as we have seen in ChapterXIII) proved hopelessly insufficient to contain the captives; yet in 1393 the Inquisitor is said to have burned 150 at Grenoble in one day; in 1432 the hierarchy complains that they are as numerous as ever; in 1475 they are again preaching their faith openly. In 1478 Louis XI's answer to the Pope's remonstrances was to issue an edict in French, speaking contemptuously of the Inquisition and accusing the Inquisitors of exaggeration and fraud, and forbidding them to continue their vexations among his subjects of Dauphiné. Thus, after a war of 250 years, orthodoxy has so little advanced that the Pope dares not risk an open breach with a king who shows far more resistance than what had cost the Counts of Toulouse their throne, and Provence its civilisation. The Waldenses had by this time, in many places, made common cause with the Hussites of Bohemia; and here they survived until the Reformation enabled them to merge in that greater movement. In Dauphiné and Piedmont they survive to the present day, having outlived a Crusade on a large scale in 1488, when the French and Italian authorities joined hands to destroy them and raised an army computed at 18,000 men, with the full crusading Plenary Indulgence which gave each orthodox soldier the martyr's passport to heaven. They survived that massacre of 1686 which drew from Milton his "Avenge, O Lord, thy slaughtered saints"; and, if they are nowadays more interesting to the historian than influential in Christian theology, that is because so many of the points for which they suffered have become either commonplaces accepted, if only tacitly, by orthodoxy itself, or matters too unimportant to divide men seriously.

CHAPTER XIX

The Friars: Action and Reaction

DOMINICANS and Franciscans were the most active among Inquisitors, but we must not forget that this was far from their only activity. It may be called their negative side; and the positive was the more important. The ordinary friar was better than the Inquisitor, inasmuch as he sowed the wheat while the other was struggling to uproot the tares.

We might well wonder, comparing the Vaudois and even the better among the Catharists with the ruck of contemporary clergy, whether it was possible to live a truly evangelical missionary life in that age without coming into conflict with the hierarchy. But the answer is simple: one man, at least, did so; St. Francis of Assisi. He showed an almost unique combination of two qualities most difficult to reconcile; originality and obedience. St. Dominic was a figure of far less originality, but superior in business qualities. Both were consumed with zeal for men's souls and with devotion to the Church. St. Francis laid far the greater emphasis upon poverty; St. Dominic upon theology. Not, of course, that these things fall in life, as in thought, into separate compartments; yet the difference of emphasis was very real and very important. St. Francis would help the poor, primarily, by becoming like them; his motto was to follow, naked, the naked Christ. Mr. Ralph Bennett shows conclusively that poverty in this sense was by no means a Dominican ideal.[1] On the other hand, St. Francis's ideal of complete poverty, rigidly maintained, was practically irreconcilable with any but the most rudimentary theological learning, in an age when, for instance, a copy of the Bible cost at least as much as the whole yearly income of an average parish priest.

Thus the two Orders learned gradually from each other. Dominicans were so like the Franciscans that they lived almost altogether without settled endowments beyond their actual buildings, which themselves, in the earlier days, were of the plainest and cheapest. Both Orders, with the Austin Friars and White Friars who obtained definite papal confirmation of their Rules in the same generation, lived mainly from hand to mouth by begging: they were the Mendicants, who often proudly contrasted themselves with the Possessionates, i.e., the Bene- dictines and other older Orders who, though vowed to extreme personal poverty, enjoyed corporately enormous endowments. Again, whereas the Dominicans had from the first aimed high at learning for missionary purposes, the Franciscans soon followed suit, neglecting the apparent discouragement of their Rule and of their Founder's teaching. Thus, very soon after St. Francis's death, by 1230 or so, the Mendicants began to capture the Universities, where their frugality and their consuming en- thusiasm rendered them the most popular and efficient teachers. In 1260 St. Bonaventura, then Franciscan Minister General and Professor at Paris, set the official seal upon this intellectual movement. A dozen years later, Roger Bacon can speak of the Mendicants as "the Student Orders," in contrast with the comparative intellectual inertia into which the monks had sunk by that time. Until the very end of the Middle Ages the majority of Schoolmen, and the best Schoolmen, were friars.

Here, then, was a true step forward in civilisation, very different in principle from the Inquisition, even though nearly all Inquisitors are Mendicants. Men had been attracted to the heretics by their poverty and self-denial. The Vaudois, for instance, acquired a certain reputation as folk-physicians, but would take no money; only food and drink. But here were orthodox missionaries poorer still and still more serviceable. The legend that monks first, and then Franciscans, were the physicians of the Middle Ages is contradicted by the most definite evidence; but in fact St. Francis and his earliest disciples did make it part of their extreme self-sacrifice to tend

lepers; and a compassionate friar had incomparably more
freedom of ministration among the poor than a compassionate
Vaudois. Even in 1348, when the friars were admittedly far
sunk from their first fervour, one monastic chronicler extols
those of Sicily and another those of Paris, side by side with the
nurses of the Hôtel-Dieu, as showing an honourable contrast
with the great majority of the clergy, whom they accuse of
panic fear and neglect during the Black Death.[2] To the last, the
better friars may have been as ready to help with simples as
they were to mix in nearly all other social activities; but from a
very early date the formal study of medicine and of law was
definitely forbidden to them, as liable to distract them from
theology, and tempting them to receive money. Thus, studying
theology first and foremost, and for the most practical purposes, they were now far better able to meet the heretics on their
strongest ground, that of the Bible. There was, in their convents, an elaborate ladder of theological education; at the
Universities, friars of conspicuous ability lectured on the whole
Bible text. Others were certificated as preachers: the chronicler
Salimbene is an excellent example of this class; he shows great
familiarity with all parts of the Bible text. Towards the end of
the thirteenth century, the Dominican Hugues de St.-Cher
headed a company which produced that Concordance to the
Vulgate which, essentially, is still used at the present day. The
friar could thus bandy texts with the most fluent heretic; and he
had this enormous advantage, that all men believed in the
special and incommunicable virtue of the "original" Latin.
For, by this time, Jerome's version, the Vulgate, was treated as
inspired; and laborious explanations would have been needed to
make the villager, or even the townsman, understand that this
Latin was removed by one very definite step from those words
which the Holy Ghost had dictated to the Hebrew or Greek
writers. The friars, therefore, cut the ground from under the
heretic's feet in a large number of cases; and it is mainly owing
to Francis and Dominic that religious revolution was postponed
from the thirteenth to the sixteenth century.

Yet, orthodoxy being as inelastic, and heresy as restless, as both essentially are, it was natural that the new life thus infused into Western thought should breed new heresies. As the century which saw the White Robe of Churches saw also nascent Catharism, so that very poverty with which Francis had won his victory, and to a great extent the other Mendicants, bred a new and most formidable heresy, that of the Fraticelli.

Francis had done the hardest thing in the world while insisting that it was the easiest, if men would only set themselves to it in earnest. He imitated the Christ of the Gospels more closely than any other man of whom we have record. But, like all imitators, he distorted involuntarily, exaggerating here and minimising there. The hierarchy of his day needed as plain speech as that which Christ gave to the hierarchy of His own time and land; yet Francis never spoke out with such plain rebuke as other saints have permitted themselves. The later years of his life diminished his influence as ecclesiastical, apart from social, reformer. He had not resisted unto blood. Not, of course, that the stake would have deterred him; his actual bearing under the cruel cautery of his eye-doctor would assure us of that, if we had no other evidence. What restrained him was the overwhelming reverence for his own High Priest; and this, much as it added to his personal charm, detracted proportionally from his efficiency as reformer. He was not more loving than Christ, or more tender towards men's weaknesses; but he did stop short at that which brought Christ to the cross— that irreconcilable war against the sinner, so long as he remained inseparable from his sin. There St. Francis minimised; but in the matter of poverty he exaggerated; his never-sleeping self-consciousness on this point amounted almost to idolatry. And, as the faults of a man's followers are always his own short-comings writ large, so both these distortions came out fatally not only in the next generation, but even before the Saint's death, with a crudeness which embittered his last years. He himself had shown an almost miraculous combination of self-denial and cheerfulness. That his whole Order should have been

able to maintain such an even balance could not be expected;
but the divisions which actually happened were greater and
more rapid, perhaps, than in any other great religious revival.
In 1228, when Gregory IX was canonising St. Francis, two
years after his death, there were ascetics in the Order and there
were cheerful friars; but already the two parties were often at
daggers drawn, and the cheerful majority was quite ready to
persecute the ascetic minority, with the natural result of driving
them into still more exaggerated asceticism. Thus there were
soon two definite party names: *Spiritual* for the few, *Conventual*
for the majority. The magnificent basilica which we now see at
Assisi was erected over St. Francis's bones by a Minister General
who had been his close personal friend, but who collected money
in cynical violation of the most emphatic command of the Rule.
Leo, a still closer friend, protested by breaking the money-box
placed at the door to receive those forbidden offerings; but he
had to flee almost for his life.

The quarrel soon became one of the most serious questions in
all ecclesiastical politics. Gregory IX, though he had been a
close personal friend of St. Francis, issued a bull in 1230 which
freed the Order from obedience to the Saint's solemn *Testament*.
Brother Elias scourged St. Antony of Padua to the blood for
differences on this question; while the no less saintly Cæsarius of
Speyer was chained in prison for two years, and finally clubbed
by a brutal gaoler. Thenceforward the control and policy of the
Order oscillated between these conflicting parties. The few
leading Franciscan Doctors of Divinity at Paris attempted
vainly to draw up a compromise. In 1248 a determined Spiritual
became Minister General; John of Parma, the most truly
Franciscan of all St. Francis's successors. But, in the meanwhile, what might have been called mainly a question of
discipline was becoming more and more definitely doctrinal.
Abbot Joachim of Fiore, whom Dante puts among the most
conspicuous saints in Paradise, had written a strange series of
apocalyptic treatises which, pursued to their logical conclusions, would have revolutionised the Church. The world (he

calculated) had existed for 1260 years under the Old Dispensation: for that was the space of time which theologians
reckoned from Adam to Christ, on the basis of Revelation
xii, 6. It would exist for the same space under Christ's Dispensation: i.e., down to A.D. 1260 or thereabouts; Joachim made
allowance for possible error of a few years. Then would come
the Dispensation of the Holy Ghost, in which Old and New
Testament alike would be read with new and clearer eyes; and
this would be the Everlasting Gospel of Revelation xiv, 6.
The world would then become, in a sense, one great monastery
of self-denial and devotion and contemplation; and, just as the
Last Supper superseded the Paschal Lamb, so the Eucharist
itself will become superfluous in this world so directly ruled by
the Holy Ghost, the Comforter. Here was, indeed, a revolutionary conception, far more solvent of strict orthodoxy
than even Newman's Theory of Development in its ultimate
implications. The Church, in Joachim's idea, was not so much
that static and monumental temple which we see in St. Thomas's
Summa, but a tabernacle accompanying the journey of the
Chosen People through the wilderness, pitched here to-night,
but to be dismantled with to-morrow's dawn and pitched one
stage further on. The conception is as bold as Lessing's famous
Education of the Human Race. Yet, though another of Joachim's
theories on the Trinity was indeed condemned by Innocent III,
he himself had died uncondemned, after a long life of flattering,
if only passive, patronage by three popes. Doubtless they had
not read his writings, but only respected his person and knew his
open profession of readiness to correct anything of which the
Holy See might disapprove. But, in conjunction with what we
shall presently see, how a Franciscan might be burned alive for
wearing pertinaciously the wrong frock or refusing to beg for oil
and wine, this Joachism illustrates the fact that no contrast was
impossible in this medieval Church or State. The one regular
thing in medieval life, we may almost say, is its irregularity.

   Joachim's speculations were just of the sort to ferment with
intoxicating force among these freshly-trodden grapes of the

Franciscan vintage. Here was a Brave New World coming; and they, the Brave New Order, were its pioneers. Abraham had been the central figure of the First Dispensation; Christ, of course, of the Second; but Joachim had naturally left a blank for the third. Who could be the most obvious figure here but St. Francis, that most intimate of all Christ's followers, upon whom, by a miracle then extolled as unique, Christ Himself had imprinted all His own five wounds? As the dove had come to Noah with the message of salvation after the Deluge, and as the Holy Ghost had descended in the form of a dove, who could be so fit for the New Age as these dove-like Friars Minor, whose grey frocks contrasted so strongly with the raven-black of most of the older Orders? If this sounds puerile now, we must remember how universal in those days was what may almost be called the Religion of Clothes. It was not only that special garments were essential accompaniments of all Church functions, but in the Monastic Orders the feeling amounted almost to idolatry. Canon Law made it a mortal sin for a monk to lay aside his frock except for some really compelling cause. Rich laymen paid extravagantly for the privilege of investing that frock, if only for a few hours or minutes, at their latter end; and, as we shall soon see, a pope will make the question of the fashion of a frock into one of life or death.

Joachim's writings caught especially the fancy of those more enthusiastic spirituals who populated the mountain hermitages of Central Italy, and of those Southern French populations among whom so many heresies had already been bred. It intensified their already extreme other-worldliness, and therefore it widened the division between them and that majority which was conforming more and more to the world by reason of the irresistible pressure which the mass of humanity always exerts upon any movement, whether in attraction or in repulsion. It intensified their apotheosis of their Founder. Long since, Benedictines had looked upon their own Rule as divine. Franciscan zeal outdid this; and, in 1279, Nicholas III, a great lover of that Order, issued his bull *Exiit qui seminat*, which described theirs as inspired by the Holy Ghost through St. Francis. Therefore the Joachites, among whom were some of the ablest and best Franciscans, were more and more opposed to the increasingly frequent and open relaxations of the Rule. At the same time, and in the same proportion, they themselves became increasingly irksome to the Conventuals, as self-righteous extremists who lacked the spirit of compromise; men "gey ill to live wi'." Presently, too, one extreme Spiritual committed a gross blunder which compromised the whole party. This was Gerard of Borgo San Donnino, a Franciscan Professor of Divinity at Paris. In 1254, after four years of teaching, he published a treatise called *Introduction to the Everlasting Gospel*, in which he pushed Joachism to its extremest logical and, we may add, even imaginary consequences. The Friars Minor are the new Order destined to turn the whole world practically into one vast monastery. The Sacraments will be superseded as symbols; love and charity will rule all. But, as in the Apocalypse, all this will emerge only from an immense world-crisis. The Abomination of Desolation, shaking for a moment almost the throne of God, will be incarnate in a pope, somewhere about 1260, who will buy his way to the tiara and thus lay the coping-stone upon that system of simony which earnest men deplored even more plainly in the Church of that age than Glaber had seen it eight generations earlier. This, of course, could not be tolerated. A papal commission, next year, suppressed the book as quietly as possible, for fear of scandal and in consideration of the unique services which the friars in general were rendering as a papal militia. But the episode ruined John of Parma, in spite of his conspicuous abilities and virtues: enemies even accused him of having written the book himself. Eighteen months later he resigned, to live thirty-two years longer "the life of an angel" in retirement, during which he refused a cardinalate with the words: "I could give wholesome counsel if there were anyone to listen to me; but in the Roman Court there is little discussed except wars and triumphs, and not the salvation of souls." The miracles wrought at his tomb earned him a popular cult;

and in 1777 he was formally beatified, though he had died in Joachism.

Thenceforward the see-saw continued between strict and relaxed interpretation of the Rule. In 1279, Nicholas III had prepared and published his bull *Exiit qui seminat* with almost unexampled care and solemnity. Among his collaborators on the document were two Franciscan cardinals and the future Pope Boniface VIII. Excommunication *ipso facto* was pronounced against any man who should gloss it, comment on it, discuss it or explain it away: its minute and clear provisions as to property and economics were to be taken only in their literal sense. It pronounced clearly against all the worst relaxations that had crept into the Order, yet it followed the legal fiction already adopted by Innocent IV and Alexander IV, of allowing the friars to vest their possessions in the name of the Papacy, while enjoying themselves the usufruct. If any compromise had been possible, this bull would have succeeded. But none such could really be found between a majority with whom relaxation had become habitual, and a minority to whom the strict observance of the Rule was, literally, a question of life or death. This became even more obvious when St. Bonaventura succeeded John of Parma as General. He, again, worked for compromise; and his intellect and piety were such that, if any man could have succeeded, it might be expected of him. Yet, while on the one hand he rebuked the Order as a whole, in a solemn circular letter, with a plainness and circumstantiality which from the pen of a modern historian might arouse suspicions of anti-clerical bigotry, yet by the other party he was regarded as a traitor. He complained of the conventuals' importunate begging: "the wayfarer fears to meet a friar as he would fear a robber." He describes idleness and vagrancy, greedy appropriation of legacies and burial-fees to the disadvantage of the parish clergy, and extravagances which belied their profession of poverty. He is recorded to have said that he would willingly be ground to powder, if by such sacrifice he could bring the Order back to what he remembered in his boyhood. Yet he had not the stubborn resolve of a great practical reformer; and in one matter he supported relaxation. As one of the most distinguished philosophical theologians of the Middle Ages, he was conspicuous in the fight for educational advance in the Order, and for such university studies as would have been impossible under the strictest interpretation of St. Francis's commands; indeed, such as the Saint seems, by implication at least, to have despised as he despised beautiful architecture, and all things which do not lead us straight to Heaven. Thus St. Bonaventura became a bugbear to the Spiritual extremists. The *Fioretti* records a vision in which a certain recreant friar, black in heart and with huge claws as keen as razors, was seen to fall upon the saintly John of Parma. In the Italian version this traitor is unnamed; but in the original Latin there is no concealment; St. Bonaventura is definitely specified. That such a man should have appeared in this light to honest and orthodox fellow-friars is a testimony to the demoralising effects of this civil war. There were some extremist Spirituals to whom even the bull *Exiit* seemed insufficient in its defence of the Rule; and these were treated by their fellows with cruel severity. They were condemned to lifelong imprisonment in chains, and denied the hope even of the Sacraments at their death, so that soul might die as well as body. The fact that others came and released them after a while from this sentence was no consolation to one Fra Tommaso, who was cast into prison for saying that the cruel discipline was displeasing to God, and rotted there to death in a few months.

One of the hottest points of conflict was St. Francis's *Testament*. This document, plainly expressing his distress at the relaxations which were already growing up during the last years of his life, specifically forbade them. It had not, like the Rule, received papal confirmation; and Innocent IV had ruled it out as binding in strict law; but the Spirituals clung to it all the more obstinately as their Charter, as the documentary justification of their claim to follow the true mind of Francis. To the extremists on the other side it was proportionately obnoxious:

and on one occasion, burning the *Testament* in derision, they chose for the altar of this holocaust the tonsured scalp of Brother Nicholas of Recanati. The question of the frock led to similar quarrels and excesses on both sides. St. Francis had chosen the roughest garments of coarsest cloth; he wore, so to speak, the medieval peasant's smock-frock. Some Spirituals, not content with rebuking the excesses of such Conventuals as Chaucer's Frere ("of double worsted was his semi-cope") exceeded on the other side. One would aim at making a single frock last a lifetime; another would go about in a garment shrunken "even to his buttocks," as his adversaries described it. The mendicants, like the monks, wore the same clothes night and day: it was one of the Virgin Mary's best-known miracles that she showed evident disapproval of a Cistercian who, in the heat of a summer night, slept with his garments too loosely open. Thus we need not wonder that, when one Spiritual had washed his frock and laid it on the ground to dry, Conventual enemies came and cut it in pieces, though we cannot extend the same indulgence to the vile uses to which they put those fragments.

For one moment the Testament was restored to honour, and the Spirituals, as a body, justified. Celestine V freed one group of them from obedience to the Conventual authorities, granted them Cardinal Napoleon Orsini as official protector, and thus gave them legally the status, which they already enjoyed *de facto*, of a small Order following separately its own ultra-Franciscan ideal. But Celestine was a pious unworldly hermit who had been elected in a wave of reaction against growing worldliness. Placed at the centre of this vast and complicated Roman organisation, he stumbled on from one practical blunder to another. With the best of motives, he bade fair to turn this uncomprehended machine into a weapon as lethal as a motor-car in a child's hands. He soon realised this and resigned his office in despair, thus earning a place in Dante's *Inferno* as "the man who made the Great Refusal." His successor, Boniface VIII, a pope worldly beyond even the average of his recent predecessors, quashed all Celestine's acts in a single edict; and now the Conventuals could again claim that the little group were their lawful subjects, with no right to worship Francis apart, according to their own conscience, in their own corner of the Church. Hitherto, it must be noted, there has been no question of doctrinal nonconformity. The differences, acute as they were, might fairly be described as questions of discipline.

We see this plainly in the *History of the Seven Tribulations* by Angelo Clareno, the historian and second official principal of this Spiritualist group. Briefly, these men kept their faith against every temptation to rebellion. The strength of their party lay in such little mountain hermitages as St. Francis had loved to inhabit during his last years. Such small and scattered bodies lived, naturally, only on the fringe of the great central organisation: it was the great city convents which kept discipline and ruled the Order. It would be strange if these scattered brethren had not degenerated sometimes into vagrancy, and such indiscipline as could plead no lofty ideal in its excuse. Boniface VIII, a showy and imperious ruler, had no sympathy with such indiscipline; therefore in 1296-7 he commissioned the Inquisitors to bestir themselves in the matter, but in terms which showed that he did not consider the question as one primarily of faith. Clareno's group, therefore, got no protection at the hand of this pope from their Conventual enemies. They migrated to a desert island off the Greek coast: but their persecutors scented them out after two years and accused them as heretics to Boniface, who commissioned the Patriarch of Constantinople to try them, which he did by condemning them unheard. Their appeal to Boniface never reached him. At last, in 1305, the Inquisitor at Naples began to notice them. At the first hearing, he could find no fault with them; indeed, as a Dominican, he could afford to speak his mind freely concerning their Franciscan persecutors. He said in public audience: "I swear by Him who created me that never could the flesh of a poor man be sold for the price that I could get for yours:

your brethren would drink your blood if they could." A little later, however, came the dangerous rebellion of Fra Dolcino; and, though it had not the least connection with the Spirituals, it prejudiced their cause just as, later on, Wat Tyler prejudiced Wyclif's. They were again brought before the Inquisitor, forty-two in number, and imprisoned for five months, often under torture. Two of the younger brethren confessed what the torturers required, but revoked afterwards. Some died in prison: the rest were scourged naked through the streets and banished from the kingdom of Naples. Yet these "Clareni," as they were now called, kept stubbornly to their ideal, under the official protection (for what it was worth) of Cardinal Orsini. The excuses for fastening heresy upon them were too flimsy; moreover, the Franciscan authorities were unwilling to wash their dirty linen too conspicuously in public. Thus the Clareni lasted on, resisting all temptations to the lie of the soul on the one hand, or schism on the other; protesting their unshaken loyalty both to Francis and to the Ecclesia Romana. Clareno himself lived on to 1337, obliged to live hidden in a remote mountain hermitage. "Three days before his death a rumour spread that a saint was dying there, and such multitudes assembled that it was necessary to place guards at the entrance of his retreat and admit the people two by two to gaze on his dying agonies. He shone in miracles, and was finally beatified by the Church, which through the period of two generations had never ceased to trample on him." A century after his death, St. Bernardino of Siena went far to succeed where Angelo had failed, by bringing a large section of the Order, under the name of Observantine Franciscans, back to something like its primitive strictness. These, again, had begun to lose something of their fervour before the Reformation; but the Observantines of Greenwich, with the Carthusians of Sheen, were almost the only monks or friars who dared to resist Henry VIII. The Clareni were finally merged in the Observantines by Leo X, in the year when Luther came forward.[3]

CHAPTER XX

Heresy Manufactured

ALL this time the Inquisition, as we have seen, interfered little. Dog does not eat dog; and friar hesitated long before burning friar. The heresy of the Everlasting Gospel, though quite as revolutionary as the Waldensian, had been buried, as far as possible, in decent obscurity. But now we have come to civil war among the Elect; and, as usual, this is even more cruel than ordinary war. Moreover, it rages most fiercely in the very lands which had witnessed the Albigensian Crusade. The current of human thought has all the eddies and surprises of a mountain stream; it has its unexpected shallows and rapids; its quiet circling round and round just where the water is deepest; and then its quickening over ledges of sunken rock, and at last the cataract.

Southern France was now under the Northern heel; but it was never truly and continuously quiet. As time went on, the names on the Inquisitors' registers amounted to thousands and thousands. In the vast majority of cases, we have no reason to doubt that these folk were guilty, in that sense in which it is a crime to have lost faith not only in the mass of the clergy, but in the infallibility of a Church which in practice can produce no better ministers, and whose abstract teaching sometimes conflicts with our moral sense. Not, in most cases, her official teaching; not points upon which it is possible to prove conclusively that the Ecclesia Docens was committed; but points held by the ordinary priest and confessor, and therefore imposed upon the multitude with a pressure which they had no means of distinguishing from an infallible pronouncement *ex cathedra*. Of that we shall see a flagrant instance in this present chapter. Further, this Bible-prohibition in process of time inevitably increased the doubts of simple yet thoughtful folk, who could get a few glimpses of what lay behind that veil in the forbidden region, and could see how far, sometimes, the Ecclesia Romana had advanced beyond Apostolic Christianity, by that process which, since Newman's famous Essay, has been called Development. Therefore, if the secrets of all hearts could have been revealed, for one formal heretic there would have been found perhaps a hundred who cherished, if only vaguely, some material heresy. Even of the formal heretics, as we have seen, only a small fraction were actually burned; perhaps as few as one in fifty. Under torture and fear of the stake, which was always plain enough in the background if not imminent here and now, the vast majority preferred to recant and abjure. But their return to actual orthodoxy was very doubtful in many cases. Inquisitors noted a difference here between the Cathari and the Vaudois. If a Catharist Perfectus abjured, you could generally trust his perseverance; his differences from the Church were fundamental, and his was the nature that "moveth altogether if it move at all." But the Vaudois, in essence, strove merely for a return to primitive Christianity; he repudiated only Newman's Developments; and those were not so fundamental and unnatural that he should be willing to assert his nonconformity through thick and thin, through torture and down to the stake. His conformity, therefore, was easier to secure, but more superficial. We have seen how Inquisitors describe the Vaudois as worshipping frequently with the rest in the parish church. Thus the population of Southern France, at the back of its plain and combative heresies, had still a mass of potential heresy in 1300, after two centuries of organised persecution and of counter-reformation through the friars. Moreover, it was from the masses that these friars themselves were mainly recruited from the very first, and in increasing proportion as the earliest flame of enthusiasm slackened.

The struggle between Spiritual and Conventual in Italy had mainly been guerilla warfare; the minority were able to flee from place to place, and could not be effectually dislodged from this multiplicity of mountain hermitages. Thus Clareno could fight on for half a century, and die in the odour of sanctity among remote and simple folk who saw the man as he truly was. But in Languedoc, among busy and teeming populations, the struggle was very different; there was little chance here for the tiny minority against an enemy armed (we may say metaphorically) with all the weapons of mechanised warfare.

It is an irony of history that the leader here should have arisen in Béziers, where, earlier in this century, the papal legate had boasted one of the cleanest "clean-ups" in history; 20,000 slaughtered on one day, without distinction of age or sex. Jean, son of Pierre d'Olive, was in no sense a heretic, though his persecutors created a heresy by insistently treating him as such. He was a friar specially distinguished for learning and piety, but also (and this was his main crime) for strict observance of his Rule. He was so intensely devoted to the Virgin Mary that this brought him the most definite official condemnation of his whole life: Nicholas III condemned him to burn with his own hands a Mariolatrous tract which he had written, and he obeyed without hesitation or protest. His deathbed confession of faith was irreproachable; and so many miracles were worked at his tomb in Narbonne that his festival became one of the great solemnities of the year. But he had Joachitic leanings, and enthusiastic disciples not only exaggerated these but interpolated his writings with frankly unorthodox Joachism; and thus he became the centre of a movement which, under persecution, drifted naturally into rebellion. Two Ministers General in succession condemned his writings as heretical, and demanded their surrender for burning. Brother Pons Botugati, celebrated for piety and eloquence, refused to sacrifice his own copies; he was thrown into a foul dungeon and chained there in filth, so that when his body was cast into an unconsecrated grave, it was already half-eaten with vermin. Thus there grew up a new heresy, inspired partly by the Everlasting Gospel, but originating among the Franciscans and spreading especially among their Tertiaries. This is what

Bernard Gui stigmatises as the heresy of the Béguins and
Béguines, and to which he gives considerable attention.

Another movement for independence of thought became
conspicuous in 1300, the year of that first Jubilee Indulgence in
the Roman Church in which Dante places the action of his
Commedia, and which inspired the Florentine Villani to write
his great *Chronicle*. Here again, the main actor is a Franciscan
equally remarkable for intellect and force of character. Bernard
Délicieux, Lector at the convent of Carcassonne, was on
friendly relations with such distinguished contemporaries as
Raymond Lull and Arnaud de Villeneuve, the Pope's physician.
He was remarkable for eloquence in public, and persuasiveness
in private negotiation. The Dominican Inquisitors at Carcassonne were about to pass post-mortem judgment upon one
of the richest citizens, one Castel Fabri. Doubtless the rivalry
which had long been working between the two Orders had
something to do with the ardour of Bernard's championship: for
Castel Fabri had died in the arms of the Franciscans and had
been buried in their cemetery. Bernard undertook the office of
advocacy in the dead man's defence; the Dominican Inquisitor,
on reflection, refused to hear him. Castel Fabri was condemned,
and his wealth duly confiscated.* Thence sprang a quarrel
which had even important political consequences. The story of
Bernard is lengthy and intricate.[1] He negotiated long with the
King and the Pope, with many vicissitudes of fortune; the one
thread that ran through all his labours was the arraignment of
these Dominican Inquisitors in the South. In the Inquisitorial
depositions against him it is recorded how "Once, at Toulouse,
he constantly and publicly asserted that Saints Peter and Paul
would not be able to defend themselves from heresy if they were
now alive and if they were examined in the fashion followed by
the Inquisitors."[2] He was greatly responsible for that movement already described in Chapter XIII, for the reform of
prison conditions and the repression of Inquisitorial illegalities.[3]

* It will be seen how great a temptation this law of confiscation was to the
Inquisition, and how it explains the frequency of post-mortem trials upon
rich folk.

But, disappointed finally of the King's help, he committed the fatal error of joining a party of citizens who were willing to go all lengths against the Inquisitors, and of negotiating with the son of the King of Majorca for the political independence of the South and its freedom from that Northern domination which had been the net result of the Albigensian crusade. The plot failed, and he was lucky to escape from the King with his life. But at last, in 1316, came the election of John XXII as Pope, in many ways epoch-making, and to Bernard frankly disastrous.

For this John was he who, after so many papal vacillations, at last decided the quarrel of the Rule with unmistakable clearness, and practically hereticated all the Spirituals within a few months. He was above all things a lawyer and a politician, in spite of the theological attainments of which he was proud, and the unusually assiduous performance of religious ceremonies which it would be unfair to suspect of hypocrisy. His ambition and avarice were excessive. Of his wars against the Visconti of Milan we are told by a contemporary that the blood shed would have incarnadined the Lake of Constance and the bodies of the slain would have bridged it. Here we have the most definite corroborative evidence in his surviving account-rolls, which show that the military budget amounted to an enormous proportion of the whole, taken over the course of his reign.[4] He was doubtless one of those of whom Marsilius and Machiavelli were thinking, when each asserted in turn that the popes had been the main authors of wars in Europe. To meet these vast expenses and those of his court at Avignon, he tightened existing methods of taxation and invented new, to an extent which rendered the economic nexus thenceforward one of the main factors in papal rule and thus, after many generations, in those complaints which bulked so large in the sixteenth-century religious revolution. With all this, he was so strict in his housekeeping that he died worth 25,000,000 gold florins, in an age when the ransom of King John of France was fixed at 600,000 écus (or 800,000 florins) and when the country was, in fact, unable to pay more than 400,000. This was the pope who had now to judge; and there could be little doubt which way his verdict would go. A stubborn and inconvenient minority would have lacked his sympathies in any case; but one which took its stand upon an ideal of complete poverty—an ideal paradoxical at the best, and frankly impossible in its wildest manifestations— must be simply nauseous to him. He had dealt reasonably with Angelo Clareno and had listened with some patience to the Italian Spirituals, represented by that Ubertino da Casale whom Dante has immortalised by the mere mention of his name as leader of the party. John bade him go back to the Franciscan convent until proper provision could be made for him: to which Ubertino replied: "After one day with my brother friars here, I shall need no provision in this world from you or any other:" and John then allowed him to join the Benedictines. But the Spirituals of Provence were a more organised and enthusiastic crew than the Italians: and they were here under his very nose at Avignon. Moreover, they were now under the leadership of Bernard Délicieux, that implacable enemy of the Inquisition.

John commanded the Franciscan Minister Provincial to deal with these rebels. They appealed in a document to which sixty signatures were appended, pleading that he had been mis-informed. He answered by citing all the appellants to appear at Avignon within ten days. Seventy-four set forth, with Bernard Délicieux at their head. At Avignon, they refused to spend a night at the convent, preferring to bivouac in the open square, under the windows of the papal palace. This was not a wise move. Bearing in mind that, with each of those seventy-four, it was a point of conscience to be clothed at least as raggedly as St. Francis, and that the Pope was pretty sure to have looked down upon them from his palace, we need not wonder that the audience found him in no favourable mood. Bernard argued the case so ably that his antagonists turned to a very different point; they argued that he was excommunicate, and thus *ipso facto* suspect of heresy, for having impeded the Inquisition in past days. Here the law was definitely against him, and the Pope ordered his arrest. The next two advocates were bullied and silenced, and taken off to be put in chains. Within a short time, all the appellants but twenty-five had submitted and were put to penance by the Conventuals. John commanded the Inquisitors of Languedoc to denounce as heretics all the so-called *Fraticelli*, or *Fratres de paupere vita*; and then, in his bull *Quorumdam*, he gave to the General of the Order absolute power of determining two of the main causes of dispute: first, the vestments to be worn; and, secondly, the amount of corn and oil that might be stored in the convents. This bull ended with the words: "Great is poverty, but greater is blamelessness, and perfect obedience is the greatest good." Under this, the Inquisitors judged the twenty-five recalcitrants for heresy. Prison and torture doubtless did their work; for all but five, after a trial of six months, were brought to abjuration. One, who confessed repentance but refused to recant and abjure, was only imprisoned for life, though he had really earned the stake by Inquisitorial laws. The remaining four were burned at Marseilles (1318). The formal sentence pronounced upon them has been recorded in all its details.[5] The Court consisted of thirteen Doctors, including one cardinal and five bishops. Each separately, and all collectively, gave their judgment that certain propositions maintained by the accused were heretical, not only in their totality but singly. The question was put to each judge in turn; it began: "The question is whether these articles here following, all and each of them, are to be judged as heretical? The *first* is, to say and pertinaciously assert that one ought not to obey any superior who commands any Franciscan friars to cast off certain short and tight frocks, differently shaped from the habit of the community of other Franciscan friars; which [frocks] they had assumed of their own authority; and [to say] that no mortal man can compel them to cast off the frocks aforesaid, seeing that whatsoever is contrary to the observance of the said Franciscan Rule and to the understanding thereof is consequently contrary to the Gospel and the Faith; and conversely; otherwise it (the Rule) would not stand altogether for an evangelical Rule. . . . The *second* [article which they assert], aggravating and consonant with the first, is that the Lord Pope had not and hath not any power or authority to make that constitution which he made by advice of his Cardinals and which beginneth *Quorumdam*, wherein he committed it to the judgement of the prelates of the said [Franciscan] Order to determine and decide the length and breadth, form or figure, and similar details of the garments of those who profess the said [Franciscan] Rule; and also to prescribe in what cases, how, where, and when, and how often the Brethren themselves ought to beg, keep, or store up corn, bread and wine for the life-needs of their Brethren." Nothing short of verbal quotation could give an idea of the petty causes for which this Inquisitorial Court, in cold blood, sent four men to a horrible death. By a legal fiction, these judges argued that matters which in common sense might seem purely disciplinary were fundamentally matters of faith. For here were men claiming to follow the true Gospel life, yet rejecting the Pope's conception of it! Therefore "they impinge grievously against the glorious Primacy of the Church, which all nations must worship; nay, against Christ's Gospel itself, wherein is said to St. Peter (and through him to his successors): *Whatsoever thou shalt bind on earth shall be bound in heaven, and whatsoever thou shalt loose on earth shall be loosed in heaven:* also against the Gospel teaching which tells us that Christ had money-bags." And again: "We must decide that the aforesaid articles, and each of them, are plainly heretical, seeing that they are repugnant to evangelical truth and to the authority and power of the Pope, and especially they impinge against that article of the Creed, *Holy Church, Communion of Saints*——"

In human life, every unnatural argument is two-edged; always in due time, if not immediately, it can be turned against its first user. Just a century after this, when the assembled Fathers at Constance were faced with a Pope impossible to accept, yet refusing to resign, they declared him heretical for splitting Christendom into two irreconcilable factions, and thus contradicting in deed that same article of the Creed: "I believe in *one* Catholic and Apostolic Church."

Here, then, John has manufactured one new heresy; and within a few months he will invent another. In the meantime, however, he gave one clear and common-sense decision, sweeping away the legal fiction by which the Order was supposed to be non-possessionate because its possessions were legally vested in the Holy See. The Franciscans did not *own* these things (so ran the pretext) but had only an exclusive right of *using* them. John pointed out with remorseless logic that there was no real distinction between owning an egg or a piece of cheese and the exclusive right of eating them, and that it was mere hypocrisy to label their stores of corn and wine as papal property: therefore he would have no more of a system which burdened the Holy See with all sorts of petty questions and even with litigation. Here, for a moment, he was in line with what the Spirituals had long argued: but his next step was a fatal blow to them. They held it as a fundamental tenet that Christ and His Apostles had espoused poverty in its strictest form; that these first Christians had abjured all property whatever; not only personal property, but even the actual possession (apart from employment to relieve the poor) of any common fund. Thus (they held) the perfect evangelical life was that of St. Francis, who had repudiated not only personal possessions but also such communal endowments as the monks enjoyed. This doctrine of the Poverty of Christ had long been common to the whole Order: it was held by St. Bonaventura and all the great Franciscan Doctors: and, what is more, it had commended itself hitherto to popes. But in 1321 a specially zealous Dominican Inquisitor raised the question: his Order would not be likely to favour a doctrine which implied that the brethren of St. Francis were closer followers of Christ than those of St. Dominic. He demanded that a certain Franciscan should recant the doctrine as heretical: and both parties appealed to John. Unfortunately the doctrine had been plainly asserted by Nicholas III in his bull *Exiit*, after the most solemn deliberation, together with a rider excommunicating all who should attempt to gloss or explain it away. John, therefore, had first to issue a bull of his

own, removing this ban and thus opening the door for discussion. Thenceforward the result might be anticipated. This
Franciscan claim that the perfect evangelical life implied
renunciation of all property had been, at the best of times,
difficult to reconcile with present-day facts. It implied extreme
stress upon that characteristic medieval dualism according to
which the monk, for instance, existed in order to live a life so
pre-eminently evangelical that his works of supererogation
would overflow to the succour of comparatively unredeemed
society outside. On this principle of vicarious sanctity, then,
the Franciscan claim was encouraging: but, from other points of
view, it was awkward. Christ and His first Apostles, who had
served the world in virtue of possessing nothing, were now
represented by the Ecclesia Romana; by a hierarchy and a
clergy whose aggregate worldly possessions were known, as a
matter of statistics, to exceed beyond comparison those of any
worldly State, and (what is more) who were reputed to be
extremely tenacious of such possessions. Thus it was bound to
become, sooner or later, a question of life and death for both
parties. The spirit in which the discussion was carried on, in
face of the briefest and slenderest indications on the subject in
the New Testament or the early Fathers, may be measured by
one argument used against the Spirituals. In the famous
episode of Malchus's ear (John xviii, 11) the words run: "Put
up *thy* sword into the sheath." Here Christ, who cannot lie,
asserts at least the possession by *one* of His Apostles of *one* piece
of property! so that this pin-prick deflates the whole of the
exaggerated Spiritualist claim. Here, then, into this discussion
came a pope notorious even beyond the rest for unscrupulous
exactions and for hoarding all that could be spared from his
lavish expenses. Now that the question was forced into the
light, in face of a movement which promised to be revolutionary,
a man of John's bold and dominating character could scarcely
hesitate. He published a bull *Cum inter nonnullos*, pronouncing
the doctrine to be a perversion of Scripture and condemning the
Franciscan General Chapter which had asserted it (1323). In a

second bull, *Quia quorumdam*, he swept away all protests. Attempts have been made, from the Middle Ages onwards, to argue that John did not here contradict Nicholas III. But the whole Franciscan General Chapter, without a dissentient, complained of this contradiction; and the Inquisitor Eymeric, in the fourteenth century, explicitly admits that it exists. He only pleads that, of the two contradictors, John was right; that Nicholas does not argue the question out, whereas John does, with references to Holy Writ. He ignores the fact that Nicholas had taken exceptional trouble and time over his bull, with a future pope among his assessors; whereas John had decided with unusual rapidity and self-assertion. The result was a split in the Franciscan Order. The General, Michael of Cesena, fled to the Emperor, who was at war with John: so did their greatest philosopher, William of Ockham; and thus the Poverty of Christ became for a while one of the main factors in European politics and European wars.

The story of this chapter is important as exemplifying, in detail, the working of Inquisitorial machinery in an age when it has been going for nearly a century and is becoming somewhat worn and loose in the joints. We see how theory and practice were even less inseparable then than nowadays. Men were sometimes unable, sometimes unwilling, to enforce the strict law. Legally, that repentant but non-recantant Spiritual at Marseilles should have been burned with his four comrades. Again, Bernard Délicieux owed his life for fourteen years partly to royal favour and partly to the mercy of Clement V, who was seriously concerned to control Inquisitorial excesses; partly also, if reports were true, to the heavy bribes with which the incriminated citizens were able to nullify Inquisitorial efforts at the Roman Court. Even now, under John XXII, Bernard was not hereticated off-hand, but given formal trial before prelates, an Inquisitor and royal officers. By this time he was worn out by two years in prison; and they put him twice to torture. He threw himself at last upon the mercy of the Court, and was condemned first to a solemn abjuration, and then to degradation from Holy Orders with lifelong imprisonment in chains, on bread and water, among the dungeons of Carcassonne. Here, naturally enough, death released him after a few months.

But, if the Inquisition has lost in intensity, it has gained enormously in extension. John XXII has manufactured two new heresies, painfully wide in their sweep; and the precedent opens infinite potentialities for the repression of freedom of thought. The significance of this will come out more fully in the next chapter.

Moreover, having thus tasted blood, John proceeded to utilise the Inquisition, either directly or indirectly, for other political purposes. This has been clearly brought out at last by a German scholar, who points out that even Dante's name was dragged in as one of John's wicked adversaries.

CHAPTER XXI

The Fraticelli

ST. THOMAS AQUINAS'S definition of heresy is usually and naturally quoted as authoritative; but too often the last sentence is omitted (2ª, 2ᵃᵉ, Q. XI., art. ii, *ad tert.*). A man is not a heretic so long as his false opinion is on matters "not yet determined by the Church," but "if anyone were obstinately to deny them after they have been determined by the authority of the Church Universal, he would be deemed a heretic. *This authority resides chiefly in the Sovereign Pontiff."* The words which I have here italicised are characteristic of the frequent vagueness of medieval theologians on the most important points. To begin with, St. Thomas adduces in proof of this statement two quotations which everybody now admits to be falsely ascribed to St. Jerome; and his views on Papal Infallibility were deeply influenced by the equally barefaced forgeries of the pseudo-Cyrilline texts.* Thus by the middle of the thirteenth century, it was possible for popes to cite plausibly, if not conclusively, what seemed very high authorities for their most autocratic decisions. The great canonist Hostiensis, writing only a few years after St. Thomas, can say roundly that "he is a heretic who contradicts, or refuses to accept, Papal decretals." Here we have a far more definite decision. Yet more than a century later, when the question came at last to

* Aquinas in this passage quotes as from St. Jerome a text which the English Dominican translators, in deference to modern scholarship, confess to be almost certainly by Pelagius the heretic. Elsewhere Aquinas relies specially upon texts which had been passed on to him as from Cyril's *Thesaurus:* no such texts are there. He was, of course, in involuntary error: but Melchior Cano, one of the greatest of the theologians at the Council of Trent, was shocked to discover that these quotations, which he recognised as the strongest weapons in St. Thomas's armoury, could not be substantiated. He fell back upon the convenient supposition that the words must have been cut out by the malice of heretics. The last writer who ever ventured to maintain this was an Italian professor in 1713. (See my *Papal Infallibility*, pp. 83 ff.)

general and exhaustive discussion at the Council of Constance, the assembled Fathers decided with practical unanimity that the decrees of a General Council, even on matters of Faith, outweigh those of the popes. But, meanwhile, Papal Infallibility had been what it became again after Constance; a debatable land upon which pope or Council could at different times encroach, and, by creating an "incident," present the other side with a *fait accompli*. Boniface VIII, in his bull *Unam Sanctam*, laid it down as a necessary condition of salvation for every human being that he should be subject to the Pope— *subesse Romano Pontifici*. Here he took up a position which has been compared with that of Louis XIV. The King of France could say: *"L'Etat, c'est moi!"* but this pope had practically said before him: *"L'Eglise, c'est moi!"* Thus, whereas hitherto the heretic had been a man who dissented from what, at least, was the tradition of many centuries, he is now one who clings to tradition against the Papacy. He appeals from John XXII to what saints and popes had said, and what the whole Franciscan Order had believed since its first foundation. John might have answered any objector in the words with which Pius IX met the mild protest of Abbot Tosti: *"I* am Tradition!"—*la Tradizione son io!*

So far as the clergy were concerned, and even the vast majority of the Franciscans, this bold stroke was at first thoroughly successful. In ecclesiastical, as in other politics, the *fait accompli* has always been one of the strongest possible moves. A single precedent may easily consolidate into custom; and custom will gradually become law: *Consuetudo optima legum interpres*. So it was in this case. Even after Michael of Cesena had been deposed from the Generalate, and the General Chapter "purged" by the expulsion of about sixty per cent who were more or less of his opinion on the Poverty of Christ, the new General Chapter of 1329 could not be persuaded to vote a declaration condemning that doctrine. But to disbelieve is one thing; to go to the stake for one's disbelief is quite another. By passing seventy-four men through the Inquisitorial prisons of Marseilles, and burning four of them, John was able to silence nearly all the rest. He could have boasted, like others as courageous and ruthless as himself, that he had accomplished a great revolution with very little bloodshed. In districts accessible to the Inquisitors, the worst was to show itself later on. But, even at this moment, when the Emperor's war with the Pope in Germany made it convenient for him to protect them, Michael and Ockham and Marsilius of Padua were able to carry on polemics which shook the Papacy to its foundation. Of these men, Marsilius was by far the most significant for us. He brought to the dispute that freedom of mind which the Italian citizens had developed during their many generations of political discussion and practice: for, compared with a city such as Padua, the French themselves were children in political sense. His historical and theological criticism is surprisingly modern. He saw clearly, what all scholars came to admit three centuries later, that the spurious Epistles of Pope Clement must be a forgery, although they occupied an honourable place in that collection by the so-called "Isidorus Mercator" to which Nicholas I had given full juridical force.[1] He traced equally clearly the steps by which the Petrine claims had grown from the most uncertain beginnings to their present greatness. He proved that the Pope's present claim to confirm Imperial elections was contradicted by historical records; and that, on the contrary, the early bishops of Rome had been frankly subjected to the Emperors. Basing himself on these and similar criticisms, he argued that no single man has power to excommunicate justly; it must be for the Church body as a whole to decide whether the accused is to be cast forth from its communion. Coercive jurisdiction is unfit for priests: their jurisdiction should be only moral. The laity should reduce their revenues to a reasonable salary in each case, and employ the surplus on more useful purposes. The supreme power in Christendom should be no single man, but a Council of the whole Church. Ockham, at this point, went one step further, and hinted that women might have votes for this assembly, since they have souls to save as well as men. John condemned all this, as well he might; but the pronouncement was merely on his own authority. He had indeed consulted certain Doctors of Theology, whose opinions coincided with his own. But his bull appeals to no Conciliar decree: in that sense there is no question of Aquinas's condition, that a man is no heretic unless he contradicts a thing "defined by the authority of the Church Universal." The only authority at the back of this bull was the Pope's: he bases his case upon his own interpretation of the Bible, upon which he condemns as heretical (for instance) Marsilius's denial to the clergy of the right of coercive punishment, except so far as the State may commit it to them. He tells Marsilius that it is a specially merciful concession to grant him four months for complete recantation. But the heretics could afford to defy all this; and they lived out the rest of their lives mainly at Munich, where the Inquisition could not reach them. Meanwhile John himself fell under grievous suspicion of heresy; and this is one of the most piquant incidents of its kind. He preached a sermon to the effect that the souls of the Saints are still only under the Altar, and will not enjoy the Beatific Vision until the Last Judgment. This, apparently, rested upon the narrowest and most literal interpretation of the Apocalypse (Rev. vi, 9). At first, John maintained it so seriously that he imprisoned an English friar who preached against it, and would have punished Guillaume Durand, the celebrated Bishop of Mende, for the same cause, but that the French King and the University of Paris acted with the greatest promptitude and decision. The latter condemned John's doctrine formally; and the former wrote to him that his University, with its posse of Doctors in Theology, must know better than the Pope and his lawyers. The Pope's denial (he said) was practically destructive of belief in the intercession of the Saints, even including the Virgin Mary. A chronicler records further that he said publicly: "The Pope shall recant, or burn!" The Emperor also seized the occasion, and posed now as Defender of the Faith against his enemy. John answered Philippe de Valois almost in the humble tone of a boy before his master; the doctrine (he said) had not been positively asserted, but only thrown out for discussion: he was ready to be corrected by anyone who could give better reasons than his own, were it only an old woman. This, of course, was in flat contradiction to his former actions: but death came before the question could be regularly settled. A sudden flux left him only three days to settle his accounts with the world and with God. After his death, a bull was promulgated in his name recanting his doctrine, and submitting all his words and deeds to the judgment of the Church. Many doubted its genuineness, but without sufficient reason. In any case his successor Benedict XII, who, as Bishop of Pamiers, had been one of the most active agents of the Inquisition, left no doubt about the doctrine. Two days after his election he stepped in; within a few weeks he had decisively contradicted John in a public sermon; and a year later (1336) he decreed formally that the Saints do enjoy the Beatific Vision and that to contradict this is heretical. This decree passed thenceforward into the formulas of the Inquisition. Here, then, was a fresh heresy. Though not quite so novel as those of John's manufacture, it rested no less constitutionally on the sole authority of a pope: this time on Benedict's. Therefore if John, having resigned his tiara as Celestine did, had continued to assert his doctrine of the Beatific Vision, he would thenceforward have been a branded heretic. Thus he, the autocratic inventor of 1317 and 1323, becomes the scapegoat of 1336. When Pegna, in the sixteenth century, cast about for "a conspicuous example" of a papal pronouncement which binds on pain of heresy, he instances this of Benedict XII. "To assert the contrary [of Benedict's doctrine, as John had done until his very deathbed] will be impious and heretical, as Eymeric teacheth excellently in the eighth question of his second part."

The impulse thus given to the disquiet of the Spirituals, and especially to the extremists, may easily be imagined. From this time forward, at least, there was a quite definite Left Wing Party, with a hierarchy of its own in many places. St. Francis had called his brethren Friars Minor; and now these, the elect among the *Fratres Minores*, call themselves in Italy by the still more homely and humble title of *Fraticelli*, Little Brethren. In France, men call them *Béguins*, from the common appellation of the Third Order of St. Francis, to which so many of them belonged. Bernard Gui, writing about 1323, describes their rise in about the year 1315, when the Spiritual quarrel became acute, and emphasises their wide extension already (Bk. V. ch. 5). He goes minutely into their tenets and manner of life; and we see how much they had in common with the Waldensians, whom however they repudiated as vehemently as the orthodox did. Both sects were recruited mainly from the poorer classes, and owed much of their popularity to their free criticism of hierarchical capitalism. Again, the Béguins objected to oaths: not absolutely, but wherever the Faith or the Creed are not in question. They had their little tracts in the vulgar tongue: not, indeed, translated from the Bible, but from the Spiritual Pierre de Jean d'Olive and similar sources. They had their own little conventicles in which they read and expounded these, with Lives of the Saints. This, says Gui, they do "in order that the school of the devil may seem, under a show of good, to imitate in some fashion the school of Christ; although the Commandments of God and the Articles of Faith should be preached and expounded in the Holy Church by the rulers and pastors thereof, and by doctors and preachers of God's word, not by simple layfolk; moreover, it should be done not in secret, but publicly." The Fraticelli almost deify St. Francis and take their stand upon the Poverty of Christ. John XXII (they say) unlawfully contradicted the Gospel and would have changed St. Francis's sacred Rule; he was a heretic, and the First Antichrist of Revelation. The four friars burned at Marseilles were as truly martyrs as St. Laurence and St. Vincent; their relics are holy, and we pray to them in heaven. The prelates and cloisterers who live luxuriously and persecute the poor are mere Pharisees. Their Church, the Carnal Church, is the Scarlet Woman of Babylon. Armageddon is at hand—some say, as early as 1325, others as late as 1335. Then the whole world will be a changed place. "After the death of Antichrist, the said Spiritual men shall convert the whole world to faith in Christ, and the whole world will be good and benign, so that there shall be no wickedness or sin in the men of that age, except perchance venial sins in a few of them; and all things shall be common so far as use is concerned: none shall offend another or solicit him to sin, for the greatest love shall reign among them and there shall be one Fold and one Shepherd." Some hold, however, that this will last for only a hundred years, after which the world will grow evil again, and then the Last Judgment.

Here, then, is the sect at a comparatively early stage of development, seen through unsympathetic eyes. Let us now see how they bore persecution a century later in Italy, where the multiplicity of remote mountain villages or little towns had enabled them to maintain themselves from generation to generation, and even to develop a rudimentary hierarchy of their own. At this time they found their bitterest antagonists in three saintly men, strict Observantines: St. Bernardino of Siena, St. Giovanni Capistrano and Blessed Giacomo della Marca. These outdid the heretics in poverty and asceticism and magnetic eloquence; the two latter braved all risks of assassination in wild country among a sometimes unfriendly population; and they wielded torture and the stake always to back them up in the last resort. Martin IV, in 1428, supported them by commanding that Magnalata, one of the village strongholds of the Fraticelli, should be razed to the ground; he decreed that heresiarchs are to be tortured till they reveal the names of all confederates; the children of heretics are to be deported to other districts where they may be brought up in the Faith. Of this torture we have clear details from a later year, 1468. The Fraticelli, like the Vaudois, when once they had been driven underground, were credited with unnatural abominations. Men accused them of promiscuous lust in their secret conventicles; or of an abomination called *barilotto*, which added to this promiscuity the crime of roasting a new-born child in public at a fire and drinking a sacramental cup mingled with the ashes. One unhappy Italian peasant, Antonio da Sacco (A.D. 1466), persistently denied complicity in this crime, until torture extorted a confession from him. Then, "as soon as he was taken off the rack, he denied that he had ever been at the *barilotto*, but he had indeed heard talk [of it]." He recognised now, however, that he had previously obeyed the devil; he was willing now to make his confession to the orthodox priests, and to serve the Pope "in any service, even in the stable and in double chains." This crawling surrender, said his judges, was an evident victory for the truth: "for the holy martyrs, who suffered for the true Faith, not only feared no torments, but laughed at them and overcame them; yet this Antonio, at the very first stage of torture, was conquered by the truth." However, even in this, his deepest humiliation, the man protested against his previous confession of infamy. "He said of his own accord: 'See, my lords! yesterday, on the rack, I said that I had twice been at the *barilotto*; this is not true. I have a wife, young and fair, and a comely daughter here in prison at Santo Spirito; and for that cause I would never have permitted [such a thing].' Moreover, coming nearer and nearer, he said humbly: 'My lords, pardon me!'" So runs the persecutors' official record; and there is perhaps no document which throws more painful light on what might be done at any moment in the name of Christ's religion.[2]

Still more significant are the Blessed Giacomo's own words in that treatise which he wrote against the public manifesto of the Fraticelli. He is obliged to admit the possibility of a heretical Pope; for, in the Middle Ages, not even the most orthodox apologist ever attempted to explain away the case of Honorius I: that Pope's heresy was plainly asserted in the Breviary, the book which every priest was bound by law to read daily and study. But Giacomo pleads: "I say unto thee that, although some supreme Pontiffs have died in faithlessness (*in infidelitate*), yet shalt thou always find that, when a Pope hath died in heresy, a Catholic Pope hath immediately succeeded. Thus, in the whole succession of Supreme Pontiffs, we do not find that there have ever been two Popes heretical in immediate succession." Moreover, even if what the Pope proclaims does happen to be heretical, God will pardon those who believe this falsehood out of reverence to Papal Authority. Then Giacomo falls back upon that undeniable argument of the *fait accompli*. All Catholic doctors teach us that true Faith grows in power and dignity under persecution. Every fresh martyr in the Early Church brought in a hundred new converts. The true Faith of St. Peter has brought to its orthodox followers the blessings of wealth, dignity, wisdom, virtue and multitude. We are the Catholic Church. Contrast this with the sect of these Fraticelli, which "under oppression," fails and becomes more discredited. It began with powerful and dignified patrons: it is now socially despicable and moribund. Moreover, through the Catholics God works miracles; the fact that St. Bernardino recalled twenty-three different dead folk to life hath been approved by a commission appointed by the Supreme Pontiffs of the Roman Church. . . . Yet of you, who pretend yourselves a Church, it is never found or heard that any one of you ever wrought any miracle, except that when they are burned* they stink like rotten flesh. Take, for example, Fabriano.† When, during the visit of Nicholas V, some heretics were burned there, the stench filled the whole city for three days long; and this I know, because I smelt the stench of those men for three days as far as our convent. And yet‡ I had persuaded all [at the last moment] to return to the Faith; and all had come back and made confession and communicated, in tears and compunction; and thus these, who had relapsed, were justified [at the last]. But one, who was called Chiuso of Fabriano, the heretics' treasurer, would never return. I bear witness before God that he never called upon God or the Virgin

* Reading *comburuntur* for *corrumpuntur*, as the context seems plainly to require.

† A little mountain town which was one of the heretics' headquarters. Here, in 1447, Nicholas V himself assisted at an *auto de fe*.

‡ Here, again, *dum* seems a plain misreading for *tamen*.

or any of the Saints to help him, nor besought God to spare his sins, nor ever said *mea culpa* for his sins; but, as one desperate and dried up, he kept saying 'The fire cannot burn me.' And I bear witness before God that he burned three days long, though wood was added again and again." He goes on to accuse the Fraticelli of moral abominations.[3] It would be difficult to find a better instance of the mischief that false history may work, even in the best minds. No legend could be more pardonable and more apparently harmless than those which recounted the superhuman constancy of all orthodox Catholic martyrs; or, again, that legendary "odour of sanctity" which commonly takes the place of ordinary putrefaction in a saint's grave. Yet here we have a pious and charitable man steeling himself against his natural pity for human suffering by the consideration that all folk who are unwilling to be burned, and who stink in the fire, thus confess themselves tacitly to be the devil's martyrs!

In contrast with this, let us now see the story of a martyred Fraticello, told by one of his disciples in simple popular Italian.[4]

In January, 1389, a missionary came from the Fraticelli of the Mark of Ancona to comfort those of Florence. This Brother Michael stayed until Easter Tuesday, when, just upon the point of returning, he was betrayed by two Béguines and three widows who had professed to be of his sect. Thus, "as the day was beginning to break, there came forth from a house over against them many soldiers and constables, and fell upon our brethren; there were sixteen among them, all armed, and raven friars among them."* They haled Michael and his companion to the Bishop's prison and took his breviary from him. At vespertide "the Chief of the Pharisees" [i.e., the Bishop] sent for him and examined him. He confessed himself an ordained priest and a believer in the Poverty of Christ. "Then said the Pharisees, with many scoffs and gibes, 'So the Church has

---

* I.e., Dominicans, who wore a black scapular over their white frock. We have seen how the Joachite Spirituals took the grey Dove of Noah's Ark as prefiguring the grey Franciscans. As the orthodox looked upon the Dominicans as God's sheep-dogs, so the Fraticelli were tempted to identify Black friars and Black monks with Noah's Raven.

remained among you!' And thus they sent him back to prison.
Next day the Bishop called together his college of Pharisees,
among whom were many university masters; and, when these
were gathered together in the council chamber, Brother Michael
was again sent for and drawn forth and brought before them.
Then, after many insults and scoffs, his confession of the day
before was read aloud, with the addition of many false conclusions, whereunto he answered, saying: 'Wherefore have ye
written falsehoods which we never said? Ye shall render
account for this at the Last Day.' But for all that he could say,
they wrote down whatsoever they would. Then, after reading
his confession (as his companion told me) they asked him
whether he would cleave to the doctrines which were held by
such solemn masters and by all the people of Florence. Whereunto he made answer that he held Christ crucified to have been
poor, and that John XXII was a heretic, since he had asserted
the contrary; and that all his successors who had held and still
held and defended John's decretals were heretics also. Then,
alleging the decretal of Pope Nicholas III, they began to answer
confusedly, saying: 'We will show you how the words of
Nicholas III may be accorded with John XXII.' And, as they
thus spake with much confusion among themselves, Brother
Michael alleged the Rule of St. Francis (for there were certain
professors of that Rule in the judgment-hall), saying to them:
'See ye not that ye deny the very words whereunto ye have
made profession?' One of the friars, writhing under these
words, said: 'I will render no judgment that is against our Rule,'
and would have gone on to speak; but they suffered him not,
but the Chief of the Pharisees turned upon him with great force
and fury, saying: 'Tell the man to abjure his error.' And he,
being afraid to see such fury, said: 'Son, I pray that thou
acknowledge thy faults before God, and I pray God to give thee
a true understanding'; and therewith he held his peace. Then
one of the masters alleged a certain point of the Gospel concerning the poverty of Christ; but Brother Michael made answer:
'We will not interpret Holy Scripture from our own head, but

let us come to what Holy Church hath determined on this point
and what the saints have said.' And, when he would have
alleged the decision of the Church and a text from the saints,
they mocked at him and said in great fury: 'Dost thou believe
thyself deeper in understanding of the Scriptures than we, who
are Masters of Divinity?' And thus, mocking the holy man with
many scoffs and gibes, they said unto him clearly and without
more ado: 'It is our will that thou shouldst hold that Christ was
proprietary, and Pope John XXII a catholic and holy man.'
Unto this our holy brother, as one standing among wolves,
answered: 'Nay, but he is an heretic,' making no account of
their words and threats." They took him back to prison and
put his feet in the stocks. Here he remained for three days
longer, under the warning that this respite was given him for
repentance and that the law must take its course after that date.
The narrator describes at some length his ill-treatment in prison
and his re-examination on the fourth day, under the same unjust
conditions as before, his evidence being further falsified in order
to prejudice the general public against him. He was handed over
to the secular arm and "afterwards, about the third hour of
night, came a certain proselyte of these Pharisees, saying: 'Alas,
vouchsafe now to repent, and know that the Bishop sendeth
you word how that to-morrow at ten o'clock ye shall be given
over to the magistrate to be burned; and I give you to know
that the mitres and cloaks are already made, with Fraticelli
painted on them in company with devils.' The holy man, rather
refreshed than dismayed at this speech, made answer: 'I will
hold no otherwise than as I have said.' . . . Then he fell upon
his knees with his companion and said: 'Methinks our father
St. Francis will be there by the stake; and, more than that, I
believe Christ's Apostles will be there, and those glorious
martyrs, Brothers Bartolommeo and Antonio'; and then again,
with words that seemed of consuming fire, he said: 'I tell thee
yet more; I believe Jesus Christ will be there.' This he said with
such fervour that it seemed to burn him up. After this he added:
'I doubt sore of myself lest, seeing myself doomed to such a fate,

I should waver somewhat in my mind, apart from such waverings as I might have at the stake.' And again: 'May God keep His hand on my head!' And thus he spent all that night, between confession and prayer unto God, with very little sleep." Instead of burning him that day, they went through the ceremony of degrading him from his priestly office. Then "the magistrate bade that he should again be shackled and cast into prison, wherein were folk who vexed him by day and night with many insults, for that he would not believe in the Pope. And in that prison there was but one plank whereupon a man might sleep, and they suffered not the holy man to lie there, but on the earth in a corner that was wet with the continual dripping of water; and he was barefooted and bareheaded, nor had he his mantle. And withal he must continually answer the brutalities of the people, who, under cover of great compassion, tormented his soul by day and night. . . . One citizen said unto him: 'Why dost thou not as others do?' to which the holy man made answer: 'I would rather suffer myself to be cast among lions.' " Next day, at last, they burned him, amid a concourse of people unusual even for busy Florence. On his way to the stake, "he walked with somewhat lengthy strides and with his head down, saying his prayers as he went; and he seemed in truth one of the [old] martyrs, among such a crowd of folk as was scarce seen before. And all the people, moved with compassion, cried unto him: 'Alas! why wilt thou die?' And he ever made answer: 'I will die for Christ!' 'Nay,' said they, 'but thou diest not for Christ'; and he: 'I die for the truth.' Then said one: 'Ah, thou believest not in God!' 'Yea,' said he, 'in God and the Blessed Virgin and Holy Church.' Then said another: 'Wretch! thou hast a devil, who draweth thee with him.' 'Nay, God forbid!' said he. And thus he answered oftentimes as he went; yet, even so, only to such things as seemed to need an answer, and oftentimes raising his eyes to meet theirs.

"When they came to the Canto del Proconsolo, there was a great rumour of people that pressed to see him, and one of the faithful, seeing him, mingled with the rest and said: 'Brother

Michael, pray God for us!' To whom he made answer, raising his eyes: 'Go with God's blessing, Catholic Christians.' Again, at the Fondamenti di Sta Liperata one cried to him: 'Fool! believe in the Pope!' Then he raised his head and answered: 'Ye have made a God of your Pope, even as they still seduce you!' A little farther on, in answer to the same cry, he said with a little smile: 'These goslings of yours have fooled you well!' whereat many marvelled, saying: 'He goeth merrily to his death!'

"When he came to San Giovanni [the Baptistery], one said: 'Repent, repent, and choose not to die!' to whom he made answer: 'I repent me of my sins.' And to others, saying: 'Escape with your life,' he answered, 'Escape ye from your sins.'

"Just beyond the Bishop's Palace, one said: 'Thou dost not ask a soul of us to pray God for thee.' Then he cried aloud: 'I beseech all faithful Catholic Christians to pray God for my soul!'

"Between the Mercato Vecchio and Calimala, one cried: 'Escape, escape!' and he answered: 'Escape ye from hell, escape from hell, escape from hell!'

"When he came to the Mercato Nuovo, some said: 'Repent, repent!' And he made answer: 'Repent ye of your sins, repent of your usuries and your false bargains!'

"Then, on the Piazza de' Priori, one said: 'Repent of this error, choose not death.' And he said: 'Nay, for it is the Catholic faith; nay, for it is the truth, whereunto all Christians are bound.'

"And at the Cornmarket there were many ladies at the windows and tables whereat folk played, who looked up from their play and said unto him: 'Repent, repent!' Then said he: 'Repent ye of your sins of usury and gambling and fornication.' And, a little farther on, some said: 'Fool, wherefore wilt thou die?' And he: 'I will die for Christ.' . . . Then said another: 'O! ye say that we are not baptized, nor true Christians.' Then Brother Michael looked him in the face and said: 'Nay! I say that ye are baptized Christians; but ye do not as Christians should do.' Then said the other: 'The people's voice is God's voice.' 'Nay,' said he, 'but it was the people's voice that crucified Christ and slew St. Peter.'

"When he came to Sta Croce (the Franciscan convent) they showed him St. Francis's statue hard by the gate of the friary; then he raised his eyes to Heaven, saying: 'Saint Francis, my father, pray to God for me!' Then he turned to the brethren who stood on the church steps, crying with a loud voice: 'The Rule of St. Francis, whereunto ye are sworn, hath been condemned; and this is how ye deal with all such as will observe it!' These words he repeated as often as he thought the Brethren needed them; of whom some shrugged their shoulders, and others drew their cowls over their faces.

"Then, when he turned the corner and went towards the Porta alla Giustizia, many folk vexed him sore, saying: 'Recant, recant; wherefore wilt thou die?' To whom he made answer: 'Christ died for us.' Then said some: 'O, thou art not Christ and hast no need to die for us.' 'Nay,' said he, 'but for Him will I die.' To which one made answer: 'O, thou art not among heathen folk!' 'Nay, but I will die for the truth.' 'Let us grant, then, that this be the truth; why shouldst thou die on that account?' To which he made answer: 'For the truth died St. Peter, and St. Paul lost his head.' . . . And when another alleged Holy Scripture, saying that Christ fled more than once from death, and other holy men, then Brother Michael turned round and looked upon him and said: 'Thou also art answerable, and thou shalt one day render account of these words that thou hast spoken.' . . . And, being dry with much speaking and for the throng that pressed upon him, he oftentimes lapped the rain-water as it fell. And, seeing that one of the faithful rebuked those who would have had him recant, one of the sergeants and other folk began to take note of this, saying: 'These are of his disciples'; wherefore he fell apart from him for a while.*

---

* Was not this the narrator himself, who tells us in the next paragraph that he did not hear Michael's next words?

"When he was come to the Gate a faithful woman cried aloud: 'Stand fast, martyr of Christ, for thou shalt soon receive thy crown!' I know not what he answered; but there arose much talk of this thing. . . .

"When he came to the stake (so far as I could see, and as I heard from others) he went boldly into the hut;* and, while he was being bound to the stake, many thrust their heads in to pray him to recant; but he stood firmer and firmer. And, as one told me for certain, he asked him: 'What is this for which thou wilt die?' and Brother Michael made answer: 'This is a truth which is lodged in my soul; so that I cannot testify to it except in death.' Then, to affright him, they made smoke twice or thrice around the hut, and many other frightful things; and the people round besought him all the while to change his mind, save only one of the faithful who comforted him. Moreover, I heard that a youth was brought unto him, with certain of the Prior's servants, sent by the Ten† to bring him back safe and sound if he would recant. And one of the captains, seeing his constancy, said: 'What perversities hath the Devil put into this fellow's head?' and the youth made answer: 'Perchance this is of Christ.' At last, having besieged him with many arguments, they set fire to the hut from above; and then Brother Michael, having finished his *Credo* (which he began as he entered into the hut), began to sing the *Te Deum*; and, as one told me, he sang perhaps eight verses, and then made a sign as though he sneezed, saying those last words: 'Lord, into thy hands I commend my spirit.' When the bonds were burned, he fell dead to the earth upon his knees, with his face to Heaven and his mouth wide open.

"When he was dead, many (even among his adversaries) said: 'He seemeth like unto a saint.' Then some besought of the Captain of the Horse, as a favour, that they might bury his body. And the captain, having drawn up written evidence of

---

* Apparently the pile was enclosed in a sort of wooden hut, as the narrator always calls it a *capannuccio*.

† The Ten Priors were the regular committee of government.

his death, gave them leave and departed with his sergeants. And those young men took away the body, and wrapped it in a linen cloth, and carried it and buried it in a grave at some distance from the stake; and folk returned to their homes; and it was the twelfth hour when he left the palace, and he died a little before the thirteenth hour. And, while folk went homewards, the greater part thought it an ill deed, and they could not say enough evil of the clergy. One said: 'He is a martyr,' and another: 'He is a saint,' and another the contrary. And thus there was greater noise of this deed in Florence than there ever had been.

"And on Friday night the faithful went, the one not knowing what the other did, and found themselves together at his grave and carried him away secretly. Wherefore on Saturday morning many who went to see him found him not; and, when this was noised abroad in Florence, certain preachers found matter to say thereof in the pulpit, saying that they would fain have set guards, lest folk should canonise the dead man and hold him for a saint."

CHAPTER XXII

Politics—The Templars

RELIGION and politics are seldom separable in practice, whatever logical distinctions we may make. Therefore, just as the Inquisition's revival of the Old Roman torture system caused a similar revival in civil courts also, so its machinery for the suppression of religious nonconformity lent itself easily to employment against the political nonconformist.

Philip IV of France—Philippe le Bel—is a somewhat enigmatical character. He was so, evidently, even to his own contemporaries; and one historian has suggested that, since they could not call him *The Good*, and dared not call him *The Bad*, they took refuge in *The Fair*, since his handsome person was indisputable. He made himself more absolute than any of his predecessors in France or of his contemporaries in Western Europe. The Papacy was by this time definitely victorious against the Empire; but this rise of the French despotism was destined to create a still more formidable rival. From 1305 onwards, the Popes lived at Avignon and therefore, politically, were very much at the mercy of the French Kings. When all exaggerations are set aside, the fact remains that their wealth and their claim to temporal as well as spiritual sovereignty rendered them often helpless in the hands of the most powerful and aggressive, at that time, of European sovereigns, who, being as it were at their door, had their persons terribly at his mercy. During these seventy years of the so-called "Babylonian Captivity," the cardinals were preponderantly of French nationality; they elected French Popes; and, in that sense, the Papacy was almost as definitely French as it is now Italian, under the system by which only one non-Italian Pope has been elected during the last 500 years.

Philip was just the man to recognise the political value of having the Supreme Pontiff, so to speak, in his pocket. The main motive of his attack upon the Templars is sometimes ascribed to greed, sometimes to fear of their political rivalry; for this was one of the richest and most powerful institutions in Europe. From whichever cause, it is acknowledged on all hands that he resolved on their destruction and bullied Clement V into lending him the Inquisition as a fit instrument for the purpose. He had surrounded himself with unscrupulous ministers; and, here again, we need not attempt to solve the historical question how far he used them as tools and how far they used his immense prestige as a battering-ram. Both he and they saw very well that, when a nation has enormous natural advantages and military force, or even when it has only the reputation of such force, its best policy is always to attack rapidly and present the world with a *fait accompli.*

The records of the trial are voluminous, and they speak more eloquently, perhaps, than any other records for the efficacy of torture as a foundation-stone of Inquisitorial procedure. One abomination after another was suggested by the Court to these helpless prisoners; and, soldiers though they all were by profession or in reality, large numbers confessed. Yet we have, for the falsehood of these suggestions, evidence which may almost be called scientifically complete. To take two instances only. The Inquisitors procured confessions as to a certain idol which Templars adored at their admission, by way of denying God for the Devil. Yet, although Philip had seized and sealed all Templar houses and property from the very first, no such idol was ever found. So also with the story of a charter of treasonable import, kept in copy at every Preceptory for the acceptance of candidates for admission: none such was ever found. True, the torturers were helped here by the undoubted unpopularity of the Order (until the flagrant injustices of the trial awoke a certain movement of popular disgust and sympathy) and by the general belief in its moral decay and comparative uselessness since the loss of Palestine. But Philip was

as bent upon the destruction of these monasteries as Henry VIII
in sixteenth-century England; and he adopted methods to which
Henry, at his worst, did not even approach. In all this he worked
through Rome; not only indirectly through this pope-made
machine of the Inquisition, but by forcing Clement to take
personal part in the crime. The Pope was, for a long time, really
anxious to protect the Templars. But Philip had two ways of
forcing his hand. When he hesitated, Philip renewed his threat
of calling upon Christendom to condemn his predecessor,
Boniface VIII, as a heretic and criminal of the blackest dye,
thus dragging the Papacy through the mire again. But,
normally, that threat was not needed; the King took the simpler
course of setting the Inquisition to work first and consulting
Clement afterwards. In this way he soon made him so definite
and public an accomplice in the proceedings, that Clement
could not retrace his steps towards justice without the most
humiliating self-condemnation. He had to choose between the
lie of the soul and political ruin.

Therefore, in 1311 he prepared to deliver judgment at the
Ecumenical Council of Vienne; or, rather, prepared to justify
solemnly the condemnation to which he had already committed
himself in 1307, and which he had repeated publicly since. In
prevision of this, he now moved all Europe to a fresh campaign
of torture, in order to confront the assembled Fathers with the
greatest possible number of "confessions." We have seen how
far intelligent Inquisitors were willing to admit, like intelligent
Roman jurists in the past, that torture was regrettably liable
to elicit falsehood. But this consideration was entirely out-
weighed by the plain experience that it brought out, in nine
cases out of ten, what the Court wished to believe. Therefore
nobody hesitated about the application of a principle so obviously pious in its results. In England, no conclusive evidence
could be found by normal means. and the prisoners evidently
enjoyed a certain amount of popular sympathy. Therefore
Inquisitors were sent over from France—the first and last
appearance of the Inquisition proper in this country until

Mary's reign. These men, formally commissioned to elicit evidence "in accordance with ecclesiastical law" (which, of course, freely admitted torture), were met by the incompatibility of torture with English law. Only three runaways, when apprehended, were induced in prison to confess what was wanted: otherwise, the Inquisitors drew blank. Thereupon the Pope wrote to Edward II in great impatience. This prohibition of torture made it impossible to get true evidence; neither law nor custom must be permitted in England to override Canon Law; Edward and his officials, as impeders of the Inquisition, would render themselves *ipso facto* excommunicate. To this threat the Pope added a bribe; a Plenary Indulgence for all Edward's past sins if he would permit the papal judges to torture these suspects. He sent similar letters to all the Bishops, rebuking them at the same time for not having resisted this "unjust" royal prohibition. Edward gave way; he sent a series of missives permitting Bishops and Inquisitors to employ "ecclesiastical law," or, as the later missives said with brutal plainness, "torture"; and in every case he explained carefully that he was prescribing this change "out of reverence for the Holy See."[1] No direct evidence has been published for the actual application of this torture in England; but the mere possibility produced its natural result: the Templars finally admitted that they were defamed for heresy and unable to purge themselves as law required; therefore they besought mercy and promised to perform whatever penance might be enjoined.

To Aragon, which had then as free a constitution as England, special Inquisitors were similarly despatched and found the same difficulty; the law did not allow torture. The Inquisitors induced the King to put the prisoners in irons and treat them more harshly; still no success. Then Clement wrote commanding that torture should be applied. Apparently this was not done thoroughly enough; for in 1312 the Council of Tarragona, pretty evidently in sympathy with popular feeling, declared the Order in Spain innocent of the crimes imputed to it.

Meanwhile Clement had sent a series of bulls to realm after realm, pressing the need of obtaining confessions by torture, which in some places had been negligently and imprudently omitted. He even commissioned his legate at Rhodes to go over to Cyprus and make sure personally that the order was carried out. All were to send him, as soon as possible, the evidence thus collected. The result was, not only that some were racked who had been hitherto spared, but others were brought from prison to be "questioned" afresh and more severely. The episcopal prison at Nîmes held now twenty-nine prisoners, four having died meanwhile. "Some had already been tortured three years before; but now all were tortured again, with the result of obtaining the kind of testimony required, including demon-worship."[2]

The full abomination of these proceedings cannot be realised except in the light of some of the victims' recorded protests. In April, 1310, nine of the imprisoned Templars petitioned the Council to give them a fair judicial hearing, without the presence of layfolk who might overawe the witnesses. "For all the Brethren, generally speaking, are stricken with such fear and terror that there is no marvel whatever concerning those who lie, but rather concerning those who maintain the truth, while they see the tribulations and anguish suffered continually by the truth-tellers, and the threats and contumely and other evils which they sustain daily, together with the comforts and delights and liberties enjoyed by the false witnesses, and the great promises which are daily made unto them. Wherefore it is marvellous, or rather stupendous to all men that greater credence is given to those liars who, thus corrupted, testify thus for their bodily profit, than to those who, as Christ's martyrs, have died in torments with the palm of martyrdom for their maintenance of the truth, and also to that larger and saner number of those still living, who in defence of the truth, impelled by conscience alone, have suffered, and do still suffer in prison so many torments, pains, tribulations and anguish, revilings and calamities and miseries. Moreover, your petitioners say that, outside the realm of France, no Brother of the Temple, in all the world, will be found to say, or to have already said, these lies; wherefore it is plain enough why they have been said in the realm of France, since those who have said them gave their evidence under corrupt influences, fear or solicitation or bribery." Lizerand quotes aptly an illustration of this last point the case of "Humbert Blanc, Preceptor of Auvergne, who managed to escape to England, where he was arrested and questioned, but never confessed anything."[3]

After this general protest, let us take the particular protest of one sufferer, "aged fifty years or thereabouts," who now retracted his former confession. "When the Lords Commissary explained to him the articles whereupon they were to examine him, then this witness, pale and in great terror, said upon his oath and under peril of his own soul (invoking upon himself, if he lied in this matter, sudden death, and that he might be forthwith swallowed by hell in the presence of the said Lords Commissary; beating his breast with his fists and upraising his hands towards the altar in reinforcement of his assertion, and bending his knees), that all the errors attributed to the Order were utterly false, although he himself had confessed some of them by reason of many torments inflicted upon him, as he said, by the Lords G. de Marsillac and Hugues de la Celle, Knights of the King, who examined him. He said that he had seen, the day before, fifty-four Brethren of the Order carried in wagons to be burned because they would not confess the said errors, and then he heard that they had been burned; so that he, doubting that he could not keep good endurance if he were burned, through fear of death confessed and deposed upon oath before the said Lords Commissary and certain others, that all the errors imposed upon the Order were true, and that he would [have confessed] if he were examined, even to have slain the Lord, if this were demanded of him. He besought and adjured the said Lords Commissary, and us the notaries who stood by, that what he had said might not be revealed to the King's men nor to his own [prison] guards; for (as he said) he feared, if they knew this, that he would be given over to the same punishment as those fifty-four Templars aforesaid."[4] These men had been burned as "relapsed" heretics, for having revoked their confession of guilt. The burning was done by Philip, illegally, since the Inquisitors had not yet formally condemned them, and he thus trespassed upon the Church's powers. But in this he only took abusively into his own hands what the Church was bound by her own principles to do: the burning of these "relapsed" was in strict accordance with Inquisitorial law, though the secular arm had done it upon its own responsibility.

CHAPTER XXIII

Politics and Witchcraft—Joan of Arc

JOAN OF ARC'S case was no less scandalously political.[1] Here we have one of the saddest conjunctures, though one of the most frequent; civil war, with a third party whose interest it is to seek its own advantage in this fratricidal strife. The treacherous murder of the Duke of Burgundy at the bridge of Montereau had divided France into two irreconcilable factions, and English troops now poured again over the Channel. The Duke was buried among the Carthusians at Dijon; and, centuries later, when his skull was sometimes shown as a relic, a monk laid his finger on the gash made by the murderer's axe, and said: "This is the gate through which the English marched into France!" Henry V won Agincourt and was crowned King at Paris; after his death, the Regent Bedford was in effective occupation of all north of the Loire; France seemed lost, when Joan relieved Orleans and turned the tide. At last, by ill fortune, she herself was taken prisoner. It was perfectly natural, given the ordinary mentality of the age, that the English should attribute her almost miraculous victories to witchcraft; and, since sorcery came legally within the competence of lay magistrates as well as ecclesiastical, they could have condemned and burned her off-hand without violating medieval conceptions of justice to any very scandalous extent. But, for her complete discredit and for the world-wide justification of their own cause, they needed her solemn condemnation by the Church; and this they obtained as easily as Philip had done with the Templars. Prisoners, under the rules of chivalry, were regularly bought and sold; and the Regent Bedford, after hard bargaining, purchased Joan for a sum roughly equivalent to more than £30,000 modern. She was now his property; and he kept her in his own

prisons under guard of his own soldiers. This was the first
injustice; a person suspected of heresy should have been kept
in the Inquisitor's or the Bishop's prison. Next, they chose as
judge the Bishop of Beauvais, a bitter partisan of their own.
The excuse was that she had been taken prisoner in his diocese;
but there was no legal excuse for his trying her at Rouen, not
only outside his own diocese but in a different province. The
English had brought her thither, to their own military headquarters; they also paid the expenses of Bishop and the Inquisitor—for, however reluctantly, the Inquisitor of Rouen
agreed to attend and thus to give special authority to the whole
proceedings. She was brought chained into court, under guard
of English soldiers; and, when at last the judges had practically
made up their own minds against her, they sought confirmation
from the University of Paris. This body was, at that date,
practically recognised by custom as a sort of Court of Appeal
for spiritual questions throughout Western Christendom; we
have seen how naturally the King turned to it in the matter
of the Beatific Vision, and how confidently it condemned
John XXII's view as heretical. But the University at that
moment was as bitterly pro-English as the Bishop. Paris had
suffered from the blockade caused by Joan's continuation of
the war of national defence; it had been reported (no doubt
falsely) that she had promised her soldiers freedom to plunder
and slay if they could recapture the city from the English.
From the first, the University had shown the utmost hostility
to her; and now it permitted itself to send a unanimous corroboration of the twelve fatal articles by which the Bishop and
Inquisitor had condemned Joan, with only the feeble proviso
that their assent was conditional on the fact that these contained a true presentation of the case. That, of course, was the
whole point at issue; were the Rouen accusations true? The
trial lasted nine months in all; Joan was completely in her
enemies' power, though she claimed her right of transference
to the Bishop's prison. One of the main points made against her
was her insistence on wearing the same male costume in which

she had led the soldiers to victory: her refusal to change this for women's clothes at her judges' bidding was counted against her as heretical disobedience to the Church; yet we must remember how she was at the mercy of her guards in prison. The judges, however, were guided here by an instinctive realisation of her weak point. She was convinced of the sacredness of her mission; convinced of the reality of her visions, of the voices which had guided her to victory and which she still heard from day to day. They tried to bind her—and perhaps to ensnare—with a multiplicity of oaths; she was constantly obliged to protest that she would not swear on the Gospels, to entirely irrelevant questions, under possibility of involuntary perjury. "I promise to answer you truthfully that which touches your case; and the more you constrain me to swear, the longer I shall take to tell you." "Asked if she would swear, simply and absolutely, she answered: 'You may well do without it, I have sworn enough, twice.' . . . She said that of her coming to [the Ile de] France she would willingly speak the truth, but not the whole truth: and a week would not be enough for that."

Again, throughout this interminable trial, with a prisoner in that enfeebled condition, everything possible was done to wrest her deeds and her words to evil. She had had constant visions; these were reckoned as the most suspicious points against her; yet in thousands of ascetics before her such visions had counted as proofs of sanctity. Some men attributed to her the recalling of a sick child to life; this afforded suspicion of witchcraft, though her contemporary St. Bernardino of Siena was half-deified for having revived twenty-three dead folk. She was accused of sprinkling her own banner with holy water: the charge itself was apparently invented; yet, if it had been true, it was what the faithful were regularly encouraged to do. The judges were scandalised at her making (if indeed she did make) a sort of talisman of the motto *Jesus-Maria*; yet this, again, would have been a thing which St. Bernardino did more publicly and systematically. It was made a serious accusation that she had allowed folk to touch her or her ring as holy things: yet, in the First Crusade, Peter the Hermit had seen the very hairs of his mule's tail taken by the multitude as relics. There was in her native village, as in so many others, a *Fairies' Tree*, round which the girls danced and hung flowers. Joan, often challenged on this point, denied that she had done this regularly, or more than most girls; yet, without a particle of definite evidence, they chose to ignore her denials, and made it an article of condemnation "that there, and elsewhere, she has adored them [the Fairies] and done them reverence." Or, again: "She has called up demons and evil spirits, has consulted and frequented them, and entered into pacts and treaties with them." The vaguest assertions again and again are taken as proved, e.g., "so the said Robert [de Baudricourt] affirmed, said and uttered [against Joan's reputation] in many places, and in the presence of prelates, lawyers and notable persons": but without any pretence of bringing either Robert or these notables into the witness-box, or producing written depositions from them. When she was first taken, she tried to escape by leaping from her window in a lofty tower, and was picked up seriously hurt. They attempted to prove that this was suicide, a mortal sin. Yet her own account was perfectly natural and credible: "She answered that she had heard that the people of Compiègne [where she had been taken], all of them to the age of seven years, were to be put to fire and to the sword, and she would rather die than live after the destruction of good people. That was one reason why she leapt; the other was that she knew she had been sold to the English and she would rather have died than fall into the hands of her enemies the English. . . . I did it not in despair, but in hope of saving my body and of going to the aid of many good people in need." She admitted that St. Catharine in a vision had warned her not to leap; "but I could not do otherwise." This (it was argued against her) is the heresy of fatalism. Heresy, again, was discovered in her assurance of personal salvation. Cardinal Newman, among his not infrequent lapses in medieval history, counted this as peculiar to post-Reformation pietists; yet it is recorded of more than one medieval saint. In the case of Joan, however, the Faculty of Canon Law at Paris make it their sixth article of condemnation. "This woman sins also when she says she is as certain of being received into Paradise as if she were already partaker of that blessed glory; seeing that on this earthly journey no pilgrim knows if he is worthy of glory or of punishment, which the Sovereign Judge alone can tell." Their third article is worth quoting also: "That this woman is apostate, for the hair which God gave her for a veil she has had untimely cut off, and also, with the same design, has rejected woman's dress and imitated the costume of men." The significance of that word *apostate* may be better realised when we reflect that by Roman theology, to the present moment, Popes have the right of deposing all baptized sovereigns whom they judge to be "apostate," and of relieving subjects from their allegiance to such.

A great number of the questions put again and again to this sick woman—for such she was—were indefensibly irrelevant in spite of her constant protests. As a further injustice it was decreed that any refusal to answer should be reckoned as a confession of guilt. Others, again, seem most plainly designed to catch her in her speech. They asked her which was the true pope among the three rival claimants: a question on which (as we shall see later) even canonised saints have passed diametrically opposite judgments. To the Count of Armagnac, who had consulted her by letter on this subject, she had answered cautiously: "In truth, I cannot well for the present tell"; to her judges she answered: "Are there two of them?" Again, she was interrogated as to mortal sin, a question so intricate that priests are often very shy of answering it categorically. Her reply ran: "I do not think I am in mortal sin," and that, if she were, it was for God and the priest in confession to know it.

Another time they questioned her as to "grace," a still more complicated theological question, which at one time divided the whole Catholic Church in France. Here, again, she showed simple common sense: "Asked if she knows she is in God's grace, she answered: 'If I am not, may God put me there; and if I am, may God so keep me. I should be the saddest creature in the world if I knew I were not in His grace.' "

Again, "asked if God ordered her to wear a man's dress, she answered that dress is a small, nay the least, thing." When they treated her male attire as a treacherous abandonment of her womanly commitments, she said: "There are enough other women to don them." She had caused a standard to be made for herself, with angels and other religious symbols, in which the judges tried to find proof of sorcery. "Asked which was more help, she to the standard or the standard to her, she answered that whether the victory was hers or the standard's, it all must be attributed to God. . . . Asked why her standard was borne into the church at Reims rather than those of other captains at the consecration of her King, she answered: It had been present at the perils, and that was reason enough for it to be honoured."

But she was at her best in meeting the questions which were intended to show that the so-called saints, in her frequent visions, were in fact demoniacal illusions. The judges asked: Had these visions the real saint's halo? Did the saint appear with his usual emblem according to church tradition? etc. "Asked what part of them she saw, she answered: 'The face.' Asked if the saints which appeared to her had hair, she answered: 'It is well to know that they have.' Asked if there were anything between their crowns and their hair,* she answered 'No.' Asked if their hair were long and hung down, she answered: 'I do not know.' She added that she did not know whether they appeared to have arms or other members. She saw they spoke very well and beautifully; and she understood them very well. Asked how they spoke if they had no other members, she answered: 'I leave that to God.' She said the voice was gentle, soft and

---

* The probable implication of this question seems to have been that a real saint ought to wear his halo: otherwise there is imposture.

low, and spoke in French. Asked if St. Margaret spoke in the English tongue, she answered: 'Why should she speak English, when she is not on the English side?' . . . Asked if the voices forbade her to speak the truth, she answered: 'Do you want me to tell you what is the sole concern of the King of France? There are many things that are not in the trial.' She added that she knows for certain that her king will regain the kingdom of France, as certainly as she knows that we are seated before her in judgment; and, but for her revelation, which daily comforts her, she would be dead. . . . Asked in what form St. Michael appeared, she answered that she did not see his crown, and she knows nothing of his apparel. Asked if he was naked, she answered: 'Do you think God has not wherewithal to clothe him?' Asked if he had any hair, she answered: 'Why should it be cut off?' . . . Asked whether he had his scales, she answered: 'I do not know.' "

The point of this last question is that, in the Doom which was the most usual great painting on church walls, St. Michael is always represented at the feet of Christ in judgment, with a pair of scales in which he weighs each soul in turn.

It is sometimes argued that Joan's judges acted strictly within the limits of Inquisitorial law and procedure. That is true only in the sense that, by Inquisitorial law and procedure, almost anything was permissible which should tend to bring the accused to confession or proof of guilt. When we talk of Joan's judges, we must include also all the assessors and all those theologians and canonists of Paris University who concurred in the articles of condemnation. They condemned her in sanctimonious terms as a homicide: "The said Jeanne, usurping the office of angels, said and affirmed she was sent from God, even in things tending openly to violence and the spilling of human blood, which is absolutely contrary to holiness, and horrible and abominable to all pious minds." "To this article on this Tuesday, March 27th, Jeanne answers that she first asked for peace, but if peace was not agreed to, she was quite prepared to fight." Yet Joan protested, no doubt with perfect truth, "that she herself bore the standard when attacking the enemy, so as not to kill anyone: she never has killed anyone," she said. But they charged her with grievous manslaughter in the sense that her mission had done so much to protract a long and bloody war. Thus these judges, at best, took the immoral line of assuming no distinction in justice between a country fighting for its existence and an invader who had very little excuse beyond the profit which he might reap by interfering to help one party in a civil war. That is how we must judge their conduct at its very best; yet, when we look into the evidence closely, we see that they had not even this excuse. Whenever they dragged politics in—and they did so on the flimsiest pre-texts—it was in gross partiality to the invading side. Her answers on those points show her at her best. In this field she was at the mercy of those whom she knew to be, inevitably, her bitterest enemies. Her request for a panel of judges in equal number from both of the contending sides had, naturally enough, been refused; it was not thus that the Inquisition worked, nor, except on the rarest occasions, did any Bishop's Court. Not only was she kept in a military instead of ecclesias-tical prison, but an ecclesiastical lawyer, who protested against the irregularity of the trial, was clapped into that same castle of Rouen and threatened with death. Yet she seldom flinched, and many of the judges must have felt themselves shamed by her answers. From the notorious fact of her devotion to her own King and country, they tried to argue her want of charity towards the invaders, as though patriotism were necessarily a sin. She had naturally confessed that, if she so clearly under-stood the voices of her visionary saints, that was because they spoke to her in French. "Asked if this voice, that is St. Margaret, spoke English, she answered: 'Why should she speak English? She is not on the English side.'" Then the judges write, in their Articles of Accusation: "The said Jeanne has said and publicly declared that the saints, angels and archangels speak French and not English, and that the saints, angels and archangels are not on the side of the English but of the French, affirming to their scorn that the saints in glory look with hatred on a Catholic realm, and a country given to the veneration of all the saints according to the instruction of the Church." Or, again, (in the words of an assessor, Bachelor in Theology), "when she affirms that God loves certain people, it is well: but when she says that St. Catharine and St. Margaret do not speak English, she utters a rash statement and what seems to me a sort of blasphemy, for is not God the Lord of all, the Supreme Providence both for the English and others? Thus she appears to have spoken contrary to the law of love which we should bear to our neighbour." On another occasion she gave a memorable answer which was duly recorded again in the Articles of Accusation later on. "Asked how she knew that St. Catharine and St. Margaret hated the English, she answered that of God's love or His hatred for the English, or of what He would do to their souls, she knew nothing; but she was certain that, save only those who died there, they would be driven out of France, and God would send victory to the French against the English. Asked if God was for the English when they were prospering in France, she answered that she knew not whether God hated the French, but she believed it was His will to suffer them to be beaten for their sins, if they were in a state of sin."

It was on the strength of this and similar evidence that the Bishop and Inquisitor, with assessors, drew up their Articles of Accusation against this woman, as one "restored to you [the Bishop] who are her ecclesiastical and ordinary judge, by Our Lord Christian King of France and England [i.e., by the invading enemy] . . . to the end that she should be denounced and declared by you her said judges as a witch and enchantress, a false prophet, a caller-up of evil spirits, as superstitious, implicated in and given to magic arts, evil thinking in our Catholic faith, schismatic in the article *Unam Sanctam*, etc., and in many other articles of our faith sceptic and devious, sacrilegious, idolatrous, apostate of the faith, accursed and evil-doing, blasphemous towards God and His saints, scandalous,

seditious, perturbing and obstructing the peace, inciting to
war, cruelly thirsting for human blood, encouraging it to be
shed, having utterly and shamelessly abandoned the modesty
befitting her sex, and indecently put on the ill-fitting dress and
state of man-at-arms; and for that and other things abominable
to God and man, contrary to laws both divine and natural, and
to ecclesiastical discipline, misleading princes and people;
having to the scorn of God permitted and allowed herself to be
adored and venerated, giving her hands to be kissed; heretical
or at the least vehemently suspected of heresy; in order that,
according to the Divine and Canonical Sanctions she should be
punished and corrected canonically and lawfully, as befitted
these and all other proper ends."

Joan, therefore, did not get a really fair trial, even if we make
all allowance for the spirit of her age and admit the general
justice of Inquisitorial law and procedure. The verdict of
sorcery against her was ludicrous. Yet that of heresy was indeed
established, as heresy was often understood in her time. For,
by plain Inquisitorial law, she deserved the stake on one
definite point. She had repeatedly refused to swear all that
they demanded of her. She was ready to answer, on oath, all
really pertinent questions; but she would not commit herself
beforehand to the one absolute and sweeping oath that, whatever it might please the Inquisitors to ask in future, to that she
would answer on pain of perjury—that is, of mortal sin. She
had too much experience, from the first, of their indecent prying
into her most intimate thoughts, quite irrelevant to the actual
case in court. That, indeed, was the theme of her most frequent
protests. Many of the questions they asked were on subjects
which she held most sacred as between God and herself; and she
was too honest to commit herself to an unreasonably compre-
hensive future promise, which she would almost certainly be
compelled to break, sooner or later. It is quite false to plead,
as is sometimes done nowadays, that the Inquisition did not
meddle with a man's thoughts; that it judged him only for
unnecessarily and aggressively publishing his thoughts. Neither

law nor custom prohibited this Inquisition from demanding, upon pain of perjury, an answer to any question whatsoever, so long as it could be brought within the immensely wide category of "faith"; and Joan's case shows how fatally this rule might work with a really honest suspect. Joan's refusal to swear was heretical. Again, in the course of their interrogations, they constantly brought her up against her obligations to the Church Militant. She appealed constantly to God and the Saints; but that was not enough; God and the Saints are only the Church in Heaven. The Church on Earth, the Church represented by the Pope and his hierarchy, demanded implicit obedience here below. "Asked if she would submit to our Holy Father, the Pope, she answered: 'Take me to him and I will reply to him,' and would make no other answer." That, of course, was plainly impossible; the Pope could not hear every peasant girl who insisted that she was no witch or heretic. His predecessors had created the Inquisition; and he, like them, lent almost omnipotent competence to this institution specially devised to deal with such people as Joan. The voice of the Inquisition, in this present matter, was the voice of the Church Militant. It was idle for her to protest: "I am a good Christian; and in respect of all the accusations contained in this article I commit myself to God"; or again: "I believe indeed in the Church on Earth; but for my words and deeds, as I have already declared, I trust in and refer me to God." God, for all practical purposes at Rouen, was the Church Militant, and the Church Militant was practically the Inquisition. Therefore, her judges had both law and precedent on their side when they interpreted her recalcitrance as a practical denial of one article of the Church's Creed: "I believe in one Catholic Church," a denial most plainly heretical. For month after month Joan held out against what to her was the lie of the soul: against the admission that the voice of these men here in court was the voice of God. At last she broke down and signed a solemn recantation and submission. This, she presently found, would not earn her liberation, but lifelong imprisonment, not in the hands of these ecclesiastics who had condemned her, but in an English dungeon under the double burden of condemned heretic and prisoner of war. She indignantly revoked her recantation; and thenceforward there was no hope. She was a heretic first by her own former confession; then again, by this recantation, a relapsed heretic; so Canon Law fully justified the Court in burning her.

The burning of Savonarola, an event almost equally well known, was equally political.[2] Here the Inquisition was not directly invoked; but the main agent of his death was the Pope, and he was tried by Inquisitorial methods. This Dominican friar of intense religious convictions had conceived the mission of reforming the Church and society of his day. He was no Protestant: on all essential points of dogma he accepted the Catholicism of the period: his crime was that of foretelling the future and attempting practical reform without orders from Rome. Like Joan, he claimed celestial visions and prophetical powers; and in his case, as in hers, this formed the easiest point of attack for his enemies. By his extraordinary eloquence he obtained, as other friars had obtained before him, popular permission to reform and remodel the government of Florence, which was under the despotic rule of the Medici family. In a few weeks he had changed the face of the Republic. Enemies were reconciled, men gave up their unlawful gains as conscience-money; profane amusements and excessive wastefulness of dress were abolished; the churches were crowded; and, in the words of a contemporary, "the people of Florence seem to have become fools from mere love of Christ!" Yet Savonarola himself, under this quasi-dictatorial commission, neither strove for his own personal advancement nor suffered any of his colleagues to make personal profit from this social-religious revolution. The Pope was Alexander VI, by common consent one of the most immoral who have ever sat in Rome. He offered Savonarola a cardinalate at the price of discontinuing his sermons: the friar told his envoy: "Come to my next sermon and you shall hear my reply." He fortified himself with the words of the saintly

Jean Gerson, perhaps the greatest of all churchmen in that century: "We must show humility and meekness to the Sovereign Pontiff; but, when humility fails, then we must assume a courageous freedom." Pico della Mirandola, one of St. Thomas More's favourite heroes, wrote in defence of him. But Alexander excommunicated him; and, when Savonarola defied this, he called upon the city to deliver him up upon pain of a general interdict. Famine and plague discouraged the citizens; the jealousy of the Franciscans against this Dominican increased; and Savonarola's final refusal of the Ordeal of Fire brought an unpopularity which gave full handle to his political enemies, who put him to an elaborate pretence of judicial trial. The bench was first carefully packed; one of his judges was a man who had tried to kill him with his own hands in the streets. It was decided that no full report should be published. A notary was hired to garble the documents. One of his examiners confessed these falsifications in later years; another, at the very time, threw up his office, saying he would have no share in this homicide. Yet, after eleven days of this, the commissioners were obliged to confess to the Pope: "By many and assiduous tortures, after many days, we extorted scarce anything from him by force." Only after the third application of torture did they succeed in involving him in all sorts of contradictions as to his visions and prophesies, by the same unfair interrogatories as the Inquisitor had used with Joan of Arc. By similar torture they condemned two of his fellow Dominicans; and the three were publicly burned with all solemnity on the great square of Florence in 1498. Alexander VI granted a Plenary Indulgence to all who had striven against Savonarola, "regardless of the crimes or even murders which they might have committed for this purpose."

A few words must be added here on witchcraft, the charge upon which Joan was burned and which was brought also against the Templars. Whereas, in the thirteenth century, we have seen popes and prelates sufficiently primitive in their mentality to traffic with sorcerers, yet the fifteenth had become sufficiently educated to grow ashamed of this. Therefore, since sorcerers still existed in plenty, preserving the traditions of ancient heathenism, the Church began to see here one of the most dangerous enemies, and there came a wave of panic-legislation. That mania of witch-hunting which disgraced the sixteenth and seventeenth centuries, both in the Roman Church and in an ultra-Protestant country like Scotland, had commenced in earnest only a few generations before the Reformation.

The first Pope to give a definite stimulus to witch-hunting was John XXII. In this he served the spirit of the age. The fear of poison and witchcraft haunted great folk like a nightmare. Enguerrand de Marigni, Philippe le Bel's omnipotent minister, was finally hanged because his wife and sister had made waxen images to bewitch Louis X. A cardinal was accused of the same crime. The next King, Charles IV, was said to have been attacked through magic waxen images. A little earlier, the Bishop of Coventry and Lichfield was accused of rendering homage to the devil by kissing him on the posteriors, a proceeding which soon afterwards formed one of the charges against the Templars. Boniface VIII (who himself had been accused of keeping a Familiar Spirit) allowed the bishop to purge himself with thirty-seven witnesses who testified on his behalf. In 1308 women were burned in Paris for attempting to kill the Dame d'Ulmet by sorcery, and Bernard Délicieux was accused of similar attempts upon the life of Pope Benedict XI. John XXII made frequent use of witch-trials for political purposes: one may almost say, systematic use of them, as Dr. F. Bock has shown with convincing evidence in his *Studien zum politischen Inquisitionsprozess Johanns XXII*. Even Dante's name is mentioned by a witness in connection with a supposed attempt to destroy this pope with the usual wax-image magic (p. 33). Nor were these merely political excuses; there is abundant evidence that John, sharing all the superstitions of his time and conscious of his many bitter enemies, regarded himself as a special target for such perils. In 1317 the barber-surgeon and some clerks

of the Sacred Palace were executed on the usual accusation
(among others) of waxen images. At the very outset of his
reign, he had condemned the Bishop of Cahors for identical
attempts upon his life. The bishop was formally degraded
and handed over to the secular arm, by which (writes Bernard
Gui) "he was partly flayed, and then drawn through the
town to the stake and finally burned."[3] Upon this sorcery-
craze and the prevailing brutality and superstitions of this
period Lavisse comments pertinently: "When we read the
literary works and the official acts drawn up in the language
of the Schools or the Chanceries, we easily forget that the
men of that time were barbarians; but the [legal] procedures
remind us of the fact."[4] John took wholesale and excited
measures which helped naturally to increase the public sense
of danger; and the witch-craze intensified steadily to the
end of the Middle Ages and beyond. Other popes followed
with similar enactments in 1374, 1409, 1418, 1437, 1445
and 1451. Prominent theologians wrote fervid appeals to
the public, and backed up their words with deeds. The earliest
of these, the Dominican Nider, a contemporary of Joan,
deals with her case at some length; he implies a general belief
in her guilt and classes her with other "political" witches.[5]
In 1487 the University of Cologne warned the public that
to argue against the reality of witchcraft was to incur the
guilt of impeding the Inquisition: a guilt which ranked as
constructive heresy. Thus, when the sixteenth century came,
"Protestant and Catholic rivalled each other in the madness of the hour. Witches were burned no longer in ones
or twos, but in scores and hundreds. A bishop of Geneva
is said to have burned five hundred within three months,
a bishop of Bamburg six hundred, a bishop of Würzburg
nine hundred. Eight hundred were condemned, apparently
in one body, by the Senate of Savoy. . . . Paramé [in his
History of the Inquisition] boasts that in a century and a
half from the commencement of the sect in 1404, the Holy
Office had burned at least thirty thousand witches who,

if they had been left unpunished, would easily have brought the whole world to destruction."[6] It is common knowledge that John Wesley himself ranked belief in witchcraft as almost essential to the Christian Faith.*

---

* The account-rolls of the Bishop of Utrecht, in 1409, testify to the encouragement given by the hierarchy to the grossest superstitions on this subject. The bishop took a fine of 96 pounds and 5 shillings from Ghysbert Vleming "for that he bought the soul of Jan Botterbroec," and another of 134 pounds 15 shillings from "Jan Janson, *alias* Botterbroec, citizen of Amersfoort, for that he sold his soul to Ghysbert Vleming for a sum of money."—*Rekeningen van-Het Bisdom Utrecht*, 1378–1573, Pt. II (1932), p. 19.

CHAPTER XXIV

England

WE have seen how slightly England was affected by those heresies which swarmed on the Continent in the eleventh, twelfth and thirteenth centuries.[1] Speculative unorthodoxy seems to have been practically unknown at our universities. It was two great Oxford teachers and archbishops, Pecham and Kilwardby, who found even St. Thomas Aquinas deficient in orthodoxy.[2] In 1311, as we have seen, there was no Inquisitorial machinery beyond the ordinary power of bishops to watch over purity of doctrine; torture was threatened or applied to the Templars only by way of exception and as a special favour of Edward II to the Pope. The first serious symptom is the case of a certain deacon named Ralph de Tremur. In 1355 Bishop Grandisson of Exeter fulminated against this man at great length and with extreme solemnity.[3] He was already M.A. (of Oxford, in all probability) in 1331, and was still on leave in 1332 to absent himself from his living of Warleggan in Cornwall for the purposes of study. But now in February, 1355, he has been "for a long while" preaching flat heresy, especially in denial of Transubstantiation. Therefore Grandisson denounces him in a letter which the archdeacons are to publish in their chapters, and the parsons to their congregations. He writes: "O detestable tongue, more poisonous than that of any mad dog, which should be cut away by the physicians of the Church and by the King's ministers, and cut into small pieces and cast unto the hogs and sows, since it knoweth not to speak rightly and learneth not to refrain from uttering so execrable a heresy." All who, from henceforth, are guilty of speaking, sitting or eating with this man must know that they incur the major excommunication. Shortly afterwards,

Grandisson presses this case upon the notice of the Bishop of London, into whose diocese Tremur had evidently wandered. The man, he says, has now added evil deeds to evil words, and is all the more dangerous because he is an able philosopher and excellent grammarian, with ready command of four languages, Latin, French, English and "the Cornish or British tongue." Not content with depreciating St. Peter and St. John, he preaches to the people that they are idolaters, worshipping as God a particle of bread made with their own hands; moreover, on one occasion he has carried it from church and cast the Holy Wafer into a fire. If the Bishop of London does not take energetic measures, Grandisson will liberate his soul by reporting the matter to Rome, "lest by remissness or negligence I fall under the canonical penalties specially (as you know) proclaimed at the [Fourth Lateran] Ecumenical Council; or lest (what is last and most terrible of all) I be cast into the outer darkness wherein is weeping and gnashing of teeth, where the fire is not quenched, nor shall the worm of conscience die." We hear no more of Ralph de Tremur; but Grandisson's letter asserts that he was making disciples; and he was very likely still alive when Wyclif came forward in 1377.

Meanwhile, as we have already seen, one of the greatest of English philosophers had ripened into heresy, though not in England. William of Ockham, "the Invincible Doctor," took his B.D. at Oxford and passed on to Paris, where he took his D.D. Here he became intimate with Marsilius of Padua; and the epoch-making *Defensor Pacis* (1324) testifies to much community of thought between the two men. From 1321 onwards Ockham strongly espoused the general Franciscan opposition to John XXII's doctrines concerning the Poverty of Christ; and he was one of the group which could not be frightened or cajoled into later conformity. In 1327 he was imprisoned; in 1328 the Pope published a bull charging him with errors and heresies. He escaped to Munich, where, under protection of the Emperor, he wrote a series of attacks upon papal despotism which were almost as formidable as those of Marsilius. In his eyes, "no human institution is absolute or final, and neither Pope nor Emperor can claim exemption from the general law of progress and adaptation."[4] Meanwhile, his strictly philosophical work at Paris had been equally epoch-making. Though his doctrines were more than once forbidden from Rome and, in 1339, the Faculty of Arts at Paris formally forbade the teaching of them, yet they carried all before them, until by the end of the century they were victorious throughout Europe. In the main his teaching was sceptical, and could easily be used against (for instance) the dogma of Transubstantiation. Yet here—a not uncommon phenomenon—Ockham himself kept his faith in a water-tight compartment: the miracle can neither be discovered by reason nor proved by logic, but apprehended by the believer's mind. Others, naturally, were not so compliant; and Ockham's philosophy, quite apart from his denial of John XXII's orthodoxy and of papal omnipotence, worked gradually for the downfall of much that the Middle Ages had so laboriously built up. Luther, in later years, referred back to Ockham as "My dear Master." And Wyclif, whom Gregory XI solemnly condemned for teaching "the ignorant doctrine of Marsilius of Padua of accursed memory," himself claimed Ockham as a precursor in his struggles for moral reform.[5]

John Wyclif is too well known to need detailed treatment here.[6] He did not share Ockham's views altogether; on the contrary, he reacted from Ockham's pronounced Nominalism in metaphysics and taught a moderate Realism. But he cannot have avoided the influence of Ockham's critical method; and it has been suggested that his main philosophical work, the *Trialogus*, was suggested by Ockham's great *Dialogus*. Beginning thus purely as philosopher-theologian, Wyclif was brought into politics by the rising tide of protest from England against papal exactions and undue interference. In 1374 or 1375 he wrote a pamphlet against the claim of Gregory XI, who wanted 100,000 florins from us in aid of his wars in Italy, and demanded a renewal of the yearly tribute which John Lackland had promised under oath to Innocent III, but which had not been paid since 1333. Wyclif, in this pamphlet, sketched the argument which he developed afterwards in that book *De Dominio Civili* which earned him papal condemnation as a heretic of the school of Marsilius. *Dominium*—"Lordship"—in medieval parlance included both persons and property: both dominion over other men and ownership of land or office, as we still speak of a "landlord." The gist of Wyclif's teaching, which he inherited and amplified from his old Oxford master Fitzralph, Archbishop of Armagh, was that "Dominion is founded upon Grace." No man has a strict right to lordship over persons or land except in so far as he himself is in God's grace: the unjust man who stands in such a position is, from the point of view of abstract justice, a mere usurper. Wyclif drew no violent practical conclusions from this revolutionary doctrine; his attitude was rather that of a Fabian Socialist in our day. There is the distant goal we are to aim at: we must approach it how and when opportunity offers. Circumstances might well render a sudden upheaval more mischievous than the patient endurance of patent anomalies. We see all round us unjust and wicked men abusing their *dominium* over men or money: but this must often be suffered: for a while, "God must obey the Devil"; an epigrammatic phrase which his adversaries naturally turned against him. But (argued Wyclif), when such an unjust man talks of his "rights," or argues from the assumption that any attack upon him is an attack upon Divine Providence, then he must be given to understand that he is saying the thing that is not: *right* would demand his expropriation, and it is only *expediency* that still keeps him, on sufferance, in possession. Thus, though Wyclif argued against serfdom as a matter of justice—the only medieval philosopher, I believe, who went so far as that in the direction of modern thought—yet he put forward no proposals for its abolition. The most he did was to show more definite sympathy with the Peasants' Revolt of 1381 than the peasant-born author of *Piers Plowman* did: the people's excesses were blameworthy, but they had much right on their side.[7] Again, it was only at a later stage that he began to press for considerable advances towards the disendowment of the clergy.

Yet it will be seen how inevitably that corollary would finally be drawn by a sincerely religious, logical and courageous man. In those three qualities Wyclif's strength lay: and the strength of his movement lay in that combination of qualities. Here, for the first time, were apostolic fervour, keen intellect, and the missionary spirit united with the historical experience of ten generations. Saints like Bernard had been shocked by the evil, and had prayed God to mend it, in days when there was less record of failure in the past and therefore more room for hope in the future. Wyclif was the first to meet the problem in the spirit of that dialogue which Carlyle loved to quote. "Well, well, God mend all!" "Nay, by God, Donald, but we must help Him to mend it!" If St. Bernard had been born in Wyclif's days, history might well know him now mainly as a heresiarch.

The Great Schism began in 1378, some eighteen months after the bulls in condemnation of Wyclif. Thenceforward, for nearly half a century, saints themselves were at daggers drawn between Urban VI or Clement VII and their successors. Did Urban hold the keys of the Kingdom of Heaven, and was it he against whom the Gates of Hell could never prevail? and was Clement a blind leader of the blind hell-wards, as St. Catharine of Siena thought? Or was Clement, as St. Vincent Ferrer proved by all the resources of his scholastic training, so plainly the true Christ Upon Earth that no Urbanist could escape hell except upon the plea of invincible ignorance? This contest it was that turned Wyclif from a strong critic of the papacy into its determined opponent; especially when the fighting Bishop of Norwich led an army of invasion into France on the pretext that this was a Holy War, a Crusade for the true Pope Urban. Wyclif had himself begun as a cautious and moderate Urbanist; but his conscience was outraged by the Plenary Indulgence given by this Pope to all who should join in the invasion of France. The monastic chronicler Knighton tells us how "the bishops collected an innumerable and incredible sum in gold and silver coins, with jewels, lockets, rings, dishes, pieces of plate, spoons and other ornaments, and especially from ladies and other women; for it was said that a single lady contributed £100"—let us say, £3,000 in modern terms. "And very many gave, as was believed, beyond what they could truly afford, in order to obtain the benefit of absolution [of their sins] for themselves and their kindly friends . . . for they were not absolved unless they contributed according to their power and means. . . . For this bishop had marvellous Indulgences, with absolutions from pains and guilt,[8] for the said Crusade, granted to him by Pope Urban, by whose authority he absolved from pains and guilt (personally and through his commissaries) both dead and living folk on whose behalf a sufficient contribution was made. For it was told how certain of his commissaries asserted that, at their command, angels came down from heaven and snatched from their pains the souls that lay in Purgatory, and brought them straightway to heaven." The bishop began prosperously, killing 3,000 Frenchmen who believed in Clement and storming many towns and castles; but presently the tide of war turned, and he came home in disgrace.[9] Wyclif was shocked not only by this slaughter of Christian folk but by the scandal given to Christendom. He used a homely illustration. When two dogs fight over a bone, the simple course is to remove that bone altogether. In his last years he attacked, on philosophical grounds, even the doctrine of Transubstantiation, as he had long since attacked image-worship and pilgrimages. His doctrines thus became almost identical with those of the Vaudois, except on two important points. He did not share their total condemnation of blood-shed; while reprobating the bellicosity of clerics and the alleged readiness of friars to stir up civil war, he admits fighting in a just cause. Again, while deprecating the prevalence of thoughtless blasphemy, he does not forbid swearing on sufficient occasion in courts of justice, though later Lollards did some-times push their objections to that point. The one most important matter upon which he and the Vaudois agreed was the appeal to the Bible itself. We must no longer have mere snippets torn from their context and interpreted with scholastic subtlety, but a whole Bible in the mother tongue, accessible to common folk, and serving as a touchstone for doctrines which priests had so long supported not on the basis of the original Greek or Hebrew, but of a Latin version whose imperfections were confessed even by its author or reviser, St. Jerome. Though we can no longer hold that Wyclif himself wrote any part of the so-called Wycliffite Bible, yet there is no dispute as to his pressing for such a translation to be made by his disciples, or as to his appeal to the true Bible, and the whole Bible, for a rule of faith. We may indeed deplore his lapses from his own strict ideal. In 1372 or 1373 he accepted papal "provision" for a canonry of Lincoln: it never came to him in fact, but on principle he had opposed the "provision" system. Again, by accepting the living of Ludgershall and then of Lutterworth, into which for the time he put a curate to do the work while the rest of the income maintained him at his Oxford studies, he did indeed follow the regular custom. There were then no endowed Professorships at Oxford or Cambridge, and higher studies were habitually and openly supported by this system of absenteeism from the parish; but this was one of the abuses against which Wyclif himself had protested. Lastly, like St. Thomas More after him, he unquestionably took full advantage of the manners of his time, which admitted great violence of language in controversy. In one of his tracts, he acknowledges frankly his temptations to bitterness, pleading that he had struggled against it, but confessing that it had not always been overcome.

But, taking him on the whole, we may see how truly he interpreted the feelings of enormous numbers among his fellow-countrymen. Knighton, bitterly hostile to Wyclif, confesses in exaggerated language that every other man one met on the road would turn out to be a Lollard. The fact is that Wyclif crystallised ideas which had been floating in the popular mind for some time; and plain folk were stirred to serious consideration when they saw that the clergy did not dare to show their own title-deeds. For the Bible was as definitely inerrant in Catholic theory as it was to Waldo or Wyclif: the real dispute was whether the Church (which, by now, had come to mean the Pope) held from God the monopoly of its exposition. Archbishop Arundel's prohibition of unauthorised translations on pain of death, together with the Church's refusal to make any authorised version, and the Inquisitorial treatment of all Bible-reading in the vernacular as proof presumptive of heresy, steadily undermined in many minds the old implicit reliance upon clerical doctrine. Heresy was slow to grow up among us, but it struck its roots very wide and deep; the heretic might have said as Walter Savage Landor said of his own writings: "I dine late, but I dine in good company." The Lollards committed the blunder—the crime, it may perhaps be called—of allying themselves under Sir John Oldcastle with a political party. For this the cause suffered as it deserved; and Lollardy was driven underground for many generations. But there it survived and grew even in England, while on the Continent it kindled, through John Hus, the immense ecclesiastical revolution in Bohemia. There is full truth in the racy words with which old Fuller describes how the Council of Constance decreed vengeance upon Wyclif's remains, forty-one years after his death. "In obedience hereunto Richard Fleming, bishop of Lincoln, sent his officers to ungrave him accordingly. To Lutterworth they come, take what was left out of the grave, and burn them to ashes, and cast them into Swift, a neighbouring brook running hard by. Thus this brook hath conveyed his ashes into Avon, Avon into Severn, Severn into the narrow seas, they into the main ocean. And thus the ashes of Wickliffe are the emblem of his doctrine, which now is dispersed all the world over."

We cannot entirely ignore Knighton's terrified exaggeration. It is certain that there was an immense amount, when once the great question had been raised, of hesitation between orthodoxy and heresy. The historian necessarily makes things more black or white than they really were; he finds it hard for himself and still more wearisome for his readers to attempt the rendering of all these half-shades which impress us more and more in proportion as we strain our eyes in the survey. Let us try, then, for once to explore that No-Man's Land of Betwixt and Between which is perhaps even more significant for social history than either pure Orthodoxy or downright Heresy.

In the intimate biographies of saints and mystics, as we find them in the *Acta Sanctorum*, for instance, nothing is more striking than their frequent unpopularity in their own time. Their earlier career was nearly always beset with opposition and misunderstandings, and some were never fully recognised until after their death. The earliest Franciscan missionaries were treated as heretics: and Jordan of Giano confesses how little he had esteemed the living Francis in comparison with Francis dead. St. Bernardino of Siena, who practically invented the cult of the Sacred Name of Jesus, as St. Mary Alacoque three centuries later practically invented that of the Sacred Heart, had to meet similar contradiction and a similar accusation of heresy. A Dominican, in 1418, thundered against him as "Teacher of Idolatry" and "Herald of Antichrist." Though he repeatedly pleaded the virtues of his sacred monogram to wean the populace from their pagan witchcrafts and incantations, yet the storm rose higher. As he says himself in a defensive sermon in the great square at Siena: "When I went to Rome, some wanted me fried, and others roasted."[10] It needed great protectors to stand boldly by him, such as his fellow-Franciscan St. Giovanni Capistrano and Queen Joanna of Naples. St. Catharine of Siena, again, is typical of many mystics whose religiosity was uncongenial to family or friends; and in England we now know one mystic of Chaucer's time, whose story is even more illuminating through her reaction upon other folk than through the psychological analysis of her own character. This religious autobiography, discovered quite recently after five centuries of oblivion, had an immediate literary success; it cannot be ignored by anyone who is deeply interested in that side of medieval life.

Margery Kempe was born at Lynn, "Bishop's Lynn" as it was then called, but "King's Lynn" now, ever since Henry VIII forced an exchange upon the Bishop of Norwich. She was daughter to John of Burnham, who had five times officiated as mayor in the old Guildhall, which was burned down in 1421. She watched how nearly the fire failed to catch St. Margaret's Church; and she flattered herself that her own prayers had contributed no little to this happy immunity. Later, she saw the present beautiful Guildhall rise from those ashes. Within her own soul, also, there had been some such burning and re-building; and it seems that few contemporaries doubted her supernatural powers, however strenuously they might dispute whether she owed them to God or to the Devil. Her husband, John Kempe, was in all probability son to John Kempe of Norwich, a Fleming whom Queen Philippa had imported to create a weaving industry in England. Margery characterises him as "a worshipful burgess" and gives her own age at marriage as "twenty years or some deal more": this was in 1393, when her John was probably about twenty-seven. Between that date and 1414, when the pair took a solemn vow of separation and chastity, she would seem to have borne fourteen children: but it is difficult to fit them in to her very incoherent autobiography. Somewhere about 1430, as she seems to imply, only one son was still alive: infant mortality did even more than famine and fever to work against increase of population in the Middle Ages. As daughter to this five-fold mayor, and daughter-in-law to "the Patriarch of the Woollen Industry" at "the Manchester of the Middle Ages" (as Norwich has been called), Margery in her unregenerate days was as dressy and proud as Mine Host's wife in the *Canterbury Tales*. She tells this with the relish with which Bunyan recounts his own youthful errors: but, presently, like Bunyan, she became hysterically set upon fleeing from the wrath to come. Like him she suffered imprisonment, though only occasional; her trials were not more severe, apparently, than those of the earliest Franciscan missionaries in France and Germany.

Let us take one matter upon which she herself laid exaggerated stress and which her contemporaries treated with almost equal over-emphasis: that of her white dress. Here, as everywhere in the book, it is almost impossible to make out a chronological sequence; but the logical sequence is plain enough. White clothes were naturally unusual in the Middle Ages; washing was a serious matter. They might also suggest certain spiritual implications: several Religious Orders wore white; so did certain penitents, by official command; again, there was the priest's white surplice, and the thirteenth-century author of *The Owl and the Nightingale* sums up the clergy generally as "all that weareth linen cloth." Margery, whose vainglory of dress had been one of her worst sins, now at her first conversion exchanged that vanity for another: "This creature" (for thus she always writes in the third person) "was smitten with the deadly wound of vainglory and felt it not: for she many times desired that the Crucifix should loosen His hands from the Cross, and embrace her in token of love"; that is, as He did in that thirteenth-century story of the Merciful Knight recorded in art by Burne-Jones. When therefore she had become a precious brand plucked from the burning, and folk discussed her religious talk very freely, whether in praise or in blame, it was very natural that she should be fascinated by the idea of a distinctive dress, just as her predecessor and master in mysticism, Richard Rolle, had made himself conspicuous by fashioning a sort of hermit's dress out of two frocks borrowed from his sister. God, she was soon convinced, willed that Margery Kempe should wear white. This divine will became more and more certain, at least in the sense of the French proverb: *Ce que femme veut, Dieu le veut.* Therefore, for God's love, Margery determined to wear white. A well-intentioned anchorite went quite the wrong way to dissuade her: he pleaded "God forbid it, for she would then make all the world wonder at her!" The Bishop of Lincoln disapproved and bade her consult his brother of Canterbury; but God forbade this to Margery. The Mayor of Leicester suspected her of heresy and witchcraft. The Archbishop of York "commanded his retinue to fetch a pair of fetters and said she should be fettered, for she was a false heretic." "And there came many of the Archbishop's retinue, despising her, calling her 'Lollard' and 'heretic,' and swearing many a horrible oath that she should be burnt. And she, through the strength of Jesus, spoke back to them: 'Sirs, I dread ye shall be burnt in Hell without end, unless ye amend in your swearing of oaths, for ye keep not the commandments of God. I would not swear as ye do for all the money in the world.' Then they went away, as if they had been shamed." For indeed Margery, once marked for public notice by her garments and her thousand other eccentricities, was naturally suspected of heresy in medieval England. One of the most definite notes was precisely this horror of oaths which comes out repeatedly in Margery's pages. It was in her lifetime that Chaucer had painted that inimitable scene, which, like so many more of his pictures, might seem a mere caricature if we had not abundant corroboration from episcopal Registers and similar formal documents. When the Man of Law had ended his pathetic tale of Dame Constance, then

> "Oure Hoste upon his stiropes stode anon,
> And seyde, 'Good men, herkeneth, everichon!
> This was a thrifty tale for the nones!
> Sir Parish Prest,' quod he, 'for Goddës bones,
> Tell us a tale . . . by Goddës dignitee!'
> The Persone him answérde, '*Benedicite!*
> What eyleth the man, so sinfully to swere?'
> Our Hoste answérde, 'O Jankyn, be ye there?
> I smelle a Loller in the wind,' quod he.
> 'Nowe, good men,' quod our Hostë, 'herkneth me,
> Abydeth, for Goddës dignë passioun,
> For we shul han a predicacioun;
> This Loller here wol prechen us somwhat.'
> 'Nay, by my fader soule, that shal he nat!'
> Seyde the Shipman; 'herë shal he nat preche;

He shal no gospel glosen here, ne teche.
We leven alle in the grete God,' quod he,
'He wolde sowen som difficulte,
Or sprengen cokkel in our clenë corn."

Margery, moreover, added to her suspicious horror of oaths a still more suspicious, however partial, knowledge of the Bible, of which she had picked up a smattering in oral converse with friendly priests and friars. When she was examined before the Archbishop of Canterbury, then she reports how the assistant clergy said: "Ah, Sir, here wot we well that she hath a devil within her, for she speaketh of the Gospel" against swearing. Books written from the Protestant side, such as Foxe's *Martyrs*, give less convincing evidence than this orthodox autobiography for the extent to which in those days religious eccentricity carried its very life in its hand. Margery may have met Chaucer, who had certainly many Eastern Counties' connections: and to her book we may apply, in its minor degree, Dryden's praise of Chaucer: "Here is God's plenty." Almost every reader may here find something to his own particular taste. One man will note the events which "befel on a Friday on Midsummer Eve in right hot weather, as this creature was coming from Yorkward and carrying a [leather] bottle with beer in her hand, and her husband a cake in his bosom." He will say: "Here is the good old England of my dreams! a land flowing with beer and hikers, a land of honest stone-milled flour and of Chaucer's moist and corny ale." "It was full merry" (he will say) "in Chaucer's England." Yet, in that England itself, and in so choice a spot as Bishop's Lynn, the converted Margery spent all her life "with great sobbings and sighings after the bliss of heaven . . . so much, that she could not well restrain herself from speaking thereof: for whenever she was in any company she would say oftentimes: 'It is full merry in heaven!' And they that knew her behaviour beforetime, and now heard her speaking so much of the bliss of heaven, said to her: 'Why speak ye so of the mirth that is in heaven? Ye know it not, and

ye have not been there any more than we.' And were wroth
with her; for she would not hear nor speak of worldly things as
they did, and as she did aforetime."

There we have a mystic tottering on the verge of unorthodoxy,
but saved by her intimacy with priests and friars, and by her
passion for pilgrimage: indeed, the adventurous story of her
many travels surpasses even the psychological story of her
religious experiences. Let us now compare with her a namesake
and contemporary, of rather humbler social rank, whose
religious feelings took her over the narrow line which so often
divided orthodoxy from heresy.

Margery Backster was wife to a carpenter at Martham, on
the Norfolk Broads. In 1428 a neighbour deposed before the
Bishop of Norwich that another neighbour had seen in her
house, one day in Lent, "the said Margery being therein, a brass
pot standing over the fire, with a piece of bacon and oatmeal
seething therein"; which of course was a mortal sin. To fhis she
added heresy, saying that the Church had no right to impose
fasts, and "that it were better to eat the fragments left upon
Thursday at night on the fasting days, than to go to the market
to bring themselves in debt to buy fish"; for, in fact, fish was
generally much dearer; so that Erasmus very truly stigmatised
these "fasts" as the rich man's indulgence and the poor man's
pain. She had spoken against Transubstantiation and image-
worship and the cult of the Cross and pilgrimages; the much-
worshipped St. Thomas of Canterbury was "a false traitor,
damned in hell." The Pope and his hierarchy are tyrants,
deceiving and fleecing the people; especially the Bishop of
Norwich and others who "have most cruelly slain the servants of
God" and protected themselves by "false pardons . . . falsely
obtained" from Rome. Moreover, "the said Margery Backster
did inform this deponent that she should in no case swear;
saying to her in English: "Dame, beware of the bee, for every
bee will sting; and therefore take heed you swear not, neither by
God, neither by Our Lady, neither by any other Saint; and if ye
do contrary, the bee will sting your tongue and venom your

soul. . . . Also, this deponent saith that the said Margery
desired her that she and Joan her maid would come secretly in
the night to her chamber, and there she should hear her
husband read the law of Christ unto them, which law was
written in a book that her husband was wont to read to her at
night: and that her husband is well learned in the Christian
verity. . . . Moreover, that she should not be burned, although
she were convicted of Lollardy, for that she had a charter of
salvation in her body."[11]

Here is a typical Lollard case; yet it is not sufficiently
recognised that Margery's feelings on most of these points were
repeatedly expressed in effect, though in more cautious language
by Erasmus, especially in his letter to his friend the Bishop of
Basel and in those Bible commentaries and prefaces which were
patronised by Pope Leo X. As Dr. P. S. Allen, his latest and
greatest editor, puts it, Erasmus "gave utterance to what all
felt, but none dared to whisper but he." Yet even with him it is
often a mere whisper; for many of these utterances, if he had
raised his voice and proclaimed them from the housetops,
might have brought even Erasmus to the stake. Though
England had escaped the Inquisition in its fullest and most
brutal form, yet real freedom of thought and speech were
impossible. Parliament, indeed, had twice shown considerable
sympathy with the Lollards (1382 and 1395); but their cause
was ruined by political implications, true or false; and the
bishops had strong royal support when, in 1397, they pressed
for the execution of impenitent heretics, "as in other realms
subject to the Christian religion." Therefore Henry IV, in
repayment for the clerical support which had helped him to his
throne, enacted the statute *De Hæretico Comburendo*. This was
followed by a series of decrees from Archbishop Arundel at the
Lambeth Council of 1407-8. From that time forward the lay
magistrates were bound to seek out and punish, with the stake
in the background for cases of obstinate impenitence, the
following ecclesiastical offences: (1) To preach religion without
definite official authorisation from the bishop. (2) For an

incumbent to preach, even to his own flock, on religious subjects outside the very elementary points which the Lambeth Council of 1279 had prescribed as a minimum. (3) The licensed preacher may preach to the laity only against layfolks' sins; he may preach against clerical sins only in select clerical assemblies. (4) Schoolmasters must not permit their pupils to discuss the Faith, even in private. (5) No Bible translation is to be made or read except with express licence from the Bishop or a Diocesan Synod. (6) None may doubt or reject any portion of Canon Law, or the [papal] Lawgiver's powers. On all these points, as in matters of High Treason against the King, the authorities have power to arrest on suspicion and proceed to a summary trial. These decrees lack, of course, many of the worst features of the Inquisition proper. Here in England there may be secret tale-bearing, but there is no secret examination of witnesses, and the accused will be heard more or less publicly. There is no torture, nor is there a whole pack of *Domini Canes*, privileged beyond all other officials in this immensely-privileged Church, whom merely to impede is *ipso facto* heresy. On the contrary, Mr. H. G. Richardson has brought out the jealous care with which the English State kept these matters in its own hands. Yet, even in this milder form, such legislation worked terribly against any healthy interchange of thought except within the old traditional limits. For one victim of *De Hæretico Comburendo* in the body, we must reckon hundreds whom it marred and stunted in intellectual, or even moral, growth. A distinguished scholar, Pecock, Bishop of Chichester, died in prison [1460] for having been rash enough to argue against the Lollards on their own ground, instead of burning them. And, while we regret the execution of St. Thomas More as one of the darkest tragedies in our history, we must not ignore the fact that, if Henry had not decapitated him, it was by no means impossible that some pope would have burned him. His contemporary Julius II was even more cynically political and more unscrupulously violent than John XXII had been. It might have happened in his time that the Poverty of Christ should again have become a major

politico-social issue, shaking the papacy to its foundations. If
More had then fulfilled his serious intention of taking the
Carthusian vows, and had lived in the Charterhouse not for four
years only but for forty of earnest contemplation, might he not
have come to believe deliberately and deeply that Christ and
His Apostles had included moneylessness in their rule of life?
In such a case, that theory which men often attempt to explain
away as a mere *jeu d'esprit* in More's *Utopia* would have become
deadly earnest with him; and Julius need not have troubled to
invent any fresh legislation. John XXII, speaking to all
Western Christendom, had already condemned this idea as
heretical, and many men had already been burned for it. If it
be pleaded that such a More as we are here assuming, the
contemplative and visionary Carthusian, would at once have
given way and abjured whatever a pope condemned, then we
must deduct something considerable from his intellectual or
moral stature. Men of all creeds admire him now as a man who
died because he would not commit the lie of the soul. Savonarola
was almost, if not quite, as saintly a man; but he was thrice
tortured and then burned for "proving his contempt for the
Holy See by neither asking absolution nor yielding obedience."
Or, again, we may take More's friend Colet. His life was not
such as to make it credible that, having come to any prayerful
and definite conclusion for himself in his Bible study, he would
ever have abjured his belief. No doubt Erasmus would, but only
with a disdainful smile. It is difficult to believe that More, if
matters had ever come to that point, would have renounced "the
liberty wherewith Christ hath made us free." Therefore, since
the wind bloweth where it listeth, we must recognise that it
might have blown upon him from the Pope instead of from
Henry VIII; and that he would have found himself against the
more dangerous of the two totalitarian rulers, since popes had
asserted from time immemorial an absolutism which Henry and
his contemporary princes were only now striving to imitate.
When Paul III called upon the English to wage civil war against
Henry VIII, and exposed us as a prey to any foreign invader of

his own party, and proclaimed further that all English prisoners should become the lifelong slaves of their orthodox captors, in all this he was only asserting that which his predecessors had claimed for centuries past, and which princes or magistrates had often suffered and sometimes actively agreed to. Thus, whereas it is one of the worst blots upon Henry's fame that he hanged and disembowelled the seven Carthusians who were unalterably loyal to Papal Supremacy, yet Carthusians no less holy than they might well have been burned with Savonarola and his two fellow-friars at Florence, after application of torture, in defence not of Papal claims but of the inalienable rights of conscience. And in their case, as in Savonarola's, the fickle mob would doubtless have amused themselves by stoning the roasted corpses until "it rained blood and entrails."[12] It is unhistorical to ignore that the principles upon which Innocent III acted in handing over Southern France to a foreign soldiery and to an alien sovereign were not only still maintained in More's day, but have never since been retracted by the Ecclesia Romana.[13]

CHAPTER XXV

Spain

THIS country must be treated in special detail, because by common agreement the Spanish Inquisition stands in a category by itself, both as to its constitution and in its effects.

As England was least Inquisition-ridden among all the great countries of Europe, Spain at the end of the Middle Ages was worst: so much so, that modern apologists commonly attempt to draw a clean line of demarcation here. Elsewhere, they admit, the Ecclesia Romana was definitely responsible for this institution; but in the Peninsula it was a State machine; whatever ill was done must be reckoned not to the Church, but to Ferdinand and Isabella, the enlightened despots who created modern Spain.

This is a deceptive half-truth. The instrument which, confessedly, Spanish sovereigns abused had been constructed by the papacy. It was specially adapted to the purposes for which Ferdinand and Isabella used it; and popes themselves had often tried to employ it with equal severity; in so far as they failed, it was for lack not of will but of power. Finally, the Spanish abuses claimed papal protection, and nearly always got it, tacitly if not explicitly: the rare papal protests were never clinched with deeds. Civil authorities were threatened, and sometimes punished with the gravest penalties, for neglecting to back up the Inquisition, but never for excessive and misguided severity. Thus the Inquisition became one of the principal features of national life. The modern Spaniard owes as much to this institution, whether by attraction or by repulsion, as Britain does to her parliamentary constitution.

Yet whereas, from 1480 onwards, all this is true, up to that

date Spain had been one of the least Inquisition-ridden countries.
There had been plenty of heresy, such as we have seen in
Priscillian, countered by plenty of combative orthodox enthusiasm, as in Dominic. This country which had produced
some of the finest pagan Latin writers under the Empire, and in
which Latin was never quite the dead language which it became
among the general population of more Northern countries, had
never slumbered under the comparative intellectual apathy of
the ordinary Englishman during the last five centuries of the
Middle Ages.* We may again recall Boccaccio's line: *"Hispanus
et Gallus, studiis tardusque Britannus."* Moreover, even though
there had been no remnants of Latin culture, the Moor and the
Jew have kept Spain alive. For in this Peninsula there was such
a mixture of different races and creeds, side by side, as could be
found in no other great country of Europe. That, indeed, is one
of the most instructive features in this Spanish story. It shows
how, when men must needs live together, there is a natural
process of adaptation and compromise so long as no great
cause of friction and no aggressive proselytism come in to
interfere with the ordinary man's inclination to live and let live.
Such comparative harmony may be due in great part to mere
indifference; but it does, in fact, come about.

At first, the Spanish problem was comparatively simple:
there was only the question between Christian and Jew. The
first conquerors, the Visigoths, were Arians and comparatively
tolerant of religious differences. They enforced less of the
Roman Imperial law in favour of Christianity than they might
have done. But with their conversion to Catholicism a change
came at once. The Third Council of Toledo (589), held to
condemn the Arian heresy, increased Jewish disabilities. The
next Toledan Council (633) passed a decree which was later
incorporated in Canon Law, with lamentable results. A Jew
who had been forcibly baptized in infancy, or forced to accept
conversion for fear of death, was thenceforward a Christian

* We must say this in spite of the distinction of our Anglo-Norman satirists
and chroniclers: those men are not a fair indication of the general intellectual
level.

subject, so that relapse might bring him to the stake. The
country was thus filled with *conversos*, converts by force
in most cases, half-way between the real Jew and the real
Christian.

Then, in 711, came the Saracen invasion; and the problem
became three-cornered between Moslem, Christian and Jew. It
seems paradoxical at first sight that this should have simplified
the question of toleration: but so it was. Religious persecution
is always based on the hope of exterminating one's opponent:
or, if not completely, at least of paralysing all his energies.
Under Saracen rule in Spain there seemed less chance of such
success; moreover, Islam was not hypnotised by the belief that
disbelievers are doomed to an eternity of torment, and therefore
that all free interchange of thought is deadly. They allowed the
Christians free use of their religion; thus grew up the so-called
Mozarabic community, in which Latin was so completely
forgotten that its Scriptures and Liturgy were translated into
Arabic, while it kept its Latin rites and hierarchy. When
Mozarabic zealots abused this tolerance by publicly decrying
Islam, persecution followed; but normally the relations were
quite friendly. When the Cid conquered Valencia (1096), the
capitulation was signed by the principal Christian as well as
Moslem citizens. Lea writes truly: "Natural attrition, so far
from inflaming prejudices, led to natural toleration; so that
fanaticism became reduced to a minimum precisely in that
corner of Christendom where *a priori* reasoners have been
tempted to regard it as especially violent." Even in the wars of
reconquest, "brave warriors learned to respect each other; and,
as usual, it was the non-combatants, Christian priests and
Moslem faquis, who retained their virulence. . . . In the
adventurous career of the Cid, Christians and Moslems are seen
mingled in both contending armies; it is for the most part
impossible to detect in the struggle any interest in race or
religion."[1] During the frequent civil wars in Northern (i.e.
Christian) Spain, Moors were sometimes employed by both sides;
on the other hand, Christian knights would sometimes seek

service under Moorish generals. By Canon Law, to aid the Saracens was to become a "fautor" (abettor) of heresy and a subject for burning; yet "in spite of the thunders of the Church, the traders continued trading and the princes made offensive and defensive alliances with the infidel." The Jews, though usually tolerated, were less fortunate. Their skill as physicians, financiers and administrators frequently brought them to great wealth or high position; but this exposed them to envy and unpopularity; and favour alternated with massacre.

In proportion as the Christians reconquered Spain, they were at first as tolerant of religious differences as the Moors had been. The conquered people were allowed to retain their religion and property: this began at least as early as the tenth century. These Mudéjares, as they were called, supplied most of the agricultural and artisan class, while the Jews did most of the trading. The conqueror was a feudal lord who exploited his lands with slave labour. This tolerant policy was not altogether continuous, and there were such individual cases of oppression and injustice as we might expect from this rough feudal society: but the two races and religions lived together in comparative harmony until the twelfth century. Then in Spain, as elsewhere, the revival of intellectual interest brought heretical activities also. There are no indications of the same Catharist organisation in the Peninsula as in Languedoc; but, especially when we come to the thirteenth century, there are serious outbreaks at many points. By this time the Mudéjares were numerous and prosperous: exploited by the dominant classes, but surviving through their superior industry, thrift and sobriety; "they were slaves to their word; their reputation for probity and honour was universal and their standing as merchants was proverbial." Naturally, however, they suffered from anything that tended to emphasise religious differences. The clergy were professionally bound to do all they could for the conversion of these infidels who, under tolerance, had been rapidly increasing. Therefore, among other disabilities, a badge of infamy was decreed for them. The Lateran Council of 1215

had already prescribed this for all Jews; and in 1371 Henry II of
Castile prescribed it for Moors also: a red circle on the left
shoulder. In 1266 Clement IV wrote to the King of Aragon
urging him to expel all his Mudéjares: it is disgraceful in him to
suffer this religious anomaly for the sake of mere temporal
advantages. At the Council of Vienne (1311), Clement V
ordered all princes to forbid the Moors from allowing the
Muezzin to make his public call to prayer from his minaret. But
the princes took no notice; the population in general was
tolerant enough; so the decree was vainly repeated at the
Council of Tarragona (1329); and again, with despairing emphasis, "by the bowels of divine mercy," at that of Tortosa
(1429). It was not till the reign of Ferdinand and Isabella that
the decree of Vienne was at last enforced.

On the other hand, its prescriptions against the Jews fell
upon far less stony ground; for cupidity was here strongly
interested, apart from religious motives. The Spanish prelates
now came back from that Ecumenical Council of Vienne with
the instruments they needed for a systematic antisemitic
crusade. In their own Council of Zamora (1313) they invoked
the curse of God and St. Peter upon the long-standing privilege
whereby Jewish witnesses were required against Jewish
defendants: and they enacted decrees designed to cut off all
intercourse between the two communities. The churches must
no longer be profaned by attendance of Moors or Jews at Mass:
and, as their apparent skill as physicians and surgeons is often
used for the malicious murder of Christians, the ancient canons
forbidding employment of Moors or Jews are to be enforced
under threat of excommunication. This was repeated in 1335
and 1412. Yet about 1462 a Franciscan preacher complained
that all nobles and prelates were keeping Jewish physicians,
who boasted to each other as to who has caused most Christian
deaths! In 1469 a Jewish cure was permitted to the King of
Aragon of a double cataract; and though Ferdinand and
Isabella renewed the prohibition in 1480, the Dominicans
obtained permission to violate this law in 1489, on the ground

that there were few non-Jewish physicians in Spain. In 1412 it was decreed that Jews and Moors should everywhere be segregated in their own ghettos, behind an impenetrable wall with only one gate. They were also forbidden to attend Christian weddings or funerals. The repetition of such laws shows the impossibility of enforcing them strictly; yet, as Lea ironically says: "they answered the purpose of inflicting an ineffaceable stigma upon their victims and of keeping up a wholesome feeling of antagonism on the part of the population at large."

In consequence, Spanish Judaism shows more painful alternations than elsewhere between comparative prosperity on the one hand and robbery and massacre on the other. The Jews were too numerous to be eliminated wholesale until Spain became a Totalitarian State under Ferdinand and Isabella; but the Church did all she could to keep them in the position assigned to them by Canon Law; that of slaves to the Christians. One noteworthy exception here must be emphasised. The Black Death, with its general panic, gave rise to the idea that the wells had been deliberately poisoned. Sometimes the lepers were accused of this crime, but more often the Jews, and there were general massacres; in Germany the cry ran "Baptism or Death!" But Clement VI pointed out this absurdity; he showed how the plague raged in districts where there were no Jews; and he ordered all prelates to proclaim to their flocks that Jews were not to be beaten, wounded or slain on this plea, and that all offenders in this matter should be excommunicated. But a single instance of this kind availed little to counterbalance the steady pressure of the ordinary clergy. A few years earlier, in Navarre, a zealous Franciscan had preached revolution against the Jews and had initiated a reign of pillage and slaughter. In 1391 the Archdeacon of Seville, Martinez, started a still more terrible "Holy War against the Jews." He tore down synagogues, and the mob at his instigation stormed the ghetto: the survivors escaped alive only by accepting baptism. The slain were reckoned at 41,000. This must be discounted for the usual medieval exaggeration in large figures;

but the fact is that two of the three synagogues were converted
into churches and that the third sufficed for the small Jewish
remnant. The flame then spread to Valencia, where the ghetto
was sacked and several hundred slain; thence to Barcelona,
where also the choice was between baptism and the sword;
again to Toledo, Palma, Saragossa and other cities. In other
places the Jews did not wait for slaughter, but crowded to the
churches for baptism. The myth of the Ritual Murder was
revived or invented, with the parallel story of a consecrated
Host stolen and cast into a boiling cauldron, from which it
miraculously emerges. Under sufficient torture, victims were
found to confess these things. Moreover, all this physical
violence was backed up by the fiery proselytism of St. Vincent
Ferrer. This man was one of the greatest mission-preachers of
the Middle Ages, and (as we have seen) a theologian so orthodox
that, under the Great Papal Schism, he wrote a scholastic
treatise proving that his own pope must needs be the true one
and the Italian pope so false that all who believe in him must go
to hell unless excused by invincible ignorance; a conclusion most
unflattering to St. Catharine of Siena, who was unshakenly loyal
to her own Italian.[2] Legend recounts that he baptized 4,000 at
Toledo in a single day. "It is to be hoped that in some cases, at
least, he may have restrained the murderous mob, if only by
hiding its victims in the baptismal font."[3] Thus, inevitably
there arose again a definite class in Spain, that of the *Conversos*.
These renegades, naturally, were more bitter than others
against those whom they had quitted; and their more dubious
sincerity was cloaked under a special show of orthodox zeal. As
early as 1449 many of the noblest houses had Jewish blood in
them; for these *Conversos* were men of more than average
ability. King Ferdinand the Catholic himself was of such a
family; so was the Inquisitor Torquemada and his next successor in the Inquisitorship General; so was a contemporary
Archbishop of Granada. Such was the natural result of lynch-
law, continued sporadically from generation to generation, with
effects so demoralising both to culprits and to victims that the

Inquisition, with all its injustices, did yet betoken a step forward in law and order.

Ferdinand and Isabella were confronted with the gravest difficulties. Her right of succession was disputed. Long misgovernment had split both Aragon and Castile into factions headed by powerful nobles: it was one of their earliest acts to raze forty-six castles of robber-barons. Laws and treaties had been so habitually violated that no man could trust another. The Church was corrupt and the clergy little respected. The Archbishop of Toledo, Primate of Castile, wasted his enormous revenues in war and upon schemes of alchemy: one of the most magnificent tombs of the period was that of his bastard son in the Franciscan Church at Toledo. Among the ordinary clergy, concubinage was even more common than elsewhere in Europe; and this same primate was compelled to decree that none should henceforth be ordained to the clergy who could not speak Latin, the language of the Liturgy! The multitude of *Conversos* entailed frequent insincerity among priests and prelates. Bribery was almost universal in the law-courts; and the statute-law, never properly codified since 1348, was by this time a mass of confusion and contradictions. Against all these difficulties the two sovereigns fought with the boldest promptitude and, on the whole, with conspicuous success. At the end of their long reign, they had conquered the last remaining vestige of Moorish sovereignty in the Peninsula, and had brought the too independent nobles to heel. With the help of Cardinal Ximenes, one of the greatest European churchmen of that age, the clergy had been sufficiently reformed to rank among the best, instead of the worst, in Christendom. Civil justice, again, was no longer more corrupt than elsewhere; and the ecclesiastical courts were overshadowed by an enormously more powerful—one might almost say, a new—Inquisition. Spain was now the most efficient Totalitarian State in Europe, or in the world.

Though both sovereigns prided themselves upon their orthodoxy, yet in face of the papacy they stoutly maintained that comparatively independent attitude which had long been characteristic of kings and nobles in the Peninsula, on all matters except the most definite questions of dogma. But here, in the Inquisition, was a matter where papal and royal interests coincided in the main. When once Ferdinand and Isabella had established it, Royalty and Papacy formed an alliance which, despite all domestic friction on matters of detail, was invincible. From this time forward "no Church could be more arrogantly national than the Spanish, fenced round as it was with exemptions, royal, episcopal, monastic. But none was ever more Catholic. It bred neither heresy nor schism."[4]

The most serious problem was that of the *Conversos*, who filled many of the most important posts at the court. Friars and other orthodox preachers had long conducted a fierce campaign against this state of things; and naturally it was among the first to engage royal attention. The Pope, Sixtus IV, had already hoped that the Inquisition would be introduced; and in 1478 the sovereigns procured a bull from him to that effect. One important point upon which he must have hesitated was that here, in Spain, the sovereigns insisted upon earmarking all confiscated property for the crown; whereas in Italy it had gone to the popes and Inquisitors, and elsewhere had been divided in varying proportions. Also, in contrast with all other countries, the Spanish Inquisitors were to be appointed and removed not by Rome but by the crown: a concession which Sixtus afterwards repented. The Spanish crown, thus provided with an immensely powerful partner upon whose support it could nearly always count, while the Concordat with the Pope might be evaded or violated at the will of Higher Statecraft, became as nearly absolute as was possible at that time and in that state of European society.

Otherwise, there is little in the Spanish Inquisition which we have not already seen elsewhere, except that at almost all points it exaggerated upon its predecessors. Here, even more than in other countries, there was the terrible temptation that Inquisitors and their officials might enrich themselves, almost

to any extent, by stretching every point for the conviction of a
wealthy suspect, or by accepting bribes for his release. Again,
the enormous extension of this machinery over so large a
kingdom created a vast bureaucratic network in which even the
lowest officials were untouchable not only by civil magistrates
but even by the most exalted prelates, and therefore terribly
irresponsible in that age of comparatively lax commercial and
judicial morality. Again, the ubiquity of these officials, and the
strictness with which Spanish Inquisitors could now enforce
regulations which must often be ignored or modified by their
brethren in countries of greater social and political liberty, gave
intolerable force to one of the worst Inquisitional vices, the
encouragement of delation (i.e., statutory tale-bearing) or even
the enforcement of it by torture.* No man was safe from his
neighbours, his servants, or even his children. It was not only
that an enemy might take advantage of this secret tribunal, but
an ordinary well-wisher, or even a true friend, might fail under
threats or torments and give incriminating evidence. When it
was decided to ruin Archbishop Talavera, who, like so many
other high officials, had a strain of Jewish blood, Ferdinand
wrote to his ambassador at Rome that the testimony against
him was that of his sisters and kindred and servants. The very
beginning of the accusations against him rested upon a woman
who had been tortured as being a Jewish prophetess, and who
was threatened with further torture unless she would testify to
having seen, in Talavera's palace, things which the Inquisitor
dictated to her. The career of this Inquisitor, Lucero, should
be studied in Lea's first volume on the Spanish Inquisition,
pp. 189–211. It was only by an accident that it became possible
to bring his doings to light in his own day, and thus to compile
a body of written evidence which has survived to the present.
His predecessor at Cordova, about 1500, was prosecuted for
having defrauded the royal treasury by embezzlements which
amounted (apart from such trifles as precious pearls) to some
300,000 maravedis, at a time when six maravedis formed the

* Compare the case of the Dutch Consul at Barcelona in Chapter XXVI.

ordinary wage of a day-labourer. Lucero himself was a criminal
of larger scope: he invented the existence of a vast conspiracy,
supposed to have ramifications throughout Spain, for abolishing
Christianity and replacing it with Judaism. Some of these
conspirators were witches, riding by night on demon goats;
others, named side by side with these, were well-known
ecclesiastics. He primed his prisoners to bear witness to such
stories; and, having convicted one well-known preacher on the
strength of such evidence, he burned in a single batch 107 poor
wretches who were testified as having attended his sermons.
This went on from 1501 to 1507, when a noble of Cordova
complained to the royal secretary that Lucero, and his fellow-
Inquisitors, "were able to defame the whole Kingdom, to
destroy, without God or justice, a great part of it, slaying and
robbing and violating maids and wives, to the great dishonour
of the Christian religion."[5] Yet Ferdinand, who often took real
pains to see justice done even by the Inquisitors, favoured this
villain down to the very end. It can scarcely have failed to
weigh somewhat with him that Lucero was always able to pour
enormous sums into the Treasury; but jealousy for his
Inquisition was probably the main motive. The scandal was
so great that the Supreme Committee, greatly influenced by
Cardinal Ximenes, tried Lucero publicly before a committee
including many royal councillors. After full enquiry these
decided that the supposed plot was fictitious, and that the
"evidence" for it should be expunged from the records. But
little was done to restore the property confiscated, or the houses
pulled down as nests of the "conspirators." He himself, with
some accomplices, was sent in chains to Burgos; yet Ferdinand
still defended him so stoutly that the Supreme Committee
ventured to do no more than dismiss him from the office which
he had disgraced for eight years. He retired to a rich canonry,
which was one of his Inquisitorial earnings, and ended his days
there in peace.

Lucero was, of course, an exceptional criminal; and doubtless
we may set against him others of exceptional piety and zeal for

justice, in so far as even the best natures can resist the ghastly temptations of irresponsibility. There were official visitors who went on rounds of inspection and reported disorders; but the Supreme Committee very rarely punished the offenders themselves, while they steadily defended them from outside punishment. Lea gives a most significant concrete example (I. 528). "There is no reason to suppose that the Barcelona tribunal was worse than any other; and a series of reports of visitations there gives us an insight into the evils inflicted on the people. In 1544 Doctor Alonso Perez sent in a report in consequence of which the Suprema roundly rebuked all the subordinates, except the judge of confiscations. All but two were defamed for improper relations with women; all accepted presents; all made extra and illegal charges; all neglected their duties and most of them quarrelled with each other. . . . Yet the Suprema was too tender of the honour of the Holy Office to dismiss a single one of the peccant officials. It ordered them to be severely reprimanded, a few debts to be paid and presents to be returned, and uttered some vague threats of what it would do if they continued in their evil courses."

In 1482 Sixtus IV issued what Lea characterises rightly as "the most extraordinary bull in the history of the Inquisition; extraordinary because, for the first time, heresy was declared to be, like any other crime, entitled to a fair trial and simple justice!" He complained that the Inquisitors of Aragon had been moved for some time past not by zeal for the Faith but by cupidity; and proceeded to decree amendments of procedure which were to override all conflicting papal decrees and must be followed henceforth under pain of excommunication, or even, if need were, by appeal to the secular arm. These new provisions set aside some of the most important and characteristic points of Inquisitorial procedure. Slaves and unfit witnesses were no longer to be heard against the accused; evidence for the defence must be freely admitted; counsel must be allowed for defence; and any heretic freely acknowledging past guilt under seal of confession to Inquisitor or bishop should be penanced only

secretly and given a certificate to free him from further
molestation for the past. This bull, which would have revolutionised Inquisitorial procedure, had almost certainly been
procured by the *Conversos*, wealthy and able men, who saw a
very profitable speculation in bribery at the fountain-head of all
Church legislation. In any case, Sixtus's own subsequent
behaviour shows how little he was in earnest. To begin with, the
execution of this bull would have introduced some real justice
into Aragon alone; nothing was said about Castile, where
Lucero and others had perpetrated some of the worst iniquities.
Again, the Pope ate his own bold words when the King braved
him to his face. If (said Ferdinand) Sixtus had yielded to the
cunning of the *Conversos*, he himself had no such intention.
Meanwhile he acted as though no bull had ever been published:
thus, of course, practically defying excommunication and doing
what, in a mere common Christian, would have justified the
gravest suspicion of heresy. Sixtus, after five months' delay,
conceded tamely on all the disputed points, and came to an
arrangement by which Ferdinand was permitted to extend his
Castilian Inquisition to Aragon and all his other dominions.
There was no further question of rectifying those crying injustices which had formed the main text of his bull; or of
indemnifying those "faithful Christians . . . tortured and
condemned as heretics, their property confiscated and their
persons relaxed to the secular arm for execution." Those bold
words of Sixtus's own bull were now meaningless, except to
show how far he was sinning against the light: "Pilate and
Herod were made friends together; for before they were at
enmity between themselves."

The natural result of all this was a gradual descent into the
most cynical corruption. "In 1560 the Córtes of Toledo
complained of the prevalence of false witness as a matter so
customary that there were provinces in which it was as abundant
as any other merchandise, and it was openly said that for money
a man could get as many witnesses as he desired. . . . The Jaen
memorial of 1506 speaks of a certain Diego de Algecira, whom

Lucero kept for five years to testify against all whom he desired to destroy, and whom the Inquisitors of Jaen borrowed for the same purpose, besides other adepts of the kind whom they employed and rewarded. When a raid was made on Arjona, the notary Barzena brought with him Luis de Vilches who, by changing his name and garments, testified repeatedly in different characters. One of the petitions of the Córtes of Monzon, in 1512, bears eloquent testimony to the same state of affairs in Catalonia, for it asks that, when a man was burnt through fraudulent testimony, the Inquisitors should not prevent the King from punishing the false witnesses."

To sovereigns who wielded such power as this, and who could count so confidently upon papal support wherever dogmatic religion came into conflict with mere humanitarian considerations, the expulsion of the Jews was almost a logical necessity, sooner or later. It was carried out even more tragically, if only on a far larger scale, than the similar expulsion from England under Edward I. Judaism itself, from its earliest appearance in history, had been marked by exclusiveness, not only religious but to some extent social. As the Law and the Prophets forbade any truce with idolatry, so the Levitical prescriptions as to food and sanitation rendered full neighbourly intercourse difficult. We see this plainly in the earliest allusions of Roman writers; Horace, Juvenal, Tacitus. Exclusiveness naturally breeds exclusion in return; by such action and reaction the gulf is widened; and thus the conservatism of Judaism brought it into conflict with that Church whose exclusiveness and conservatism were partly a heritage from Judaism itself: the enmity which began so early and has lasted so long was, in a very real sense, a civil war. And now, in fifteenth-century Spain, the problem was not only religious and social, but urgently political. Nothing resembling orthodox Judaism could be suffered in this Totalitarian State: the Jew, even more than the Moor, was an alien element. Nothing pleaded for him now but pecuniary profit; princes and nobles had found him a useful money-making machine. The two sovereigns faced this; they hesitated until the conquest of Granada, in 1492, had brought all Spain under their power. The Jews had helped in this; but the victory to which they had contributed rendered their future help less indispensable. They were always unpopular; robberies and massacres, encouraged by the clergy, had been one of the most difficult police problems. Moreover, the work of the Inquisition, now nearly twelve years old, had not only encouraged popular hatred on one side, but stiffened the resistance of those Jews to whom their religion was dearer than their life. Their leaders saw the blow coming, and offered large sums as a ransom. Ferdinand inclined towards acceptance; but Isabella was firm. A decree for complete expulsion was signed on March 30th, though in Barcelona it was not published till May 1st. It gave the whole Jewish population only till July 31st for quitting Spain, under penalty of death for delay or for subsequent return. This meant that their possessions must be sold at knock-down prices, and that in many cases they were unable to collect their debts; moreover, for those who overstayed their time, total confiscation was rigorously enforced. Export of coin or bills of exchange was forbidden; as late as 1498, Spain was still pressing England and Naples to compel emigrants to restore their own possessions illegally exported. When the Jews reached the seaports, they found themselves faced with an export duty of two ducats per head, or the daily wage of more than 120 labourers. In those circumstances these decrees were responsible for one of the most pitiful stories recorded in history. It brought out the mutual helpfulness which even the most orthodox writers of the Middle Ages noted in these Jews: but the roads to the seaports were crowded with processions of indescribable misery. Before starting, all the boys and girls over twelve were married. "There was no Christian who did not pity them; everywhere they were invited to conversion and some were baptized; but very few, for the rabbis encouraged them and made the women and children play on the timbrel . . . most of them had evil fate, robbery and murder by sea and in the lands of their refuge."[6]

Even worse is the story of the Moriscos, or Moors who had accepted the Spanish rule after their conquest by Ferdinand and Isabella. Richelieu, a fairly hardened and "realistic" statesman, characterised this business as the boldest and most barbarous in human annals.[7] Under repeated persecution by the Church, the majority accepted baptism. But the Kings suspected their loyalty; and they did indeed rebel in 1568, under pressure of intolerable penal laws, forbidding their ancestral language and amusements and dress, and even their baths, public or private. The Church had still more reason to doubt their loyalty to a faith which had been imposed upon them at the point of the sword. Charles V had, indeed, sworn to them solemnly that he would neither expel these new subjects nor make forced conversions; but Clement VII (the pope who entertained the project of allowing Henry VIII, for a consideration, to have two wives simultaneously) issued a brief in 1524 absolving Charles from his oath of 1518. "From the province of Valencia, where Moriscos were most numerous and where the Inquisitors proclaimed that all must be converted or banished, we have a letter from an enthusiastic missionary boasting the baptism of 20,000 families." But no serious attempt was made to instruct these converts, or even to provide adequate churches for them: the Venetian envoy wrote in 1526 that, since the priests cared more for taking their money than for teaching them, they either remained Moors at heart or had no religion whatever. Though Edicts of Grace were spasmodically issued, yet still under them the Inquisitorial law of talebearing, even within the same household, was explicitly maintained. Matters grew worse under the growth of that mania for *limpieza*—purity of blood—which finally became a sort of idolatry in Spanish society. Between these two millstones of political and religious persecution, the Moriscos were ground into abject slavery and irreligion. Their leaders, in despair, intrigued with Henry IV of France. Towards the end of the sixteenth century, Philip II was already contemplating wholesale expulsion. One prelate advised him that it would be easier

to appoint special Inquisitors who would so thin them out that
the miserable remnant would give no further trouble. Another
"suggested deportation to Newfoundland, where they would
speedily perish, especially if the precaution were taken of
castrating all the males, old and young."⁸ In 1607 it was
proposed to allow all non-converts to escape to Barbary; but the
Church opposed this as too merciful and too little consonant
with the claims of Catholicism as the one true religion. At last,
in 1609, wholesale expulsion was determined. All Moriscos,
under pain of death, were to start within three days of the
proclamation in their town or village, and make for the port
assigned to them. In some places they were even forbidden to
sell their goods; and, at the best, these hasty sales filled the
bazaar of Valencia with silks, embroideries, gold and silver
laces, going as cheap as the spoils of a plundered city. On ship-
board the refugees were often plundered again, or the women
and children taken for slaves. At Burgos more than thirty
emigrants were hanged for evading the prohibition to carry
money or jewels. In Africa, the Arabs fell upon those who had
managed to reach the shores alive. A trustworthy contemporary reckons the survivors at only one-third of the whole
body. The plunder which fell into the King's hands was
transferred to greedy courtiers, in far more unscrupulous
fashion than that in which Henry VIII had wasted the spoils of
the English monasteries. Yet Archbishop Ribera, the main
author and executioner of this abomination, was formally
beatified by the papacy; so that men may now as lawfully pray
to God in his name as in that of St. Peter or St. Paul.

This, then, was the crowning victory of a despotic State in
partnership with a despotic Church. Not that they worked
always in harmony: far from it. Spain was governed for more
than a century by four sovereigns of first-rate ability; and, when
Philip II died in 1598, royalty still ran on for some time with the
impetus thus gained. In spite of the theoretical concord
between Madrid and Rome, popes often found their position
very difficult. They had to endure from these Most Catholic

Sovereigns encroachments and defiances far more galling than those which had moved the strong popes of the thirteenth century to battle against weaker princes and to claim for themselves the glory of Christ's standard-bearers against Antichrist. But, in this matter of persecution, king and Pope had one mind and one aim; and they did the uncivilised job with civilised thoroughness. Kings and clergy grew more and more despotic at the expense of national prosperity. The population was estimated in 1586 at eight millions; by 1700 it was said to have shrunk to five. The contrast is very likely exaggerated: but it was certainly great. In that time the Inquisition Courts had grown to twenty-two, with an army of 20,000 salaried and privileged satellites. The institution was strong enough to defy the crown, at a pinch, more successfully than any pope; it had all the elastic impalpability of an inveterate abuse. Already, in Professor Diercks's words, it had "utterly ruined and undermined the sense of justice among the population." The *autos de fe* were among the most brilliant of popular festivals, comparable to the bull-fights of to-day. The country had nearly ten thousand monasteries, whereas pre-Reformation England, with a population of at least two-thirds, had not quite two thousand: and their proportion of the national wealth was even more remarkable than their numbers.

CHAPTER XXVI

Spain and Rome

THE repeated expulsion of so many among the most laborious and skilful workers had naturally inflicted a heavy blow upon the State; but the policy which dictated it was even more disastrous for the Church. Traveller after traveller, from the eighteenth century onwards, agrees as to the poverty of the masses and the debasement of religion. The French Dominican, J. B. Labat, who at one time was Pro-Vicar of the Holy Office, lived there in 1705-6 and paints a dark picture of religion and morals. At Cadiz, for instance, "all the monasteries, though very well off, even such as would pass for rich in France, have collectors who run about constantly in every direction." They have money-boxes with a relic or picture of a saint, which they offer first for a kiss and then for a contribution. It is difficult to resist their importunity: and even those who are firm enough to refuse money must still kiss the relic: otherwise "you would be in danger of passing as a heretic; and, if they could find any little thing to add to this supposed contempt, you would be accused to the Inquisition, which is a redoubtable tribunal in Spain." Its behaviour is easy-going with foreign traders, for filthy lucre's sake, but "with Spaniards it is different; they must kiss the relic or pay into the box." [1]

We get a similar impression from Joseph Townsend's *Journey Through Spain*. Here we have an alert and open-minded English parson, fairly grounded in physical science; one of those men who, like Malthus and Gilbert White, have done so much to enable English clergymen and laity to move gradually on together. He spent fourteen months in Spain in 1786-7 and talked with all sorts of people, mostly higher clergy, magistrates and professional men to whom his letters of introduction

recommended him. His brief notes as he passed through France
help us to understand why, three years later, that country was
aflame with revolution; and his story of Spain shows how
naturally the French Revolution enabled violent anticlericalism
to triumph there also for a while, and to abolish the Inquisition.
He deplored that, in so many places, a rich natural soil produced
only the barest livelihood, through the selfishness of the land-
lords and the throttling State regulations, with consequent
discouragement of the peasantry. All the towns swarmed with
beggars who lived on the Church doles. Only a small fraction
of the people could read or write; and, even among the highest,
there was little of modern education. "I have observed in
general that the physicians with whom I have had occasion to
converse are disciples of their favourite doctor Piquier, who
denied, or at least doubted of, the circulation of the blood. . . .
In their medical classes they had no dissections, no experiments
in chemistry, and for botany they were unacquainted with
Linnæus . . . some of the noble families agree with a physician
by the year, paying him annually fourscore reals, that is, sixteen
shillings, for his attendance upon them and on their families.
. . . Of one thing, which in Spain is required from chirurgeons
and physicians, I have never been able to find any who could
give me a satisfactory account. Before they enter into their
profession, they are obliged to swear that they will defend the
Immaculate Conception of the Blessed Virgin. This requisition
is the more extraordinary, because that point is not universally
agreed upon, even between Catholics themselves; yet many
centuries may pass before the medical tribe will be freed from
this unreasonable imposition. To give due weight to the sanction of an oath, every country should purge away those which
are become obsolete, but more especially such as are universally
regarded as absurd." The Immaculate Conception, it may be
noted, was stoutly denied by St. Bernard and, even among the
Schoolmen, by St. Thomas Aquinas and the Dominicans. In
1570, after all those generations of very violent disputation,
Pius V forbade discussions from the pulpit in the interests of

peace. Finally, Pius IX, of his own authority, decided in 1854 that the doctrine was a truth contained in the original teaching of the Apostles, and therefore an article of divine faith.

Townsend notes that this ignorance is accompanied by a low general standard of morals, especially among the clergy. Though the Inquisition was by that time comparatively dormant, and his distinguished clerical friends were free to jest with him about it, yet in the more civilised cities, such as Barcelona, men deplored its existence in private talk, while they dared not speak openly. It was still maintained, in great part at least, from confiscations, though Charles V in 1518 had recognised the vice of this system and the Cortes had frequently protested against it. Its methods were still medieval: "No tribunal has such advantages in tracing out the truth, nor can any other investigate a dark transaction with such a certainty of success as this court. Unfettered by forms, and not limited for time, they are at liberty to bring whom they please before them, to take them from their beds in the middle of the night, to examine them by surprise, to terrify their imaginations, to torment their bodies, to stretch them on the rack, to cross-examine them at distant periods."[2] Yet there were still numbers of concealed Muslims and Jews, "the former among the mountains, the latter in all great cities. Their principal disguise is more than common zeal in external conformity to all the precepts of the Church; and the most apparently bigoted, not only of the clergy, but of the Inquisitors themselves, are by some persons suspected to be Jews." Yet such was the secrecy of Inquisitorial procedure, and its relentless vengeance upon those who came seriously into conflict with it, that even such a man as the Dutch Consul at Barcelona, having been imprisoned in the distant past for not having denounced a boy who in his presence destroyed an image of the Virgin Mary, "had never been prevailed upon, in all those thirty-five years, to give any account of his confinement." The Dominican cloister there was painted with the names, offences and pains of more than five hundred heretics of both sexes, dating from

1489 to 1726. "Under each inscription there is a portrait of the heretic, some half, others more than three parts devoured by devils."* Yet, wherever he went, Townsend found lawlessness, corruption in the law-courts, brigandage and vice. His instructions to travellers on the very first page tell their own tale. "To travel commodiously in Spain, a man should have a good constitution, two good servants, letters of credit for the principal cities, and a proper introduction to the best families." One servant should be a good cook. The traveller should buy three strong mules for the necessary bedding and culinary implements. "Each of the servants should have a gun slung by the side of his mule." Townsend himself took his chance and travelled "as an œconomist"; and we sometimes get very lively pictures of his consequent risks and sufferings.

Thus the startling rapidity with which Spanish society decayed after about 1600, in spite of the natural qualities of the population, has become a commonplace of history. If Buckle's strong words in 1861 seem exaggerated in favour of his anti-religious thesis, we may turn to the German Professor Diercks in 1896, or to David Hannay in 1917, or to Rafael Shaw in 1910. All agree on the main points. Especially fatal was Philip II's edict of about 1570, forbidding study at foreign universities for fear of Protestant infection, while the universities at home were strangled by the Inquisition which rendered practically impossible any real study of medicine, natural sciences, philosophy, or the humanities in their deeper sense. The action of the Inquisition upon pure literature may be gauged by two articles of surpassing interest from Sir Sidney Lee, in *The Times* for April 10th and 11th, 1922. A Second Folio of Shakespeare's plays (1632) has been preserved in the library of the English College at Valladolid, where St. Thomas More's grandson Henry was once a student. Before any book could be admitted to a Spanish library, public or private, it had to pass the Inquisitor, who (quite apart from that *Index Expurgatorius*

* For fuller details from Townsend, see Appendix. The drawing here reproduced on page 310 was made on the spot and forms the frontispiece to his third volume.

which still exists to-day, forbidding Roman Catholics to read Montaigne's *Essais*, for instance, and Taine's *History of English Literature* and Mill's *Political Economy*) had *carte blanche* to prohibit or to mutilate it. His dealings with this second Folio (writes Lee) "lends small support to the claim of some Roman Catholic writers to identify Shakespeare's religion with their own." Sanchez, the Inquisitorial censor in this case, set out "to delete words and passages which offend either against morality or Catholic doctrine." "Especially does he try to protect Pope, priests, monks and nuns from damaging insinuations. . . . Only a single play does he wholly condemn, and that on moral rather than on doctrinal grounds." *Measure for Measure* is torn out bodily. So, again, the censor blacks out *All's Well*, II, ii. 28, "as the nun's lips to the friar's mouth," and mutilates sadly the false miracle in *I. Henry VI*. Naturally, however, he is most pitiless to *Henry VIII*, Shakespearian or pseudo-Shakespearian. All praises of Cranmer are expunged, especially such epithets as *virtuous, good, honest*. The praise of Elizabeth, as might be anticipated, is frankly intolerable, and it is so mutilated as to make nonsense of the page.*

In general, the Inquisition was far less censorious of morality than of doctrine. Sir Sidney Lee points out in his article how the novel of *Celestina*, full of gross improprieties, ran through numberless editions from 1500 to 1640, when it was at last put upon the Index. About that time the Inquisition was at the height of its power; yet the original author of *Don Juan*, Tirso de Molina, was not only a cleric but was sometimes employed as Inquisitorial censor.

Comparatively little was done on the positive side to make up for the negative working of this censorship system. Grammar schools were few, and busied with little else than superficial preparation for the priesthood. Among the monks and priests themselves there were many who could not read or write.

---

* It was in this very year 1632 that James Howell wrote to Lord Mohun: "The very name of the Inquisition is terrible all the world over, and the King of Spain himself, with the rest of his grandees, tremble at it." (*Epistolæ Ho-Elianæ*, Vol. I, sect. 5, XLIV.)

Elementary schools were almost non-existent even in 1800. The revolutionaries of 1834 and 1855, who suppressed monasteries wholesale, attempted a real educational system; yet in 1896 only about thirty per cent of the population could read and write. In 1910 not even the school law of 1857, far less stringent than that of other countries, had yet been implemented; it was calculated that, at the then rate of progress, it would take 150 years to fulfil its provisions. In consequence, there were still some 12,000,000 illiterates in Spain. As for the Universities, Diercks points out that the best books in their curriculum are either translations from, or heavily indebted to, foreign authors; and that "the Spaniards of to-day are still living mainly upon memories of their once mighty past."[3] But the most significant words of all are those which Montalembert wrote in 1855, contrasting the evolution of England with that of Spain for the past three centuries. True, he was a liberal in politics, his mother was Scotch, and he was under the spell of Gladstone's personal influence. Yet here, as everywhere, he wrote as a fervent Catholic above all else; and, if he did exaggerate in our favour, yet he had no initial temptation to think ill of Spain. But his travels there had filled him with disgust at the debasement even of that religion on which the Spaniard most prided himself. In 1843 he wrote: "What a contrast the Irish priests present with the sad downfall of Catholic ideas and Catholic institutions in Spain and Portugal, which I lately visited on my way from Madeira to France!"[4] He seemed (he said) to see clearly that this Spanish failure "establishes the intrinsic superiority" of a liberal political régime. "Let us compare England and Spain as they were at the end of the Middle Ages and before the Reformation: the former under Henry VII and the latter under Charles V; then let us see what has become of them. In 1510 England, exhausted by the Wars of the Roses, stripped of all her French possessions, not yet possessing Scotland, without Colonies and almost without a fleet, scarcely counted among the Great Powers of Europe. The Spain of 1510, freed from the Moorish yoke after seven centuries of struggle unparalleled in history, welded now into one nation by Ferdinand and Isabella, mistress of a new world through Columbus, mistress of the Low Countries and half of Italy and all Northern Africa, stood head and shoulders above all other Christian kingdoms. Ximenes governed her, St. Theresa was soon to be born of her, Gonzalo of Cordova was fighting for her. She was on the brink of a universal empire. Then, three centuries later, where did these two kingdoms stand? The England of 1800, despite her revolutions, her civil wars and religious wars, and her formidable struggle against the French Revolution, was disputing with France the first place in world affairs. She had no longer any rival on the sea; she was queen of commerce and industry. She had one foot in Gibraltar and another in Malta; she had founded one empire in India, and another in America which will perhaps eclipse her some day; she has gone on from strength to strength. She has produced, in almost every realm of thought, men of genius who have no superiors; and, finally, like Athens and Rome in their palmiest days, she is governed, generation after generation, by men in whom civic greatness is crowned with the prestige of inconquerable eloquence. But take the Spain of 1800. In spite of the virtues of her heroic population, so sober and patient and disinterested and pious, so superior on every side to the English race, this Spain, though preserved by her religious unity from one abundant source of discord and evil, no longer counts in Europe! She has lost everything—political institutions, guarantees of civic life, wealth, credit, influence, navy, army, commerce, industry, science and literature—in all these she is wanting. She has fallen from gulf to gulf, from despot to despot, from favourite to favourite. The two [contrasted] names of Pitt and Godoy sum up the destinies and the differences of these two great Christian nations at the opening of the nineteenth century. On one side life, and life in its most fruitful splendour; on the other, death, and what death! How can we explain such a difference? The Protestants, and all that crowd which looks upon Luther's reformation as

an era of progress, have a ready-made answer: 'It is Protestantism which has made England's greatness, and Catholicism
which has made Spain's decay.' For every Catholic worthy of
his name, that explanation is a blasphemy. But yet we must
manage to explain so striking a contrast. And how shall we
succeed, unless we recognise that political liberty alone has been
able to give this prodigious impetus to England? And that, in
Spain, despotism has infected, has confiscated, has annihilated
the most precious gifts that God has ever lavished on a nation
here below?"

Montalembert goes on to emphasise the liberties which Spain
enjoyed under Catholic princes in the Middle Ages, and the
courage and patience with which she finally conquered the
Moors, "until the fatal omnipotence and the stupid egoism of
her kings had condemned her to sink slowly into nothingness."
He recommends his readers to study for themselves the debasement of Spanish religion in the seventeenth and eighteenth
centuries, or to go and observe it on the spot in this year 1855.
And he concludes: "Fathom the lamentable decadence of
Catholicism in this country where the system of universal
compulsion has so long triumphed; compare it with what the
Church is doing and can yet do in countries where she has been
compelled to struggle for existence, under shelter of political
or intellectual liberty, in England and Belgium and France;
and then give your judgment!"[5] It was this, together with the
horror of judicial murder, which impelled him elsewhere to
confess that the Inquisition is the greatest of stumbling-blocks
in the path of the Catholic apologist. It destroyed the very
notion of toleration on either side, clerical or anticlerical.[6] As
lately as 1927, Carmen Alvarez Padin was sentenced at Segovia
to imprisonment "for two years, four months and a day" for
having said in public: "the Virgin Mary had other children
after the birth of Jesus." Here, of course, she was relying upon
the face-implication of such texts as of Luke ii. 7, and Galatians
i. 19. The Evangelical Alliance instructed a Spanish lawyer to
defend her appeal to the Appeal Court; but the sentence was

confirmed and she was brought to Segovia prison in July. At her daughter's motion, a petition was presented to General Primo de Rivera in the name of the Evangelical women of Spain. Hopes were vainly entertained for a pardon on the Queen's birthday; it was felt that the sovereign's English birth held out the most favourable chances.* Again hopes were vainly fixed upon the King's birthday (May 17th). At last, on July 17th, the King proclaimed, after due consultation with his Ministerial Council: "Taking into account the favourable report given by the Court which pronounced the sentence. . . . I commute for banishment the rest of the punishment which is not complied with by Carmen Padin."[7]

Rafael Shaw, in 1910, found the Virgin Mary taking Christ's place in the Trinity: folk say as they go to bed: "With God I lie down, with God I arise, with the Virgin Mary and the Holy Ghost." Large numbers of the clergy were notoriously concubinary.† A decent peasant would express regret that he did not understand the language of the Mass, and knew not why he was to cross himself at certain points. During the typhus epidemic in Madrid (1909), "it seems to be a fact that no assistance was volunteered by any Religious House." But what contributed most to clerical unpopularity was the constant interference in politics, with the natural (though not, of course, excusable) result that Liberalism was so often driven into the arms of the impossible extremist. If Spain (wrote Mr. Shaw, p. 311) is ever to be peaceful and prosperous, "first and foremost the Church should be confined to its spiritual functions, and restrained from active interference in politics, education, and

* Compare Rafael Shaw's report of clerical dislike for the King's marriage, and of the Franciscan friar who said to him: "She will do untold harm by trying to introduce her English ideas about the education of women. The women of Spain have quite as much education as is good for them. More would only do them harm." (*Spain from Within*—1910—p. 120.)

† The late Dr. Hastings Rashdall paid a long visit to Spain some fifteen years ago in order to gather fresh information for the second edition of his *Universities of Europe in the Middle Ages*. He found it spoken of on all hands, as a notorious fact, that in the ordinary parish priest concubinage is almost taken for granted. This had been so for more than five centuries: see especially the orthodox witnesses quoted in H. C. Lea, *Sacerdotal Celibacy*, II, 175 ff.

business. In a circular issued by the Bishop of Madrid in December, 1909, on the duties of Catholics in the elections, it is laid down that the Catholic voter must not vote for a Liberal as against a Catholic, and that a Liberal is, *inter alia*, 'one who

Barcelona in the Convent of the Dominicans.

Oliva Boa. Trabajador, haretico, condenadoen Persona. 17 de Octobr de 1566.

Inquisitorial Mercy.

BARCELONA DEVIL AND HERETIC
For full description see p. 325

refuses adhesion to the propositions and doctrines laid down by the Apostolic See, *principally in reference to the relations of the Church to the State.*' [Italics mine.] The attitude of Rome to what it calls 'liberalism' is so well known that there is no need to dilate upon it here. It is quite certain that unless and until the Church can be excluded from intervention in the

State, no progress will be possible. The struggle will, no doubt, be severe, for Spain is now the last stronghold of the Roman Church; but once the democracy can make its voice effectively heard, the end will not be doubtful."

In Rome itself, and the Papal States, the Inquisition was so much less prominent than in Spain that modern writers sometimes treat it as practically non-existent, and apologists even cite this in proof of papal tolerance and humanity. Shorthouse, in his *John Inglesant*, fell into this as into other historical traps; he made his Cardinal Rinuccini say: "If once they commenced to burn in Rome, they would not know where to stop." Upon this Lord Acton commented: "An account of Catholicism which assumes that, in the middle of the seventeenth century, Rome had not commenced to burn, is an account which studiously avoids the real and tragic issues of the time. The part of Hamlet is omitted, by desire. For, when Rinuccini spoke, the fires of the Roman Inquisition were, indeed, extinct, but had been extinguished in his lifetime, under the preceding pontificate, having burnt for nearly a century. Familiar instances must have been remembered by his hearers; and they had read, in the most famous theological treatise of the last generation, by what gradation of torments a Protestant ought to die. They knew that whoever obstructed the execution of that law forfeited his life; that the murder of a heretic was not only permitted but rewarded; that it was a virtuous deed to slaughter Protestant men and women, until they were all exterminated. To keep these abominations out of sight is the same offence as to describe the Revolution without the guillotine. The reader knows no more than old Caspar what it was all about. There was no mystery about these practices, no scruple, and no concealment. Although never repudiated, and although retrospectively sanctioned by the Syllabus, they fell into desuetude under pressure from France and from Protestant Europe. But they were defended, more or less boldly, down to the peace of Westphalia (1648). The most famous Jesuits countenanced them, and were bound to countenance them, for the papacy had, by a series of books approved and of acts done, identified itself with the system, and the Jesuits were identified with the cause of the papacy."

The truth is that Paul IV (1555–59) was dissatisfied with the small results which came from the comparatively mild persecution of his predecessors; he therefore reorganised and reinforced the tribunal with a severity which scandalised fairminded folk even among the orthodox. The result was that, at his death, the populace sacked the building of the Holy Office and destroyed the records. Since, again, the Holy Office at Rome refuses, even in our own day and to a scholar of such literary distinction and Catholic orthodoxy as Professor L. Pastor, all access to its intimate records, we are left in the dark as to actual statistics.[8] But one thing is plain, that the papal custom of granting pardons for money to rich folk who were attacked by the Spanish Inquisition bred finally, as might be expected, troubles in the Papal States themselves. At Ancona, in 1555, there was a "clean-up" of *marranos*, or Jews who had professed conversion. But the papal commissioner allowed himself to be bribed, did nothing, and ran away. Another more efficient commissioner was sent next year, and twelve *marranos* (or, by other accounts, twenty-four) were burned; forty-two others paid heavy fines and were only sent to the galleys.

But all this, though more severe than the French practice of that day, was certainly far less so than that of Spain. Father Labat's *Travels* show this plainly enough. He was himself by this time Pro-Vicar of the Holy Office; yet he writes with the most heretical levity concerning the four canonisations which took place at Rome under his eyes in 1712. It must be borne in mind that it is an essential of Roman Catholic faith to believe in the Pope's infallibility when he formally adds any name to the list of Saints. At the head of these four canonisations of 1712 was Pope Pius V, a great champion of the Inquisition, who by excommunicating Elizabeth had made it the moral duty of every Roman Catholic in England to rebel; a man who (in

Lord Acton's words) "held that it was sound Catholic doctrine that any man may stab a heretic condemned by Rome." Labat, though Pius was of his own Dominican Order, wrote: "It seems that the first of these four Saints, being a Pope, thoroughly deserved that his successor should bear the costs of the canonisation, and perform it without fee. This seemed all the more reasonable since the Roman Court need not fear having such an expense often thrown upon it, considering that for many centuries the Popes have contented themselves with opening Heaven's gates to other men; and if (as charity compels us to believe) they press in themselves, they do this without ceremony and without public advertisement. . . . So we were obliged either to leave our fellow-Dominican in the class of mere *Beati*, or to pay his canonisation-bill." The necessary money was collected with difficulty, together with "a little more which defrayed the expenses of the fireworks and many other things testifying to the joy and interest which we took in that celebration. . . . But it costs heavily in money to be declared Saint. Here we have an expenditure of 40,000 Roman crowns for putting four persons into the catalogue of those who enjoy that glory! This is exorbitant; and it justifies the belief that all the merits in the world would not bring a man in without money."*

Father Labat could write like this because the changing world had already begun to render the Inquisition ridiculous. The princes of different Italian States treated it more and more as an anachronism. Napoleon abolished it throughout Italy in 1808; but Pius VII restored it on Napoleon's fall; and it was active in Tuscany and the Papal States until the lifetime of living men. It still exists under the title of Holy Office; and though the 1917 *Code of Canon Law* has at last abolished corporal penalties for

---

* Henry VII worked hard to procure the canonisation of Henry VI, and built the magnificent chapel at Westminster for that saint's relics as well as for his own tomb. According to the contemporary chronicler Hall, himself educated on Henry's foundation at Eton, the fatal barrier lay in the exorbitant fees demanded at Rome. It has been reported that the canonisation of More and Fisher in 1936 cost £17,000: it would be interesting if an exact statement of accounts could be published.

questions of faith, yet the principle has never been abandoned. In the present century two separate professors of distinction in Rome, with Papal encouragement, have taught that the Pope possesses the *right* (as apart from *expediency* or *present power*) of punishing all baptized Christians (Protestants included) for pertinacious nonconformity, either in goods or in body. And, since the *Code of Canon Law* is the Pope's own creation and may be altered by any succeeding Pope with a single stroke of the pen, therefore Roman authority reposes still upon this principle which we have traced all down the Middle Ages. Thus, if any State ever became again a hundred per cent Catholic, it is difficult to see how it could avoid not merely the possibility, but even the moral compulsion, of reintroducing the principles, if not the whole methods, of the medieval Inquisition.

EPILOGUE

THE foregoing chapters may explain why some of the greatest Roman Catholic writers have judged the Inquisition as severely as any reasonable Protestant. We have seen how Cardinal Richelieu stigmatised the expulsion of the Moriscos as *"le plus hardi et le plus barbare conseil dont l'histoire de tous les siècles précédents fasse mention."* Montalembert, the enthusiastic champion of liberal Catholicism, confessed to an English public: "I grant indeed that the Inquisition in Spain destroyed Protestantism in its germ; but I defy anyone to prove that it has not given it throughout Europe the support of public opinion and the sympathies of outraged humanity. It has created in both worlds inexhaustible nourishment for impiety, and for the hatred and discredit of Catholicism."[1] Lord Acton, most learned and politically-minded of all English-speaking Catholics, repeatedly expressed himself in still stronger terms. He wrote to Mary Gladstone: "The principal obstacle on the way to Rome [is] the moral obstacle. The moral obstacle, to put it compendiously, is the Inquisition. The Inquisition is peculiarly the weapon and peculiarly the work of the Popes. . . . No other institution, no doctrine, no ceremony is so distinctly the individual creation of the papacy, except the Dispensing Power. It is the principal thing with which the papacy is identified, and by which it must be judged. The principle of the Inquisition is the Pope's sovereign power over life and death. Whosoever disobeys him should be tried and tortured and burnt. If that cannot be done, formalities may be dispensed with, and the culprit may be killed like an outlaw. That is to say, the principle of the Inquisition is murderous, and a man's opinion of the papacy is regulated and determined by his opinion about religious assassination."[2] And again, to W. E. Gladstone: "There is much to deduct from the praise of the

315

Church in protecting marriage, abolishing slavery and human sacrifice, preventing war and helping the poor. No deduction can be made from her evil-doing towards unbelievers, heretics, savages and witches. Here her responsibility is more undivided, her initiative and achievement more complete. . . . It was the negation not only of religious liberty, which is the mainspring of civil, but equally of civil liberty, because a government armed with the machinery of the Inquisition is necessarily absolute."[3]

Though we must grant that Montalembert was, above all things, a great orator, yet we must insist, on the other side, that Acton was an historian trained in the most scientific school, and a man of most exceptional learning. If he wrote so strongly, it was because he was convinced of the historian's duty to judge between conflicting claims; he had as little sympathy with the trimmer in literature as in politics. An apologist has recently pleaded, in face of criticism upon the eschatology of St. Thomas Aquinas: "I think the reason must be that many think in their hearts that the Middle Ages must have been cruel and superstitious and quite inferior to ourselves in thought and conduct, and so they seize upon this text without reflection."[4] But surely this is putting the cart before the horse! It is because modern readers find their ancestors unquestionably doing and saying things that shock us now, that they condemn these men, judging not *a priori* but *a posteriori*. We must not, of course, measure the men apart from the society of their own age; but neither can we separate the society from the men who composed it. St. Louis was no barbarian, far from it; yet he was capable of giving very barbarous advice to his courtiers about religious discussion. Herein he followed the doctrines of his Church; we must here look upon him less as legislator than as mouthpiece. Yet, on the other hand, if that Church was occasionally capable of such barbarous teaching, this was because it had absorbed, and only partly civilised, millions of separate semi-barbarians. Where wrong exists, the root must be sought either in the individual or in his society, or in both.

For, if the story of the Inquisition reads sometimes like a tale

from a madhouse, we must remember that men do not act thus
without some cause. In its own day, apologists laid overwhelming stress on the religious side. To the Spaniard, these
bonfires were among the greatest of popular festivals because
they were Acts of Faith—*Autos de Fe*. But it is seldom that the
modern apologist emphasises that side; few could be found in
this twentieth century to echo heartily those words of the Jesuit
Civiltà Cattolica which, in 1853, extolled the Inquisition as "a
sublime spectacle of social perfection." Instinctively, defenders
appeal nowadays to our social feelings. They admit and regret
the cruelties; they admit even gross and almost fundamental
blunders; but they palliate these as natural incidents in a
righteous Armageddon. Europe, they argue, was sinking into
a slough of social filth, and one cannot purge Augean stables
with clean hands: and thus the Inquisitors, even at their worst,
were saviours of society.

Those of us who most strongly repudiate this plea in its
totality are therefore most bound in duty to consider what
truth there may be at the bottom of it. Intolerance is our
enemy; but the first condition for getting the better of an enemy
is to understand him. In all ages, men have sometimes rushed
in masses upon each other, either in blind panic or under the
settled conviction that their own party is the only social safeguard from things that are worse than war. Yet to condemn
such movements off-hand and absolutely is to share the very
sin of unreason which we attribute to them. Let us ask, then,
what are the symptoms which made so many men believe in the
Middle Ages, and some even to-day, that the pitiless surgery of
the Inquisition was necessary? Why was independent thought
so often treated as an unforgivable crime? Was it not, in one
word, mainly because crudity or unthinking levity too often
debased the currency of serious thought, and then the innocent
suffered, as they constantly must, for the guilty?

In a brilliant French comedy, *Le Voyage de Monsieur
Perrichon*, a candid young man is shocked to find himself
suddenly faced with a piece of mean ingratitude. His cynical

friend is rather amused at all this fuss: what, after all, is *ingratitude*? "It is a variety of pride. As an amiable philosopher has said, 'ingratitude is the independence of the heart'; and this M. Perrichon is the most independent carriage-builder among all the carriage-builders of France."

From that angle, we see at once that independence is not, in itself, necessarily a virtue: it is not a thing to be proud of without further qualification. It may, in fact, be simply one of the baser forms of selfishness; it may come from the grossest over-estimate of our own individual value, and under-estimate of the claims which society has upon us. Yet every psychologist knows that this desire for the assertion of one's own individuality often attracts and dominates a man as completely as money, or wine, or women, or ambition. Indeed, the fiercest lust to go on our own way is very commonly bound up with the lust of sway over others. Thus a boasted independence of mind often becomes independence of heart; one of the most fatally disruptive forces of society.

Man is not, and cannot without absurdity even aspire to be, a wholly independent creature. His perfection consists in a right proportion between dependence and independence: between collectivism and individualism. However ferociously he may assert his own individuality, 99 per cent of the things he thinks and says and does will be the same as what other sane people think and say and do. In proportion as we can manage to march with our fellows in the main, we shall be heard, and be probably worth hearing, whenever conscience compels us to preach something different. Eccentricity, posing as originality to itself and to the public, is one of the worst anti-social forces. Not, of course, that there is any clear line of demarcation between true and false independence. Yet here, as elsewhere, man's superiority over the brute beasts resides in his struggle to draw the difficult distinction more and more clearly and justly. As far as possible, we must seek for practical tests. Of these there is one, applied constantly and instructively in business, and even by children among themselves, which is now finding its way into politics: the principle of the forfeited deposit.

Macaulay noted long ago that two children dividing an apple will sometimes adopt a test which no grown-up man has ever bettered: "You cut, and I choose: or *vice versa.*" The essence of this is, that it calls forth the fullest sense of responsibility. That sense of personal responsibility is what every self-appointed Saviour of Society needs to have brought home to him. We do it nowadays in parliamentary elections, to the full satisfaction of 999 persons out of 1,000: the candidate who cannot get a reasonable proportion of the votes ought to have known that his claims on society were not considerable enough; he must forfeit his deposit. Is it not equally just (as apart from mere expediency, to which we may come later) that every candidate for a public hearing on the weightiest subjects should either show a full sense of responsibility or be liable to forfeit? Is not this an obvious and civilised way of reminding him that he is a social animal, owing in all probability immensely more to his human environment than that environment, which he now claims to control, is ever likely to owe him? Irresponsible talk is a debasement of the moral currency, all the more mischievous in proportion to its colourable truth. Men appreciate obvious banter and good-humoured paradox; but the sham independence of thought which claims serious freedom from social control is no more virtuous in the thinker, or profitable to society, than M. Perrichon's "independence of the heart."

In fact, such extreme claims to independence are suicidal; they are, essentially, confessions of their own unreality. There is general agreement that actual wrongdoing must in strict justice be punished, though expediency may prompt us to condone it. But we cannot here draw a definite line between words and deeds. Every sincere word is a potential deed; therefore, in so far as a man's words are such as he is not ready to implement in action, he is a mere windbag. To claim absolute immunity for words is, by the clearest implication, to plead their unreality. Therefore the men who declare war on existing

society or on that State from which they are most willing to
accept all that they can get, have in strict justice no appeal
against those who take them at their word.

We must, of course, lay every possible stress upon that
limitation "in justice." For, as a matter of expediency, there
may be the strongest reasons for giving this potential war-
monger, this man who preaches war against his social environment, as much rope as possible. To begin with, in a small
minority of cases, such men do turn out later to be far more in
the right than that majority who would gladly punish their
words. Yet what does such a man's cause lose, in the long run,
by a forfeit such as reasonable fine or imprisonment? So long
as there is no question of capital punishment or life-imprison-
ment—and here all the non-totalitarian states have separated
themselves clearly from the principles of the Inquisition—it
may well be that the man's cause will actually gain by this
conflict with society. The most conspicuous among those who
protested, often with considerable justice, against the strong
current of popular feeling in the Great War, are now increased
in position and influence in proportion as the pacifist reaction
of to-day can discover solid truth in their contentions. The
Conscientious Objectors have now published a co-operative
volume, under the title of *We Did Not Fight*. Their own
descriptions show plainly how little they suffered even at the
time, in comparison with those others who went into the
trenches in order to resist what they regarded as a threat to
democracy. Of the seventeen British subjects who contributed
to that volume, nine are now high enough in the social scale
to be in *Who's Who*, though not all these were there before the
War. One, since the War, has succeeded to his hereditary
peerage; another has risen to the Lords by the ordinary political
ladder; others have become respectively Knight, M.P., Dean of
a Cathedral, and Extra-Mural University Lecturer. Every
one of the seventeen is probably in a better position
now than in 1914: and it may be noted that two, at least,
have modified enormously, since 1914, those very opinions

which brought them most public attention in earlier days.

When we turn to the other end of the scale, and look not at leaders but at rank and file, we see still more clearly the justice (always apart from expediency) of treating words as acts, so long as they are sufficiently public and emphatic. Claimants to originality—men who are tempted to value "independence" by quantity rather than by quality—betray very commonly a childish confusion of thought. It is true that persons of great superiority in thought or word or deed must always, in the nature of the case, find themselves in a small minority; for some time, at least. Upon that basis our pseudo-Independent (as we may call him) attempts to take this as a convertible proposition, arguing that the smallness of his own minority affords a corresponding presumption in favour of its superiority. I have heard this actually maintained even at a public meeting of "advanced" thinkers.[5] As against this, we have only to reflect that congenital idiots are in about as small a minority as those whom the Editor of *Who's Who* finds worthy of record.

Those who unthinkingly push to its extreme limits the claim of immunity for public utterances are, in fact, among the most dangerous enemies of real freedom of thought. They fall into the vulgar error of throwing out the baby with the bath. While claiming to defend intellect against illegitimate exterior control, they do in fact divorce it from inward responsibility. By abandoning self-restraint they tempt—and even to some extent justify—constraint from without. It is the tragedy of the present Spanish situation that we cannot choose either side without supporting, to some extent, men who have either committed, or at least condoned, things which carry Europe back to the horrors of the barbarian invasions. A cause which cannot restrain or eliminate its own wild men, like a mind which cannot control its own impulses or wandering thoughts, has still a long way to go in the path of civilisation. Yet sentimentality and party prejudice frequently swamp all mere common-sense considerations. There is no true Liberalism in the almost hysterical outcry which is often raised in Britain against any punishment calculated to remind "Independents," by fine or prison, of their actual dependence upon society; any punishment which takes the civil-war-monger at his word. We have recently seen a young undergraduate of eighteen sentenced under the Incitement to Disaffection Act. He had suggested to a member of the Royal Air Force that, by deserting Great Britain "on the sly" for Spain or for Russia, he might earn £20 a week; or "the other and possibly better alternative is to keep very silent and to make close friends with those underneath you, so that when you come to the time when we can have revolution, not only you and your bomber can come to help us but your whole squadron"; "us," of course, being the warriors of Soviet Revolution in Great Britain. Though the Act was three years old, this was the first charge made under it; a considerable testimonial to the mildness with which its provisions have been interpreted. But here was a clear case: not merely a matter of what one mischievous simpleton had said and written, but of what was becoming fashionable among the would-be high-brows of his own standing. As his counsel pleaded in his defence: "He is not the first young man to flirt with such advanced political views; and Leeds University is by no means the only University in the country where young men are being turned out with a similar political outlook." Therefore the judge, sentencing him to a year in gaol, said: "You are young, and I wish I could see my way to take a course that would not mean imprisonment for one so young; but it is necessary that there should be a public warning. The law is the same for a student as for anyone else." Yet thoughtless friends of liberty, even among those who are usually reflective and fair, raised a hysterical clamour against this. We were told that "Yorkshire and the country at large was stunned at the harshness of the sentence" (and again, "the savage sentence"), "for sending hot-air letters to an R.A.F. man." Need our party principles really blind us to what all history teaches, that hot air in politics plays the part of fire-damp in a coal-mine? All civilisation reposes on the sanctity of contracts. There is no more mischievous and despicable breach of contract than that of the soldier deserting his post "on the sly" and biting the hand that has fed him. As the receiver is worse than the thief, so is the seducer worse than the deserter, except in so far as we can excuse his morals at the expense of his intellect.

Almost at the same time, a University Professor thought to save his Party, and a Church Minister to please his God, by deliberate incendiarism; that is, by the most primitive form, because the most childishly easy, of physical violence. The Professor pleaded, in his printed *apologia*, that the utilisation of a specially wild and remote corner of Wales as a bombing-range "will shatter the spiritual basis of the Welsh nation." "We have put our lives in the balance against this act of Government iniquity. If you find us guilty, you proclaim the effective end of Christian principles governing the life of Wales." The Minister, again, writes: "We define our Christianity and Nationalism in terms of responsibility, and the measure of our responsibility to this nation of ours is the measure of our responsibility to God, for we believe with Emrys-ap-Iwan, and with all the great theologians of the Church, that God, who made men, ordained nations also, and the destruction of a nation is almost as great a crime as the destruction of the human race itself would be." Both of these men had convinced themselves that their incendiarism was necessary in the interests of pacifism. Ordinarily, it is nationalism which is denounced as one of the most fruitful and dangerous sources of war: but with these two pacifists nationalism is more than a passion, it is a religion. "It was in the fear of God," writes this Minister, "that I went out that night."[6] Moreover, the North Welsh jury refused to convict these two men even in the face of their open confession; and more than one newspaper cried shame upon their final conviction and sentence before an Old Bailey jury. Yet the claim of any tiny fraction of the community not only to thwart the actions of the rest, but also to use godly violence against them, must of necessity provoke the wild men among their opponents to more brutal and hysterical reprisals: "In

the name of the Lord I will destroy them." Not only is what
we commonly call despotism distressingly efficient in action,
but (what is still more distressing) believers in democracy are
sometimes unable even to claim the higher morality for
themselves.

To that extent, therefore, we must make allowance for the
general principle of the Inquisition, though not for its excesses.
In ninety-nine cases out of a hundred, the experience of later
generations suggests that it would have been wiser in the Church
to have made no appeal to force, but only to argument and good
example. Even in the hundredth case, and even when we have
made all allowance for the circumstances of the time, the
peculiar methods of the Inquisition were indefensible. But, in
face of the mistakes committed in every generation, not
excluding this of ours, we must remember that the heretics did
in fact sometimes, apart from mere hostile accusations, invite
violence by their own violent words or deeds. Pierre de Bruys
seems certainly to have preached destruction for crucifixes, and
may quite well, as his enemies asserted, have roasted his meat
at such a bonfire.[7] This it is which may go far to explain, and
even a little way to palliate, the violence of those who roasted
him in his turn. The Totalitarian Church of the Middle Ages,
generation after generation, throve upon the blunders and the
disorganisation of its opponents.

APPENDIX I

Further extracts from Townsend, *Travels in Spain*.

(1) *Vol. I, p.* 120.

At Barcelona, in the convent of the Dominicans, there is one apartment filled entirely with books prohibited by the Inquisition and, in order that no one may be tempted to peruse them, all the vacant spaces are filled with devils cracking human bones, it is to be supposed of heretics. Lest, however, this sight should not suffice to check a prying disposition, they are well secured by lock and key, and no one has access to these without a special licence. In the cloister of the Dominicans there are more than five hundred records of sentences passed on heretics, containing their name, their age, their occupation, their place of abode, the time when they were condemned, and the event; whether the party were burnt in person or in effigy, or whether he recanted and was saved, not from the fire and the faggot, for then he might relapse, but from the flames of hell. Most of these were women. The first date is A.D. 1489, and the last 1726. Under each inscription there is a portrait of the heretic, some half, others more than three parts devoured by devils. I was so much struck with the fantastic forms which the painters had given to their demons and the strange attitudes of the heretics that I could not resist my inclination to copy some of them, when no one was walking in the cloister. Some time after this, sitting with one of the Inquisitors, who did me the honour of a visit, he in a careless manner took up my memorandum book and, as chance would have it, opened precisely on the leaf which contained my drawings: I laughed; he coloured; but not one word escaped from either at the time. Fifteen months after this, when I returned to Barcelona, he smiled and said: "You see that I can keep a secret, and that we are not strangers to principles of honour." During my residence at Barcelona, I had an opportunity of seeing all the courts of the Inquisition assembled in a grand procession to celebrate the feast of S. Pedro Martyr, their patron saint, in the church of St. Catharine of the Dominicans. Happy had it been for Christendom if all their festivals had been as innocent as this! It is, however, universally acknowledged, for the credit of the corps at Barcelona, that all its members are men of worth, and most of them distinguished for humanity. Visiting the churches at all hours, whenever any service was performed, I made a party with some friends to hear a penitential service in the convent of St. Felipe Neri, on Friday evening of April 28. The first part of the Miserere was no sooner ended than the doors were shut, the lights were extinguished and we remained in perfect darkness. At this moment, when the eye could no longer find an object to distract the mind, the attention was awakened by the voice of harmony, for the whole congregation joined in the Miserere, which they sung with pleasing solemnity; at first with soft and plaintive notes—but, having laid bare their backs and prepared them for the scourge, they all began nearly at the same instant to use the discipline, raising their voices and quickening the time, increasing by degrees both in velocity and violence, scourging themselves with greater vehemence as they proceeded, and singing louder and harsher, till at the end of twenty minutes all distinction of sound was lost and the whole ended in one deep groan. Prepared as I had been to expect something terrible, yet this so far surpassed my expectation that my blood ran cold; and one of the company, not remarkable for sensibility of nerves, being thus taken by surprise, burst into tears. This discipline is repeated every Friday in the year, oftener in Lent, and is their daily practice during the holy week. I was not at liberty to ask what advantage they derived, or what benefits they expected to receive from this severity; yet, from the prevalence of vice in Spain, I fear this practice has little if any tendency to reform their morals.

(2) *Vol. III, p.* 333.

On my return to Barcelona, recommended by the minister
to the protection of the governor, feeling myself strong, I
ventured to inquire more freely [than I had before thought
prudent] into the conduct of the Inquisition. In my former
visit I had cultivated friendship with the Inquisitors, yet I had
always approached them with a degree of reverential awe; but
now I questioned them without reserve or fear. The point at
which I laboured was to converse with some who were confined
and, understanding that Mr. Howard had visited their prisons,
I pleaded for the same indulgence. To this request they answered
that I was certainly mistaken; for that no human being, unless
in custody, or himself an officer of the Inquisition, could be
admitted to see the interior of their prisons; but they assured me
in the most solemn manner that the prisoners were not merely
treated with humanity, but enjoyed every possible indulgence.
The apartments in which they are confined are spacious, airy
clean and commodious. They are permitted to send for their
own bed, with books, pen, ink and paper. They have their own
provisions and, if they are poor, they are well fed and comfort-
ably lodged at the expense of the Inquisitors. The alcalde waits
upon them four times a day to receive their orders, and once a
fortnight one of the Inquisitors visits every apartment to see
that all is in good condition and to inquire if the prisoners are
treated with humanity. To provide funds for the expense of this
tribunal they confiscate the goods of all who are condemned.
Neither their superior officers, nor yet their familiars, or lowest
servants and messengers, are amenable before the civil courts,
nor accountable for their crimes and offences to any but their
own tribunal. My friends, the Inquisitors of Barcelona, felt
exceedingly sore about the trial of the beggar at Madrid; and
assured me that the only reason why the King required the
Inquisition to take cognizance of so contemptible a wretch was
out of tenderness to the many ladies of high fashion, whose
names must have appeared, had the prosecution been conducted
in the civil courts. They likewise gave me to understand that as

long as the priesthood should be debarred from marriage, and
confessors continue liable to abuse the confidence reposed in
them, the secrecy, the prudence and, when needful, the severity
of the Inquisition would be the only effectual restraint against
licentiousness and the universal depravation of their morals.*
When a prisoner is discharged, the Inquisitors exact an oath of
secrecy and, should this be violated, the offender would have
reason to repent his rashness; for, taken from his family in the
middle of the night, he might never be released again. The dread
of this imposes silence on all who have been once confined. The
Dutch Consul now at Barcelona, through the long period of five-
and-thirty years, has never been prevailed upon to give any
account of his confinement, and appears to be much agitated
whenever urged to relate in what manner he was treated. His
fellow-sufferer, M. Dalconet, then a boy, turned grey during the
short space of his confinement, and to the day of his death,
although retired to Montpellier, observed the most tenacious
silence on the subject. His sole offence had been destroying a
picture of the Blessed Virgin; and his friend, the Dutch Consul,
being present on that occasion and not having turned accuser,
was considered as a partner in his guilt. For my own part, I am
inclined to think that in proportion as light has been diffused in
Europe, even Inquisitors have learnt humanity. But facts speaking so strongly for themselves, we must continue to lament that
darkness should so far prevail as to leave the least vestige of
Inquisitorial power; for, wherever it exists, it must be liable to
abuse, and clemency must be merely accidental.

* It was in Spain that the frequency of sacerdotal solicitation of women
in the confessional first called for the interference of the Inquisition. It was
intimated by the Archbishop of Granada to Paul IV, who in 1559 published
a bull branding this as an abuse of the Sacrament of Penance which implied
disbelief of the Catholic faith, and therefore rendered the culprit justiciable
by the Inquisition. But this, and the many later bulls, were frustrated by
theological evasions, and especially by the doctrine that absolution given to
the woman by her partner the priest is, though sinful, sacramentally valid.
Lea has analysed 3,775 cases among the Inquisition archives, of which 2,794
were monks or friars and 981 parish priests (*Sacerdotal Celibacy*, II, 294). The
records of the Toledo Inquisition (1575–1610) show this offence sixth on the
list of frequency, with 52 cases. Another of the same district (1648–1794)
gives 68 cases (Lea, *Inq. in Spain*, III, 552–3). This story is told most briefly
and convincingly in Chapter XXX of his *Sacerdotal Celibacy*.

APPENDIX II

Notes

CHAPTER I

¹ For Glaber see Migne, *P.L.*, Vol. 142, pp. 623–698. ²F. Lot. *Fin du monde antique* (1927), 452.

CHAPTER II

¹For far fuller references on this and similar points, see my *Christ, St. Francis, and To-day* (C.U. Press), 26–38. ²Tertullian, *De Spectaculis*, ch. 30. ³W. E. H. Lecky, *Rationalism in Europe*, I, 321. ⁴F-X. Godts, *De Paucitate Salvandorum quid docuerunt Sancti* (Roulers, 1899). The book is of extreme rarity, having been suppressed soon after publication, but there are copies in the British Museum, Bodley's, and the Cambridge University Library. The evidence there given is overwhelming. ⁵See my *Romanism and Truth*, I, 46 and 136*ff*, where I sum up a *Daily Telegraph* discussion of 1929, and reprint the whole of the section from St. Thomas's *Summa Theologiæ*, in the authorised Dominican translation.

CHAPTER III

¹The plate here, from the Dominican convent of Sta Maria Novella at Florence, represents St. Thomas Aquinas with Averroës, Arius and Sabellius under his feet.

There were two main anti-Trinitarian types in early Christian theology. One, which found its fullest expression in Arius, denied the divinity of Christ. He was, it was argued, the best of men, but still a man. This heresy was condemned at the Council of Nicea in 325: Arius and the two bishops who persistently held by his doctrines were banished by the Emperor Constantine. This was followed, however, by a semi-Arian reaction. Constantine recalled Arius. St. Athanasius, his steadfast opponent, was persecuted; and the doctrine was hotly contested for two generations, semi-Arianism having on the whole the ascendancy. Even Pope Liberius, under the influence of fear, communicated with the semi-Arians and subscribed to their technical formula, abandoning that term *homoousios* which was the touchstone of orthodoxy. But at last, in 381, the Council of Constantinople adopted finally the so-called Nicene Creed. Meanwhile an opposite, but equally anti-Trinitarian doctrine had grown up and found its fullest expression in Sabellius (about A.D. 260). He taught that there were not three persons in the Godhead, but three diverse manifestations of the One God. Hence this doctrine was sometimes called *Patripassianism*, since it involved the theory that God the Father hung on the Cross. It is sometimes pleaded in palliation of the lapse of Pope Liberius into heresy that he was persuaded he might otherwise seem to countenance Sabellianism. Sabellius had many followers and considerable influence, though not comparable to that of Arius: the converted barbarian invaders of the Roman Empire were mostly Arians. It is in special reference to those two types of heresy that the so-called Athanasian Creed anathematises those who either "confound the persons" or "divide the substance" of God (*vide* "Athanasian Creed"). [2]*Confessions*, Bk. I, Ch. 8 and 11. [3]Full evidence in the 16th of my *Medieval Studies*, "Infant Perdition in the Middle Ages" (Wessex Press, Taunton). The doctrine which is often saddled upon Calvin was almost universal in the Roman Church until quite modern times.

CHAPTER IV

[1]R. Coggeshall. *Chronicle* (R.S.), 121. [2]See my *Sectarian History*, pp. 18*ff*. [3]The late Dr. Rashdall went to Spain about fifteen years ago to study further in the archives for the second edition of his *Universities of Europe in the Middle Ages*. He told me that Spaniards of all classes seemed practically unanimous in regarding the majority of the parish priests as concubinaries. [4]*Carmina Burana* (ed. Schmëller, 1883), 15. [5]Compare my *St. Francis to Dante*, Ch. XXI. [6]I recount this whole story, with documentary evidence, in *Five Centuries of Religion*, II, 554–5.

CHAPTER V

[1]*Spain from Within* (reprint of articles contributed to *The Spectator* and *The Standard*, 1910). [2]*William of Newburgh*, Bk. I, Ch. 19.

Chapter VI

[1]A. Luchaire, *Inn. III, Croisade des Albigeois* (1905), p. 3.
[2]*William of Newburgh*, Bk. I, Ch. 13. [3]P. 61 of the French
edition (1907), from which I always translate. [4]Fully discussed
in No. 18 of my *Medieval Studies, The Death Penalty for Heresy*,
pp. 9*ff*. [5]*Ibid.*, p. 14. [6]*Essay on Catholic Claims* (1829), 110–111.
[7]A. Lépicier, *De Stabilitate et Progressu Dogmatis* (2nd ed.,
Rome 1910), I, 199; for other quotations see my *Death Penalty
for Heresy*, 62–70.

Chapter VII

[1]The last, and most important, sections of this book, with
Latin and French on opposite pages, has been published by G.
Mollat (Champion, 1926–7, 2 vols.). The complete book was
published in 1886 by Mgr. Douais, afterwards Bishop of
Beauvais. [2]Mollat, I, 6 (introd. to Bk. V).

Chapter VIII

[1]These scattered references, with others similar, may be
found in Douais, *Documents*, II, 191, 249, 253–4, 256, 263, 265,
269, 270, 297; Limborch, II, 3, 233, 240–2, 354, 359. [2]Martene,
Thesaurus, V. 1794. [3]Limborch, II, 377. [4]Douais, *Documents*, I,
LXXVII. [5]*Mon. Germ. Hist.*, XXXII, 31; *From St. Francis to
Danie* (2nd ed.), 274. [6]Douais, *Documents*, I, LXXXI.

Chapter IX

[1]Luchaire, *Inn. III—Albigeois*, 40. [2]I, 135. [3]These citations
will be found in Migne, *P.L.* CCXIV, 82, 904–5; CCXV, 355
(*cf.* 272, 358–9); CCXVI, 291. [4]Vacandard, 82–3. [5]Luchaire, *l.c.*,
31. [6]*Revue des Questions Historiques*, 1866, p. 169. [7]Migne,
P.L., CCXVI, 139. [8]*P.L.*, CCXIII, 566. [9]*P.L.*, CCXVI, 140.
[10]*P.L.*, CCXIII, 569. [11]*Ibid.*, 574. [12]*Ibid.*, 583. [13]*Ibid.*, 586.
[14]*Ibid.*, 609, 611. [15]*Chanson de la Croisade*, l. 3,323; Luchaire,
op. cit., 252. [16]Luchaire, *op. cit.*, 248. [17]*Chanson de la Croisade*,
l. 3,454. [18]*European Civilisation* (ed. E. Eyre), Vol. II.
[19]Vaissete, *Hist. de Languedoc*, Vol. III (1737), p. 283, *a.d.* 1216.
[20]Lea, I. 167. [21]*Ibid.*, 185.

CHAPTER X

[1]Migne, *P.L.*, CCXIII (Vaux-Cernay), 672. Lea, I, 184.
[2]Ménestrel de Reims, §145. [3]Luchaire, *op. cit.*, 247. [4]*European Civilisation* (ed. Eyre), IV, 674

CHAPTER XI

[1]Vacandard, *op. cit.*, 168. [2]See Douais, *Documents*, II, 172, 193, 214. [3]Eymeric's Directoriun (ed. Pegna, 1585), Part II, pp. 654–5. [4]Tanon, 388; Lea, I, 434. [5]Carena, *De Officio S. Inquisitionis*, 1668, p. 344, q. xiv. [6]*Vacandard*, 150–153. [7]J. Andreae, *Comment in Decret. Greg.* lib. V, tit. vii, c. xiii (fol. 31, b. col. 2). [8]*Vacandard*, 220. [9]Fuller evidence in my *Sectarian History*, pp. 103*ff.* [10]Petrus Hieremias (alias Peter of Palermo), *Quadragesimale*, Serm. XX (Lyons, 15—), f. xlii, b.

CHAPTER XII

[1]Alvarus Pelagius, *De Planctu Ecclesiae* (1517), lib. II, c. 77, f. 219, b. [2]Eymeric-Pegna, Pars. II, p. 708; *cf.* Douais, *Documents*, I, XLIV–XLV. [3]Douais, *Documents*, II, 194. [4]Limborch, II, 40. [5]Douais, *Documents*, II, 216. [6]*Ibid.*, 181, 188–9. [7]Tanon, 512.

CHAPTER XIII

[1]For this prison story see Mgr. J. M. Vidal's very valuable *Tribunal de l'Inquisition de Pamiers* (Toulouse, 1906), p. 208, and Douais, *Documents*, II, 304*ff.* Compare Tanon, 360–362 and especially Lea, II, 91*ff.* [2]Lea, II, 95. [3]Eymeric-Pegna, II, 516. [4]Vidal, 161, *note.* [5]B. Hauréau, *Bernard Délicieux*, 91.

CHAPTER XIV

[1]Mr. Christopher Hollis, in *European Civilisation* (ed. Eyre), IV, 692. [2]Tanon, 369–70. [3]*Ibid.*, 379; Vacandard, 185; Lea, I, 428. [4]Vacandard, 176, quoting from Labbe, *Concilia*, viii, 544. [5]Vacandard, 205*ff.*

Chapter XV

[1]*Summa Theologiæ*, 2ᵃ 2ᵃᵉ, q. 39, art, 1, §4. For fuller details, see my *Death Penalty for Heresy*, 17*ff*. [2]*Death Penalty for Heresy*, 19*ff* and 51–7. [3]Acton's *Letters to Mary Gladstone*, 142. [4]Lea, I, 552. [5]*Ibid.*, 553. For money values, see my pamphlet published by the Historical Association on *The Meaning of Moneys in the Middle Ages*.

Chapter XVI

[1]By far the best analysis of this side of More's character (as of many others) is in Professor R. W. Chambers's, *Thomas More* (1935), especially pp. 124, 130–1, 256, 264–5, 354. I may be permitted to refer to my own discussion of his attitude to toleration in Chapter XLVIII of a Social History of England which is now in the Cambridge University Press. [2]The first eighteen lines of this religious poem run as follows in English:

The Noble Lesson

O brethren, listen to a noble lesson
Often ought we to watch and abide in prayer,
For we see that this world is nigh unto ruin;
Very careful should we be to do good works,
For we see this world approach to its end.
Well 1400 years have been wholly accomplished,
Since the hour was written, that we are in the last times;
Little should we covet, for we are at the last end;
Every day do we see the signs come to accomplishment,
In increase of evil and in diminution of good.
These are the perils which Scripture says;
The Gospel recounts them and St. Paul also,
But no man who liveth can know the end,
Therefore should we more fear; for we are not certain
Whether death will take us to-day or to-morrow;
But, when it shall come to the Day of Judgment,
Each shall receive in full payment,
According as he has done evil and according as he has done well.

[3]See my *From St. Francis to Dante*, Ch. XXVI. [4]E. Brown, *Fasciculus*, II, 251. [5]De la Bigne, *Maxima Bibliotheca Patrum*, XXV, 261*ff*. [6]*Ibid.*, 278. [7]*Ibid.*, 281, 295. [8]*Ibid.*, 272. [9]Bk. V, ii, 5 (ed. Mollat, I, 48).

CHAPTER XVII

[1]The Book of the Knight of La Tour-Landry (E. E. T. S., 1868), pp. 62, 75, 78, 83–4, 91, 99, 117, 119, 151. The Knight puts the marriage at Cana before the Disputation with the Doctors in the Temple; and his account of the book of Ruth has scarcely any point of contact with the Bible story. [2]*Anecdotes Historiques d'É. de B.*, ed. Lecoy de la Marche, pp. 299, 307–8. [3]*Bib. Max. Patrum*, XXV, 275, F. and 298, B. [4]P. Limborch, *Hist. Inq.*, Part II, p. 263. [5]*Ibid.*, 367. [6]*Ibid.*, 264, 353. [7]*Bib. Max. Patrum*, XXV, 265, A.

CHAPTER XVIII

[1]P. Limborch, *Hist. Inq.*, Part II, 342, 346. [2]*Ibid.*, 289. [3]*Ibid.*, 264.

CHAPTER XIX

[1]*The Early Dominicans* (C.U. Press, 1937), Chapter III. [2]I give full evidence for this in my monograph on *The Black Death* (Benn's Sixpenny Series), Chapter III. [3]The story of the Spirituals and Fraticelli is well told by Lea; for a version slightly more favourable to the official Church, see A. G. Ferrers Howell's *St. Bernardino of Siena*.

CHAPTER XX

[1]B. Hauréau told it in the *Revue des Deux Mondes* for June 15th, 1868, and at greater length, with illustrative documents, in a book entitled *Bernard Délicieux et l'Inquisition albigeoise* (1877). The late Cardinal Ehrle complained that Hauréau had stretched his imagination too far: but unfortunately he did not go on to substantiate this in detail (*Archiv f. Litt.- und Kirchengesch.*, II, 145). [2]Quoted by Hauréau on p. 203 of the above-mentioned volume. [3]We need hardly wonder, then, that a partisan contemporary notes how the Dominicans, when they got him into their hands, "rent him as dogs rend the beast they have

caught; in such fashion did they tear him with divers afflictions and tortures"(*Archiv f. Litt.- und Kirchengesch.* ⁴G. Mollat, *Les Papes d'Avignon* (1912), pp. 379–80. ⁵Baluze-Mansi, *Miscellanea*, II, 248*ff*.

CHAPTER XXI

¹See his letter in Migne, *P.L.*, CXXX, 37, 57. ²*Archiv f. Litt.- und Kirchengesch.*, IV, 129*ff*. ³Baluze-Mansi, *Miscellanea*, II, 599–610. Fuller extracts in my *Life in the Middle Ages*, I, 235–8. ⁴Printed in full in *Scelta di Curiosità Letterarie inedite o rare* (Bologna, 1864) and translated at considerable length in *Life in the Middle Ages*, IV, 284–298.

CHAPTER XXII

¹Rymer, *Fœdera* (1706), III, 231, "ob reverentiam Sedis Apostolicæ." ²Lea, *Inq. Middle Ages*, III, 318. ³*Dossier de l'Affaire des Templiers*, ed. G. Lizerand, 1923, 180*ff*. ⁴*Ibid.*, 188*ff*.

CHAPTER XXIII

¹Though Mr. Shaw's *Saint Joan* is a fine dramatic success, and his picture of Joan herself is practically true to the records, his long Introduction must be dismissed as childish. The itching for cheap paradox has over-mastered him; and he flounders blindfold among the documents. An excellent translation of her trial, with a clear introduction, has since been published by Dr. W. P. Barrett (Routledge, 1931). ²Professor P. Villari's admirable *Life and Times of Girolamo Savonarola*, with numerous illustrations, has been translated into English and is easily obtainable (Unwin, 1899). ³Baluze, *Vitæ Paparum Aven.* (1st ed.), p. 187, *cf.* 737. ⁴*Hist. de France*, III, ii, 216*ff*. ⁵Nider, *Formicarius*, 1602, 385*ff*; fully translated in *Life in the Middle Ages*, I, 210–213. ⁶Lea, *Inq. Middle Ages*, III, 549.

CHAPTER XXIV

¹This chapter owes much to Mr. H. G. Richardson's valuable article in *The English Historical Review* for January, 1936. ²See R. F. Bennett, *The Early Dominicans*, 69–70. ³Grandisson's *Register*, II, 1147 and 1179. ⁴R. L. Poole, *Illustrations of Medieval Thought* (1920), 244. ⁵*Polemical Works* (Wyclif

Society), I, 91. [6]The standard biography is that of Dr. H. B. Workman (1926). Readers should also consult Mr. B. L. Manning's chapter in *The Cambridge Medieval History* (Vol. VII, Ch. XVI). [7]H. B. Workman *op. cit.*, II, 243. [8]This dangerous and misleading phrase (for an Indulgence, in strict theology, cannot remit *guilt*, but only *penalties*) was unfortunately used very commonly in the Middle Ages, not only by the vulgar but by theologians, and sometimes even by a pope. See my *Sectarian History*, pp. 38*ff.* [9]Knighton's *Chronicle* (R. S.), II, 198. [10]*Prediche Volgari*, I, 98; compare A. G. Ferrers Howell, *St. Bernardino of Siena* (1913), 114, 158*ff.* [11]Foxe, *Acts and Monuments* (Parker Soc.), III, 594. [12]P. Villari, *Savonarola*, 760. [13]See my *Malta and Beyond* (6d. post-free from 72, Kimberley Rd., Cambridge).

CHAPTER XXV

[1]Lea, *Inq. in Spain*, I, 52–56. [2]Vincent Ferrer, *De Moderno Ecclesiae Schismate* (Rome, Libreria Pontificia), pp. 96, 197. [3]Lea, *Inq. in Spain*, I, 113. [4]Dr. W. Barry in *Camb. Mod. Hist.*, I, 650. [5]Lea, *c.c.*, I, 195, 207. [6]*Ibid.*, 139. [7]"Le plus hardi et le plus barbare conseil dont l'histoire de tous les siècles précédents fasse mention" (*Lettres, &c., de R.* Soc. de l'Hist. de France, Vol. I, 1853, p. 333, note). [8]Lea, *Inq. in Spain*, III, 389–90, quoting from *Father Boronat*, I, 610–34, a book which I have not been able to consult. Buckle's description of this expulsion is easily accessible in the "World's Classics" (Bk. II, Ch. VIII, pp. 394*ff.*). There would have been about 250,000 males among these Moriscos.

CHAPTER XXVI

[1]J. B. Labat, *Voyage en Espagne et en Italie* (1750), I, 278. [2]Joseph Townsend, *A Journey Through Spain* (2nd ed., 1792), II, 347. [3]G. Diercks, *Geschichte Spaniens*, II, 651, 657, 661. [4]M. Oliphant, *Montalembert*, II, 33. [5]Montalembert, *Œuvres Polémiques*, II (1860), 409. [6]The Civil War of a century ago anticipated in almost every feature that of the present moment: see, for instance, the brief summaries in the contemporary Annual Register. The Carlist General Cabrera, after the battle of Maella, "sullied his victory by butchering in cold blood, under pretence of reprisals, 180 of his cavalry prisoners; a deed in

itself sufficiently horrible, and which gave rise to a system of similar atrocities on both sides." *Annual Register*, 1838, p. 429. [7]See the magazine, *Evangelical Freedom*, for Sept.-Oct., 1928, an article translated from *España Evangelica*. [8]See Professor Pastor's own account in his *History of the Popes* (Eng. trans., Vol. XII, p. 507). "Any description or estimate of the work of the re-organised Inquisition as it proceeded under Paul III is impossible to an historian, as no records are at his disposal. The archives of the Holy Office in Rome must certainly have documentary evidence to some extent, but inspection is absolutely refused. If the present congregation of the Holy Office still persists in maintaining a system of absolute secrecy, which has almost universally been abandoned elsewhere, with regard to historical documents now more than three centuries old, it inflicts an injury not merely on the work of the historian but still more upon itself, since it thus perpetuates belief in all and in the worst of all the innumerable charges levelled at the Inquisition." To this he adds a footnote: "At the end of 1901 I made my first request to be allowed access to the archives of the Roman Inquisition, which was followed by two other applications. The only piece of information I could obtain from the archivist, Fr. G. M. van Rossum, after fourteen months' endeavours, was that the records of the proceedings against heresy under Paul III had been lost, although the 'Decreta' of the Inquisition had been preserved. An inspection of the latter, in spite of solicitations from influential quarters, was absolutely refused me by the Congregation."

EPILOGUE

[1]*Contemporary Review* (1875), 200. [2]*Letters to Mary Gladstone*, 185. [3]Acton's *Correspondence* (ed. Figgis and Laurence), 217. [4]H. A. L. Fisher, *History of Europe*, I, 426. [5]*Verbatim Report of Debate* before the Union of Democratic Control (Hammersmith and Chiswick Branch) between Mr. Charles Roden Buxton and Mr. G. G. Coulton, Wednesday, January 24th, 1917 (Copy in British Museum), pp. 15–16. Members of that Union actually applauded the suggestion that "minorities are always right." [6]*Why We Burnt the Bombing School*, by Saunders Lewis and Lewis Valentine, published at the office of *The Welsh Nationalist*, Caernarvon, 1936. [7]See page 61 of this present volume.

INDEX

Canonized saints will be found under S.

OTHER BEACON PAPERBACKS OF INTEREST TO READERS
OF THIS BOOK